SENSING VIOLENCE

Sensing Violence

Reading with the Marquis de Sade

Will McMorran

https://www.openbookpublishers.com

©2025 Will McMorran

This work is licensed under the Creative Commons Attribution-NonCommercial 4.0 International (CC BY-NC 4.0). This license allows you to share, copy, distribute and transmit the text; to adapt the text for non-commercial purposes of the text providing attribution is made to the authors (but not in any way that suggests that they endorse you or your use of the work). Attribution should include the following information:

Will McMorran, *Sensing Violence: Reading with the Marquis de Sade*. Cambridge, UK: Open Book Publishers, 2025, https://doi.org/10.11647/OBP.0488

Further details about CC BY-NC licenses are available at
https://creativecommons.org/licenses/by-nc/4.0/

Copyright and permissions for the reuse of the images included in this publication may differ from the above. This information is provided in the captions and in the list of illustrations. Unless otherwise stated, figures are reproduced under the fair dealing principle. Every effort has been made to identify and contact copyright holders and any omission or error will be corrected if notification is made to the publisher.

All external links were active at the time of publication unless otherwise stated and have been archived via the Internet Archive Wayback Machine at https://archive.org/web

Digital material and resources associated with this volume are available at
https://doi.org/10.11647/OBP.0488#resources

Information about any revised edition of this work will be provided at
https://doi.org/10.11647/OBP.0488

ISBN Paperback: 978-1-80511-696-7
ISBN Hardback: 978-1-80511-697-4
ISBN Digital (PDF): 978-1-80511-698-1
ISBN HTML: 978-1-80511-700-1
ISBN Digital ebook (epub): 978-1-80511-699-8

DOI: 10.11647/OBP.0488

Cover image: Odilon Redon, *Saint-Antoine… A travers ses longs cheveux qui lui couvraient la figure, j'ai cru reconnaitre Ammonaria* (1889), lithograph. National Gallery of Art, Washington, D.C. Cover design: Jeevanjot Kaur Nagpal

For the students of Schools for Scandal, Brief Encounters, and Lovers and Libertines,

for Louis, Seb and Sam Blue,

and for Ian McMorran (1935–2025)

Table of Contents

Acknowledgements ix

Abbreviations, References and Translations xi

List of Figures xiii

Introduction 1

1. Looking and Touching with Eugénie 27
   Introduction 27
   Before Eugénie: Palincests 28
   Eugénie and Myrrha 36
   Lights, Camera, Reaction 45
   Beyond Eugénie: On Touching Statues 60
   After Valmont: From Fantasy to Perversion 72
   Conclusion 81

2. Hearing and Feeling with Justine 83
   Introduction 83
   Scenes of Listening 85
   Reading as Listening 98
   Justine's Scream 108
   Once More, with Einfühlung 111
   Bad Vibrations 123
   Conclusion 132

3. Translating with Sade 137
   Introduction 137
   The Translator's Body 138
   How Not to Translate Sade 145
   Smelling Silling 157
   Back to Sodom 162

From Translating to Rerererereading Sade	169
Conclusion	171
4. Teaching with Sade	175
Introduction	175
Embodied Pedagogies	178
Teaching in the Boudoir	187
Sade in the Classroom	194
Conclusion	205
Conclusion	209
Digital Appendix of resources available online at: https://doi.org/10.11647/OBP.0488#resources	219
Bibliography	221
Primary Sources	221
Secondary Sources	224
Index	243

Acknowledgements

'Writing, when properly managed', Tristram Shandy said, 'is but a different name for conversation'. This book is a conversation borne of conversation and, I hope, a book that will prompt more conversation. I would therefore like to thank the sparkling conversationalists in the School of Arts at Queen Mary, and especially those with whom I have worked so closely and so happily in the Department of Comparative Literature and Culture, and the Department of Modern Languages and Cultures. I can't name you all, but it would be remiss of me not to thank Robert Gillett for reading parts of this book in draft form and for his generous feedback. I have over the years accumulated debts to colleagues from Oxford to Oslo and beyond in the writing of this book, including a number of fellow Sadeans: Tom Wynn and Caroline Warman were there at the start and have patiently waited for me to get to the end; conversations with Stéphanie Genand, Robert Gillan, Manuel Mühlbacher, Philippe Roger and Jim Steintrager helped me along the way. Marine Ganofsky went above and beyond as a peer reviewer of the manuscript and helped me see my chapter on seeing more clearly. Adèle Kreager, and the whole team at Open Book, turned this manuscript into a book with breathtaking efficiency. I would also like to thank the very unSadean Sue Harris, Eddie Hughes, Michael Moriarty and Kate Tunstall for all their loyal encouragement and support over the last decade and more. And I would finally like to thank two scholars I know only through their research: June Downey, who asked her students many of the same questions I have asked mine but a hundred years earlier, and Anežka Kuzmičová, whose work on mental imagery has been an invaluable guide. As ever, my greatest debt is to my dearly missed mother, Edith Franck McMorran – reader, teacher and translator extraordinaire.

Abbreviations, References and Translations

The following abbreviations for Sade's works are used for in-text citations:

120J: *Les 120 Journées de Sodome ou l'école du libertinage*

AV: *Aline et Valcour, ou le Roman philosophique*

E: 'Eugénie de Franval'

HJ: *Histoire de Juliette, ou les Prospérités du vice*

Idée: 'Idée sur les romans'

J: *Justine, ou les Malheurs de la vertu*

NJ: *La Nouvelle Justine, ou les Malheurs de la vertu*

PB: *La Philosophie dans le boudoir*

Page references to *Aline et Valcour, Histoire de Juliette, Justine, La Nouvelle Justine, La Philosophie dans le boudoir* and *Les 120 Journées de Sodome* refer to the Pléiade edition of Sade's works: Sade, *Œuvres*, ed. by Michel Delon, 3 vols. (Paris: Gallimard, 1990–8). Page references to 'Eugénie de Franval' and the 'Idée sur les romans' refer to Sade, *Les Crimes de l'amour*, ed. by Eric Le Grandic (Paris: Zulma, 1995).

All translations from the *120 Journées de Sodome* are taken from Sade, *The 120 Days of Sodom*, ed. and trans. by Will McMorran and Thomas Wynn (London: Penguin, 2016). Page references to this edition are given in-text alongside references to the French edition. All other translations are my own unless otherwise stated.

List of Figures

1	Johan Zoffany, *Tribuna of the Uffizi* (1772), Wikimedia Commons, public domain, https://commons.wikimedia.org/wiki/File:Johan_Zoffany_-_Tribuna_of_the_Uffizi_-_Google_Art_Project.jpg#/media/File:Johan_Zoffany_-_Tribuna_of_the_Uffizi_-_Google_Art_Project.jpg	p. 67
2	Mean phallometric response in mm change as a function of stimulus category. From Marnie E. Rice, Terry C. Chaplin, Grant T. Harris, Joanne Coutts, 'Empathy for the Victim and Sexual Arousal Among Rapists and Nonrapists', *Journal of Interpersonal Violence*, 9.4 (1994), 443	p. 95
3	'Empathy' in Edwin G. Boring, Herbert S. Langfeld and Harry Porter Weld, *Introduction to Psychology* (New York: John Wiley and Sons, 1939), 274, public domain. Photo taken by author (2025)	p. 114
4	Matthias Grünewald, *The Mocking of Christ* (1503–5), Wikimedia Commons, public domain, https://commons.wikimedia.org/wiki/File:Mathis_Gothart_Gr%C3%BCnewald_062.jpg#/media/File:Mathis_Gothart_Gr%C3%BCnewald_062.jpg	p. 132
5	Artemisia Gentileschi, *Jael and Sisera* (1620) © Szépművészeti Múzeum / Museum of Fine Arts, Budapest, 2025	p. 134
6	*Strange Days* © 1995 Lightstorm Entertainment Inc. © 2017 Universal Studios © Mediumrare Entertainment	p. 215

Introduction

In 2015, I attended a conference in Geneva that slightly belatedly commemorated the bicentenary of Sade's death in 1814. Its title was *Les Langues de Sade* [Sade's Languages], and the conference programme included a short paragraph which elaborated on this theme. It was incontestable, our genial hosts declared, that libertinage was a 'fait de langage' [fact of language], and the conference would accordingly focus on the following three questions: 'Which languages does Sade speak? Which languages speak in Sade? How do other languages make him speak?' The talks on 'Sade's phrase' and 'Sadean phrasing' echoed those on 'Sade's diction' delivered decades earlier at previous conferences on Sade.[1] As interesting as these papers were, it struck me that we were all, still, talking about Sade's words rather that what those words were depicting. As a collective, Sade scholars have been stubbornly reluctant to talk – and write – about the most obvious features of Sade's fiction: the sex and violence. This book seeks to redress that balance by talking about the obvious, without, I hope, being too obvious. The aim in the pages ahead is to explore both the sexual violence that is at the heart of Sadean fiction, and readers' lived experience of that violence. This is, as the title would suggest, a book about Sade, but it is also a book that uses Sade to ask a much broader question: what happens to us as readers when we encounter fictional depictions of sex and sexual violence?

The reluctance of literary critics to say very much about the sexual violence in Sade has endured for decades; it was indeed discernible at the very first academic conference devoted to Sade, which took place in Aix-en-Provence in 1966. While there had been a flurry of books and writings about Sade in the years following the Second World War, these

---

1   Jacques Proust gave a talk on 'La diction sadienne' at the 1981 Cerisy confence on Sade.

had all been the work of intellectuals in the public sphere, such as Jean Paulhan, Simone de Beauvoir, Pierre Klossowski and Maurice Blanchot. Academic literary critics had come rather late to the Sade party, and were not entirely welcome when they did finally arrive. Conspicuous by their absence from the Aix conference were the very intellectuals who had led the way in introducing the French public to Sade as a significant writer and thinker: Klossowski, Blanchot, Gilbert Lely and others all turned down the invitation to attend, much to the hosts' chagrin.

Reading the transcript of that conference today, one can still sense a degree of trepidation among the organisers as they opened proceedings – understandably, perhaps, given it had only been a decade since the *affaire Sade*, a censorship trial prompted by Jean-Jacques Pauvert's first attempt to publish a 'complete works' of Sade. André Bourde, director of the research centre hosting the conference, hinted at this recent history when he affirmed in his opening speech, 'Nous ne sommes ici idôlatres ou censeurs de personne et nous sommes au premier chef scientifiques' [We are neither idolaters nor censors of anyone and we are first and foremost scientists][2] – a declaration of objectivity and neutrality. Bernard Guyon, head of the 'Faculté des lettres' at Aix at the time, made an opening speech of his own in which he stated rather enigmatically of Sade, 'Je n'ignore pas qui il est, ce qu'il a écrit, bien que, ayant trop le sens de la liberté et de la vie, je ne me sois pas condamné à lire toute son œuvre dont la principale caractéristique est peut-être l'ennui' [I am aware of who he is, and what he has written, even though, having too great a sense of freedom and of life, I have not condemned myself to reading his entire œuvre, the principle characteristic of which is perhaps tedium].[3] Backing away even further from the *divin marquis*, Guyon stressed that he himself was neither 'sadique' [sadistic] nor 'sadiste' [Sadean] before nonetheless affirming that there was 'un *fait Sade*' [a factual Sade] that merited proper study. For this task, he added, no one could be better qualified than academic scholars, who could be relied upon to approach it with 'le ton de l'objectivité, de sérénité dans le désir de rechercher la vérité, avec les armes les plus aiguës, celles des spécialistes les mieux informés' [the tone of objectivity, of serenity in the

---

2   Centre aixois d'études et de recherches sur le dix-huitième siècle (ed.), *Le Marquis de Sade* (Paris: Armand Colin, 1968), 7.
3   Ibid., 9.

desire to seek out the truth, with the sharpest of blades, those of the most informed specialists].⁴ The scientific approach to Sade was reaffirmed, with the emphasis on objectivity and the noble search for truth, but with a rather unscientific hint of antagonism: negotiating the Sadean text here is no exercise in *ennui*, but a battle the researcher conducts with a swinging blade. The imagery of combat, a commonplace ironically of libertine language, rather undermines the plea for serenity.

The scientific veneer of the Aix conference was very much of its time. George Steiner had observed a year before that 'the field of literary study reflects a large hope, a great positivism, an ideal of being something like a science'.⁵ He was doubtless thinking both of the post-war rise of the New Criticism in America and the emergence of the *nouvelle critique* in France. At the time Steiner was writing, Roland Barthes and his fellow structuralists were championing a 'science de la littérature'⁶ based on a linguistic model. Jean Marie Goulemot, an attendee at the Aix conference, indeed noted with some unease the influence of structuralism on the approach being taken by the speakers there; in a subsequent review, he condemned 'les insuffisances d'une coquetterie structuraliste qui ne fait qu'effleurer le texte et laisse le lecteur sur sa faim' [the inadequacies of a structuralist coquetry that only skims the text and leaves the reader hungry for more].⁷ For all his misgivings, however, structuralism was clearing the path for Sade's entry into the academy. In the same year as the conference, Jean-Jacques Brochier reclaimed Sade as both a classic and contemporary author in a book for the *Classiques du XXe siècle* series, following up with an essay on 'Sade et le langage'⁸ for the *Cercle du livre précieux* edition of Sade's complete works two years later. In the former, Brochier reassures the reader that the violence of Sade's fiction is nothing to worry about: 'il ne faut pas oublier que les *120 Journées de Sodome* sont une œuvre écrite, donc purement imaginaire' [one must not forget that the *120 Days of Sodom* is a written work, and

---

4   Ibid., 9.
5   George Steiner, 'To Civilize our Gentleman', in Steiner, *Language and Silence: Essays 1958–1966* (London: Faber, 1967), 77.
6   The title of a section from Roland Barthes's *Critique et verité* (Paris: Seuil, 1966).
7   Jean Marie Goulemot, '"Divin Marquis" ou objet d'études?', *Revue des sciences humaines*, 124 (1966), 417–8.
8   Jean-Jacques Brochier, 'Sade et le langage', in *Œuvres complètes*, ed. by Gilbert Lely, 16 vols. (Paris: Cercle du livre précieux, 1966–7), XV, 511–9. See also Brochier, *Sade* (Paris: Editions universitaires, 1966).

therefore purely imaginary]; later in the same volume, he adds, 'l'œuvre de Sade, c'est sa suprême contradiction, est de l'ordre du discours' [Sade's œuvre, and this is its supreme contradiction, is of the order of discours].[9] A year later, in perhaps the most influential article on Sade ever written, Barthes would echo Brochier's words in referring to 'le seul univers sadien, qui est l'univers du discours' [the sole Sadean universe, which is the universe of discourse].[10] It was this formulation that would prove decisive in bringing Sade into the literary, or at least literary critical, fold. Barthes's intervention places the Sadean text in a sanctuary – some would say prison – of linguistic codes and grammars for its own protection (rather like the royal warrants which shielded Sade from criminal prosecution at the cost of his freedom).[11] Its violence is no longer visceral but eviscerated, reduced to black type on a white page: as Barthes would put it pithily in his subsequent book on Sade,

> écrite, la merde ne sent pas ; Sade peut en inonder ses partenaires, nous n'en recevons aucun effluve, seul le signe abstrait d'un désagrément. Tel apparaît le libertinage : un fait de langage.
>
> [written down, shit does not smell; Sade can flood his partners with it, we do not get a whiff of it, just the abstract sign of something unpleasant. So libertinage appears: a fact of language.][12]

---

9   Brochier, *Sade*, 64, 98. Decades later, Camille Paglia would make a similar point, citing a gruesome excerpt from the *120 Journées* before reminding her reader: 'Remember these are ideas, not acts' (*Sexual Personae: Art and Decadence from Nefertiti to Emily Dickinson* (New Haven, CT: Yale University Press, 1990), 242).
10 'L'arbre du crime', in *La Pensée de Sade, Tel Quel*, 28 (1967), 37. Barthes's article was subsequently incorporated into Barthes, *Sade, Fourier, Loyola* (Paris: Seuil, 1971).
11 The same parallel between Sade's imprisonment and the confinement of his works to the realm of discourse was drawn by Jean-Pierre Faye a decade later: 'Dans la liste des malheurs de D.A.F. de Sade, le dernier en date est sans doute la tentative de lui faire subir l'enfermement dans les plaisirs du Texte.' [In the list of D.A.F. de Sade's misfortunes, the last to date is without doubt the attempt to submit him to confinement within the pleasures of the Text.] ('Changer la mort (Sade et la politique)', *Obliques*, 12–13 (1977), 48). Annie Le Brun also reached for the same metaphor in labelling Sade 'Prisonnier, autrefois de la Bastille, hier de sa malédiction, aujourd'hui de la critique' [A prisoner, once of the Bastille, yesterday of his curse, today of [literary] criticism] (*Soudain un bloc d'abîme, Sade* (Paris: Gallimard, 1993), 16.)
12 Barthes, *Sade, Fourier, Loyola*, 141. As Chapter 3 will make evident, Barthes rather underestimates the pungency of excremental language.

Or that old lie endured by generations of children: 'sticks and stones may break my bones, but words will never hurt me'. Here, as at the Geneva conference that drew on these lines decades later, language is stripped of any affective power, and thus of any ethical consequence. Because Barthes's readers are unable to smell words, the text can do them no harm.

After Brochier and Barthes, declarations of the linguistic and discursive nature of Sadean violence became – and have remained – a commonplace of Sadean criticism, from Phillipe Roger's assertion that Sade 'ne met à mal que le langage' [mistreats only language][13] to Laurence Lynch's reassurance that 'Sade's violence is indeed that of language'.[14] Chantal Thomas, like Roger a former student of Barthes's, thus berates Simone de Beauvoir for her failure in 'Faut-il brûler Sade?' (1951–2) to grasp the difference between imaginary and real violence: she complains that Beauvoir 'ne conçoit pas comme essentielle la distinction entre théâtre du désir et réalité quotidienne' [does not regard the distinction between theatre of desire and daily reality as essential]; she adds that, for Beauvoir, 'l'encre et le sang ne font qu'un : ce qui autorise Simone de Beauvoir à confondre Sade avec n'importe quel sadique de fait divers' [ink and blood are one and the same: something that allows Simone de Beauvoir to mistake Sade for any old sadist in the news].[15] A recent essay that chooses to analyse the word 'violence' in Sadean fiction rather than the violence itself reflects the continued reluctance of Sade scholars to abandon the linguistic terrain that made their author safe to approach.[16] The door to affect remains closed, as if there were still a lingering fear that opening it would mean exposing Sade to the kind of moral concerns that had led to the *affaire Sade*, and the decades of censorship before that.

---

13 Philippe Roger, *Sade: La philosophie dans le pressoir* (Paris: Bernard Grasset, 1976), 190.

14 Lawrence Lynch, *The Marquis de Sade* (Boston, MA: Twayne, 1984), 129. Geoffrey Bennington would similarly insist, 'the only "real" cruelty in Sade is that worked in the body of a language' ('Sade: Laying Down the Law', *Oxford Literary Review*, 6.2 (1984), 54).

15 Chantal Thomas, *Sade* (Paris: Seuil, 1994), 175.

16 See Jean-Christophe Abramovici, '« Avec une telle violence que... »: Sade's Use of the Term Violence', in *Representing Violence in France, 1760–1820*, ed. by Thomas Wynn, *Studies on Voltaire and the Eighteenth Century*, 2013: 10 (Oxford: Voltaire Foundation, 2013), 221–28.

There was an echo of Thomas's berating of Beauvoir at another conference I attended a few years ago. When a distinguished critic of Sade confessed that she found the violence in Sade upsetting, she was castigated by a male colleague for 'moralizing' and for failing to show the detachment that reading Sade required. As well as his own misogyny, the latter thereby revealed the problem at the heart of Sade studies: an Olympian detachment divorced from the practices and interests of readers outside the academy. As Annie Le Brun has moreover bemoaned, this detachment bears little relation to the practices and interests of the very author they have sought to defend:

> par la mise en place d'un réseau de plus en plus dense d'interminables analyses psychologiques, littéraires, médicales, psychanalytiques, linguistiques, on rendait Sade fréquentable en le neutralisant [...] c'était grâce à la notion d'écriture qu'on était parvenu à ce beau résultat : vingt années d'analyse textuelle aboutissaient à exclure Sade de lui-même.
>
> [by the institution of an increasingly dense network of interminable psychological, literary, medical, psychoanalytical, and linguistic analyses, Sade was made respectable by neutralizing him [...] it was thanks to the notion of *écriture* that this fine result was achieved: twenty years of textual analysis culminated in excluding Sade from himself.][17]

Little has changed since Le Brun wrote those lines, but it might now be worth adding *analyses historicistes* to her list: thirty years on, the linguistic Sade has ceded ground to an intensely historicized Sade that has situated him firmly in his own period as a reader, writer and thinker in the Enlightenment tradition.[18] As important and illuminating as this work has been, the historicized Sade and the linguistic Sade are both underpinned by the same scientific pretentions. The historicizing critic is still the clinician, calmly and objectively examining the Sadean text

---

17 Le Brun, *Soudain un bloc d'abîme*, 11–12.
18 Michel Delon's *L'Idée d'énergie au tournant des lumières, 1770–1800* (Paris: P.U.F., 1988), and his landmark *Pléiade* edition of Sade (Paris: Gallimard, 1990–8), with its prefatory essay by Jean Deprun, 'Sade Philosophe', set the tone for this kind of approach. Recent examples include Michèle Vallenthini, *Sade dans l'histoire : Du temps de la fiction à la fiction du temps* (Paris: Garnier, 2019) and Armelle St-Martin, *Sade, la Révolution et la finance* (Paris: Garnier, 2021). The numerous, and lengthy, biographies of Sade published in recent decades also reflect the burgeoning historical interest in Sade.

as symptom of its time, and still avoiding any discussion that might compromise that reassuring façade.

Trends and turns in literary theory have come and gone, from the reader-response theories of the 1970s and 1980s to the ethical turn of the 1990s and the affective and cognitive turns of this century, without leaving much of a trace on Sade scholarship. Although feminist criticism in the Anglo-American tradition has made important interventions,[19] the *réseau* [network] Le Brun identifies continues to hold. In the meantime, it has largely been left to Sade's opponents to reflect on the affective force of Sade's fiction and its ethical implications. Scholars of a humanist persuasion have watched Sade's entry into the literary mainstream with particular suspicion, if not dismay, for behind the belief that some books can be morally improving lurks the old anxiety that others may be corrupting. Wayne Booth, for whom literature is quite simply 'the good stuff',[20] generally prefers to focus on the former rather than the latter in his reflections on the ethical power of fiction, but his suggestion that we are what we read acknowledges the possibility of negative as well as positive consequences:

> Perhaps we all underestimate the extent to which we absorb the values of what we read. And even when we do not retain them, the fact remains that insofar as the fiction has *worked* for us, we have lived with its values for the duration: we have been *that kind of person* for at least as long as we remained in the presence of the work.

When Booth does come to a precise example of what he would doubtless consider 'the bad stuff', he echoes the kind of view that, for over a century, had seen Sade's readership restricted to a *happy few* of bibliophiles, sexologists, surrealists and public intellectuals respectively:

> certain other works – say the sadomasochistic novels of the Marquis de Sade and Georges Bataille – will for most people in most cultures provide a highly dubious diet. And saying *that* will not prevent my saying in turn that for some readers on some occasions – let us say the group of

---

19 Such as Nancy K. Miller's *French Dressing: Women, Men and Ancien Régime Fiction* (London and New York: Routledge, 1995) and Jane Gallop's *Thinking through the Body* (New York: Columbia University Press, 1990).

20 Wayne C. Booth, *The Company We Keep: An Ethics of Fiction* (Berkeley and Los Angeles, CA: University of California Press, 1988), 294.

> professional critics who have argued for the value of writers like Sade or Bataille (Barthes 1976; Beauvoir 1953) – they are not likely to do much harm. On the other hand it is hard to see how they could do much good, either.[21]

Not for the first time, Sade is deemed to be not 'for most people', and best kept for the expert or professional critic. While Booth chooses not to dwell on the risks Sade's fiction poses, others have been less sanguine. Roger Shattuck, writing thirty years after the Moors Murders trial, claims a causal relationship between the crimes committed by Ian Brady and Ted Bundy and their reading of Sade's works. Though the case he makes is thoroughly unconvincing,[22] suggesting correlation rather than cause, his approach at least has the merit of addressing the sexual violence at the heart of Sadean fiction in a way that acknowledges its visceral force. Describing his first reading of Sade, Shattuck tells the reader:

> Sade's narrative plunged me into feelings and reactions associated with two vividly familiar experiences of a very different kind: witnessing a major surgical operation for the first few times and participating in wartime combat fighting at close range. In watching surgery, from the moment of the first incision into the body, one fights giddily for detachment, distance, and rational justification for so unnatural an act. In combat, one may rapidly yield either to numbing fear or to surging impulses of aggression and bloodlust. In both cases, the universe has been turned upside down. What was wrong is now right in the name of some higher cause, medical or military. Insofar as I can reconstitute those distressing early experiences of reading Sade before it became a chore to continue, I sought both to withdraw and to succumb. Revulsion accompanied arousal to produce a kind of visceral trembling that resembles stage fright. Cold blood and hot blood mingled and fought one another in a state of tense paralysis. In spite of its intensity, this condition was the opposite of life, or health, or pleasure.[23]

---

21 Ibid., 41, 59.
22 As noted elsewhere, Ian Brady had already committed two of the three murders for which he was convicted before he ever read Sade (Will McMorran and Thomas Wynn, 'Introduction', in Sade, *The 120 Days of Sodom*, ed. and trans. by McMorran and Wynn (London: Penguin, 2016), xxv).
23 Roger Shattuck, *Forbidden Knowledge: From Prometheus to Pornography* (San Diego, CA: Harcourt Brace, 1997), 298.

Shattuck's account may seem melodramatic to some ears, and indeed echoes some of the hyperbolic reactions of Sade's earliest readers,[24] but its acknowledgement of a somatic response at least offers a refreshing counterpoint to the disembodied approach that continues to characterize Sade criticism. It implicitly recognizes what Sade scholars have not, which is that the lived experience of reading Sade is worthy of attention: even though the theme of the first international conference on Sade in the United States (in 2003) was *Lire Sade* [To read Sade], it was revealing that none of the speakers took up the apparent invitation to explore any aspect of the reading process or experience.

The silence maintained by critics regarding their own embodied responses to Sadean fiction should not come as a great surprise. No one, after all, wants to be thought of as a pervert. This anxiety is, I suspect, why so many who have written about Sade – from those opposed to his cultural rehabilitation to those who have played an active part in it – have described his works as 'boring'. Laurence Bongie, apparently so horrified by Sade's entrance into the academy that he felt moved to write a short biography, dismisses him as the author of 'the most monotonously egregious, long-winded pornographic novels imaginable'.[25] David Coward, whose translations of Sade's shorter fiction were the first to enter the privileged ranks of Oxford's World Classics, is similarly disparaging of Sade's 'very tedious novels'.[26] As we have already seen, participants in the first conference on Sade also alluded to the *ennui* provoked by their reading of Sade. Nicholas Harrison has noted that the same expressions of boredom were a feature of the *affaire Sade*. At one point in the trial, a letter for the defence by Jean Cocteau was read aloud which stated of Sade, 'Il est ennuyeux, son style est faible, et il ne vaut que par ce qu'on lui reproche' [He is boring, his style is weak, and his

---

24 The military analogy recalls the response of one of Sade's earliest critics, Charles de Villers: 'Un malheureux soldat, qu'on vient de passer par dix tours de baguettes, n'est pas plus soulagé de voir la fin de l'opération, que je le suis de n'avoir plus sous les yeux cet écrit exécrable' [An unfortunate soldier who has just been made to run the gauntlet ten times is no more relieved to see an end to the ordeal than I am at no longer having that execrable text before me] (*Lettre sur le roman intitulé Justine ou les malheurs de la vertu*, cited in Françoise Laugaa-Traut, *Lectures de Sade* (Paris: Armand Colin, 1973), 73–4).

25 Laurence Bongie, *Sade: A Biographical Essay* (Chicago, IL: University of Chicago Press, 1998), ix.

26 David Coward, 'Down with Sade?', *Paragraph*, 23.1 (2000), 12.

only value lies in that for which he is reproached]. When the presiding judge conceded, 'Je suis d'accord sur un point: c'est qu'il est ennuyeux' [I agree on one point: that he is boring], Maurice Garçon, counsel for the defence, was quick to concur: 'Sur ce point nous sommes tous d'accord' [On that point we are all agreed].[27] As Harrison concludes, 'saying Sade was boring was, it seems, a means of making it clear that the speaker's overall assessment of his importance was an entirely rational one, undistorted by sexual excitement or sexual repression'.[28] It is difficult not to draw the same conclusion regarding the professions of boredom made by literary critics: like the focus on language, or on history, they offer a form of reassurance that the scholar's interest is purely – in both senses – intellectual.

Whereas Shattuck invokes his own visceral response as evidence of the potential dangers of reading Sade, the exceedingly rare occasions upon which Sade critics draw on their own affective experiences conversely reflect a confidence that reading Sade is perfectly safe. When Goulemot, having been dissatisfied by the scientific approach taken at the Aix conference, had the opportunity to speak at the next major conference on Sade a decade later, he made an admission that makes him unique even now among Sade's male scholars: 'Dois-je par ailleurs le confesser, je ne suis pas de ceux que Sade a laissés indifférents, et j'entends par là sensuellement indifférents, et que n'ont pas troublés les scènes érotiques' [Should I moreover confess, I am not among those left indifferent by Sade, and by that I mean sensually indifferent, and untroubled by the erotic scenes].[29] Female scholars, however, have been a little braver than their male counterparts in acknowledging the erotic appeal of Sade's fiction. Thus, when Chantal Thomas revisits her 1978 study, *La Dissertation et l'orgie*, in 2002, she returns to her first readings of Sade as a schoolgirl and then student:

> Sade se lit de préférence au lit, et dans toutes les postures de l'abandon. Qu'en même temps ou plutôt par intermittence on soit capable de méditer et prendre des notes prouve bien à quel point est juste l'enseignement

---

27 Jean-Jacques Pauvert (ed.), *L'Affaire Sade* (Paris: Pauvert, 1957), 111, 62.
28 Nicholas Harrison, *Circles of Censorship: Censorship and its Metaphors in French History, Literature, and Theory* (Oxford: Oxford University Press, 1995), 63.
29 Goulemot, 'Beau marquis parlez-nous d'amour', in *Sade, écrire la crise*, ed. by Michel Camus and Philippe Roger (Paris: Belfond, 1983), 119.

sadien selon lequel libertinage et acuité mentale vont de pair. L'instant où l'on perd la tête, loin de nous annihiler dans un abrutissement bestial, suscite à nouveau le langage, avec une ardeur multipliée laquelle [...] reconduit doucement à l'envie de s'étourdir.

[Sade should preferably be read in bed, and in all the poses of sweet surrender. That one should be able at the same time, or rather intermittently, to reflect and take notes indeed proves the extent to which Sadean teaching, according to which libertinage and mental acuity go together, has it right. The moment one loses one's head, far from obliterating us in a bestial stupor, gives rise to language once again, with an intensified ardour that [...] gently leads back to the desire to lose oneself again.][30]

Thomas here casts her younger self as a Sadean libertine, her reading alternating between pleasure and reflection and thus echoing the familiar Sadean pattern of *dissertation* and *orgie* after which she names her book. Although she thereby potentially opens the door for an embodied approach, it is one that entirely precludes any affective response other than an erotic one: readers are free to be aroused, but not to be horrified, or disturbed, as her contemptuous response to Beauvoir's disquiet reflects.[31] In Thomas's attitude to Beauvoir there is an echo of Barthes's attitude to the fictional victims in Sade's fiction: 'Le cri est la marque de la victime : c'est parce qu'elle choisit de crier, qu'elle se constitue victime' [The scream is the mark of the victim: it is because she chooses to scream that she makes a victim of herself].[32] Beauvoir too, Thomas suggests, had a choice and made the wrong one by responding ethically rather than erotically to Sade.

With one exception, which I shall save for later,[33] admissions of erotic response by Sade scholars are confined to the margins – a fleeting aside in an introductory paragraph, in the case of Goulemot, or a preface, in that of Thomas. Separate, in other words, from the serious business of textual analysis. This is reflective of a much broader marginalization

---

30 Chantal Thomas, *Sade, La Dissertation et l'orgie*, 2nd edn. (Paris: Payot & Rivages, 2002), 8.
31 Beauvoir had said of Sade, 'Ce qui fait la suprême valeur de son témoignage, c'est qu'il nous inquiète' [The supreme value of his testimony is that it disturbs us] (Beauvoir, 'Faut-il brûler Sade?', in Beauvoir, *Privilèges* (Paris: Gallimard, 1972), 82.
32 Barthes, *Sade, Fourier, Loyola*, 147.
33 See Chapter 4, 'Teaching in the Boudoir'.

of affect that has endured in literary criticism for several decades. As suggested earlier, the ideal of being 'something like a science' that Steiner describes was not limited to structuralism and its avatars. Terry Eagleton notes that the New Criticism's 'battery of critical instruments was a way of competing with the hard sciences on their own terms',[34] and chief among those manning the battery were W. K. Wimsatt and Monroe C. Beardsley. In a landmark article published in 1949, they identified the 'affective fallacy' as 'a confusion between the poem and its *results* (what it *is* and what it *does*')', and affect itself as an unscientific and thus unwelcome distraction:

> The report of some readers, on the other hand, that a poem or story induces in them vivid images, intense feelings, or heightened consciousness, is neither anything which can be refuted nor anything which it is possible for the objective critic to take into account.[35]

As a consequence, they famously sought to bar 'talk of tears, prickles, or other physiological symptoms, of feeling angry, joyful, hot, cold, or intense' from the field of literary studies,[36] and were moreover entirely successful in doing so. Ever since, affective responses ranging from the senses to the emotions have been regarded as being beyond the purview of literary criticism. 'What has got lost', Karen Littau laments, 'is any sense that literature is also about sensations, not just about sense-making'.[37] One could add, what has therefore got lost is the very reason why most of us read fiction in the first place. This book is my modest attempt to regain some of what has been lost, and to explore those vivid images and intense feelings that Wimsatt and Beardsley dismissed.

While one can understand the reluctance to engage with affect when it comes to the erotic or pornographic, the broader failure within literary studies is more difficult to comprehend. The marginalization of affect in literary criticism and theory has extended even to those approaches that claimed to be focussed on the reader. One might be forgiven for thinking

---

34 Terry Eagleton, *Literary Theory: An Introduction* (Oxford: Blackwell, 1983), 49.
35 W. K. Wimsatt and Monroe C. Beardsley, 'The Affective Fallacy', in Wimsatt, *The Verbal Icon: Studies in the Meaning of Poetry* (Lexington, KY: University of Kentucky Press, 1954), 32, 34.
36 Ibid., 34.
37 Karin Littau, *Theories of Reading: Books, Bodies, and Bibliomania* (Cambridge, UK: Polity Press, 2006), 98.

that a form of criticism that became known as 'reader-response' would have, well, looked at reader's responses. This, however, proved not to be the case because, as Littau again notes, 'the bulk of literary theories, including those that profess to be concerned with readers' responses, are predominantly about the reader's mental activities, how a reader makes sense of a text'.³⁸ Whether a given theoretical approach has focussed on what an author means by a text, or what a text means, or what meaning a reader makes of a text, the preoccupation has remained the same. As Jane Tompkins recognized even as interest in reader-response theory was burgeoning at the turn of the 1980s, meaning remains 'the goal of critical inquiry', and the text remains 'the primary unit of meaning': 'Interpretation reigns supreme both in teaching and publication [...] virtually nothing has changed as a result of what seems, from close up, the cataclysmic shift in the locus of meaning from the text to the reader'.³⁹ Or, as Stanley Fish put it succinctly, 'interpretation is the only game in town'.⁴⁰ If the ostensible shift from text to reader ultimately made little difference, it was because the reader under discussion seemed to be an entirely theoretical construct or, as Littau puts it, 'a reader in theory':

> whether ideal (Culler), informed (Fish), implied (Iser) or textualized (Barthes), this entity is an abstraction who is neither an actual living reader, a flesh and blood being, nor a real historical person, but a transhistorical, transsubjective and transcendental receptor.⁴¹

The abstractedness of these readers is arguably what led to the demise, or at least decline, of reader-response approaches. Ultimately, the theoretical responses of theoretical readers will only ever be theoretically interesting. Real readers, I would suggest, make for far more compelling subjects.

The only prominent reader-response theorist to engage with actual readers in this period was Norman Holland, although his psychoanalytical approach in *5 Readers Reading* creates the impression that he has transformed those actual readers into fictional ones.

---

38 Ibid., 86.
39 Jane Tompkins, 'The Reader in History', in *Reader-Response Criticism*, ed. by Tompkins (Baltimore, MD: Johns Hopkins University Press, 1980), 225.
40 Stanley Fish, *Is there a Text in this Class? The Authority of Interpretive Communities* (Cambridge, MA: Harvard University Press, 1980), 355.
41 Littau, *Theories of Reading*, 107.

Given that his aim is to explore subjective response, 'using a battery of psychological tests and extensive interviews',[42] Holland ironically seems quite blind to the subjectivity of his own caricatural reading of his five readers: Sam, for example, is described as 'Good-looking, tall, talkative, cheerful and gregarious' and 'a favourite among departmental secretaries', but beneath this exterior Holland detects a 'hunger for admiration of his boyish virility and charm' and a 'desire to deal with reality by cozying up to it as a child would'.[43] His readers are all reduced to a single 'identity theme' as if they were one-dimensional fictional characters; as Jonathan Culler observes, 'to discover an identity theme is to treat a person's behaviour as a text, to interpret it as one would the accounts of a character in a traditional novel'.[44] Although Holland repeatedly questions the readers he interviews about how they 'feel' about given situations or characters, he moreover consigns the only discussion of 'Affect' to an appendix, where he admits his own principles of literary experience 'simply do not tell very much about affects'. He indeed laments the absence of any 'satisfactory theory of affect in any circumstances, real life, literary response, dreams or inner tensions'.[45] In the absence of such a theory, Holland's attempt to address affect in his appendix finds him leaving his actual readers behind and retreating into (Freudian) theory instead.

For all the limitations of Holland's approach, his interest in actual readers and their responses certainly anticipated the recent turns towards the affective and the cognitive in literary and cultural studies.[46] Inspired in part by a growing interest in neuroscience, the 'tears,

---

42 Norman N. Holland, *5 Readers Reading* (New Haven, CT: Yale University Press, 1975), back cover.
43 Ibid., 74, 68–9.
44 Jonathan Culler, 'Prolegomena to a Theory of Reading', in *The Reader in the Text: Essays on Audience and Interpretation*, ed. by Susan R. Suleiman and Inge Crossman (Princeton, NJ: Princeton University Press, 1980), 55.
45 Holland, *5 Readers Reading*, 292. The appendix echoes the similarly peripheral discussion of affect in his earlier work, *The Dynamics of Literary Response*, which also reads like an afterthought as Holland admits 'there is a great gap in this attempt to set up a model of literary response' given that he has said 'virtually nothing' about affect. The reason he gives for this omission is that 'psychoanalysis has as yet offered no fully satisfactory theory of affect' (*The Dynamics of Literary Response*, 2nd edn. (New York: Norton, 1975), 281).
46 A turn which Holland himself embraced in *Literature and the Brain* (Gainsville, FL: The PsyArt Foundation, 2009).

prickles or other physiological symptoms' that Wimsatt and Monroe Beardsley insisted were not for 'the objective critic to take into account'[47] are increasingly being taken seriously. If we as critics are willing to be subjective as well as objective, focussed on reading subjects as well as textual objects, it should be possible to arrive at a form of criticism which is less remote from the lived experience of actual readers. Writing at the height of structuralism, Culler insisted that 'The question is not what actual readers happen to do but what an ideal reader must know implicitly in order to read and interpret works in ways we consider acceptable, in accordance with the institution of literature'.[48] This book makes the opposite case, namely that the question is indeed what actual readers happen to do, not what some ideal reader might do in theory. As David S. Miall notes, Culler's statement of the question rests on two assumptions: 'first, that the nature of literary reading is necessarily decided by the theorist, who determines in advance what is to count in "the institution of literature"; second, that actual readers are too wayward in their readings to justify serious attention'.[49] Culler indeed mocks the idea that 'one should rush out armed with questionnaires to interview the reader in the street'.[50] Well, *pace* Culler, that is more or less what I have done as part of my preparation for this book – albeit not in the street but on my university campus. Miall has persuasively argued the potential of empirical research to bridge the gulf that has grown between literary studies as practised in the academy and reading as practised outside it: 'To restore contact with the reading of real readers will validate our discipline and provide it, once again, with a living context'.[51] Citing Stephen Greenblatt's dismay that literary scholars are perceived by the public to be 'cut off from the rest of the world, locked

---

47 W.K. Wimsatt and Monroe C. Beardsley, 'The Affective Fallacy', in Wimsatt, *The Verbal Icon: Studies in the Meaning of Poetry* (Lexington, KY: University of Kentucky Press, 1954), 32, 34.
48 Culler, *Structuralist Poetics: Structuralism, Linguistics and the Study of Literature* (London: Routledge, 1975), 123–4.
49 David S. Miall, 'On the Necessity of Empirical Studies of Literary Reading', *Frame. Utrecht Journal of Literary Theory*, 14.2–3 (2000), 43, https://sites.ualberta.ca/~dmiall/MiallPub/Miall_Necessity_1990.htm
50 Culler, 'Prolegomena', 54.
51 Miall, 'Empirical Approaches to Studying Literary Readers: The State of the Discipline', *Book History*, 9 (2006), 309.

in our own special, self-regarding realm', Miall argues that empirical studies might offer 'the key to unlock the door of that prison house'.[52]

Such an approach might also offer a way out of the gaol in which Sade studies continues to languish, and a way to engage more constructively with the genuine concerns and anxieties that reading Sade has provoked for generations of readers. While the physiological responses Wimsatt and Beardsley described may not have seemed particularly pressing issues for the poetry they had in mind in their influential essay, they do take on a new relevance and urgency in relation to works aimed squarely at the body as well as the mind – a dualism which, as we shall see, is untenable when it comes to describing the experience of reading. As Melissa Gregg and Gregory J. Seigworth suggest, 'affect and cognition are never fully separable'.[53] The privileging of 'sense-making' over 'sensations' in literary studies was also, until recently, a feature of cognitive science. So-called 'first-generation' approaches to cognition, influenced by artificial intelligence theory, tended to consider the mind as 'software running independently of its bodily or mechanical hardware'.[54] Increasingly, however, these have given way to 'second-generation' approaches that foreground 'the embodied nature of mental processes', and thus place much greater emphasis on 'experience and emotional responses'.[55] This shift to a more embodied view of cognition in the sciences is now starting to be felt in the humanities, as the growing number of guides and companions exploring the role played by affect and the emotions in various disciplines reflects.[56] While it is still early

---

52 Ibid., 309.
53 Melissa Gregg and Gregory J. Seigworth, 'An Inventory of Shimmers', in *The Affect Theory Reader*, ed. by Gregg and Seigworth (Durham, NC and London: Duke University Press, 2010), 2–3.
54 Alan Richardson, 'Studies in Literature and Cognition: A Field Map', in *The Work of Fiction: Cognition, Culture, and Complexity*, ed. by Ellen Spolsky and Alan Richardson (London: Routledge, 2004), 2.
55 Karin Kukkonen and Marco Caracciolo, 'Introduction: What is the "Second Generation"?', *Style*, 48.3 (2014), 261.
56 To give just a very few indicative examples in or across various disciplines: Melissa Gregg and Gregory J. Seigworth (eds.), *The Affect Theory Reader* (Durham, NC and London: Duke University Press, 2010) and *The Affect Theory Reader 2: Worldings, Tensions, Futures* (Durham, NC and London: Duke University Press, 2023); Sara Ahmed, *The Cultural Politics of Emotion*, 2nd edn. (Edinburgh: Edinburgh University Press, 2014); Sonya E. Pritzker, Janina Fenigsen and James M. Wilce, *The Routledge Handbook of Language and Emotion* (London: Routledge, 2020); Donald R. Wehrs and Thomas Blake, *The Palgrave Handbook of Affect Studies and Textual Criticism*

days, work in cognitive science is providing increasing evidence of what any reader of Sade already knows: that reading fiction is an embodied experience.

This book draws on embodied cognition to explore a form of affect that has largely been neglected in literary criticism: mental imagery. That the 'mind's eye' is a common phrase, but no one talks about a mind's ear, nose, tongue or skin, is as revealing of our ocularcentrism as the very term 'mental imagery'. While Martin Jay has revealed the long history of visual metaphors for the mind from Plato's cave to Locke's *camera obscura* and beyond, few of these have resonated as enduringly as Hume's representation of the mind as 'a kind of theatre, where several perceptions successively make their appearance; pass, re-pass, glide away, and mingle in an infinite variety of postures and situations'.[57] The same metaphor has, for example, been adopted by neuroscientists such as Bernard Baars in order to explain the nature of consciousness,[58] although Daniel Dennett has condemned the 'ghostly dualism' of what he describes as the 'Cartesian theater'.[59] According to this Cartesian theatre, as Susan Blackmore elaborates,

> We seem to imagine there is some place inside 'my' mind or brain where 'I' am. This place has something like a mental screen or stage on which images are presented for viewing by my mind's eye [...] The show in the Cartesian Theatre is the stream of consciousness, and the audience is me.[60]

While Blackmore and Dennett reject this view of consciousness, they are obliged to admit that the theatrical metaphor has a 'natural appeal'

(London: Palgrave Macmillan, 2017); Patrick Colm Hogan, Bradley J. Irish and Lalita Pandit Hogan, *The Routledge Companion to Literature and Emotion* (London: Routledge, 2022); Kaisa Koskinen, *Translation and Affect: Essays on Sticky Affects and Translational Affective Labour* (Amsterdam: John Benjamins, 2020) and Séverine Hubscher-Davidson, *Translation and Emotion: A Psychological Perspective* (New York and Abingdon: Routledge, 2018).

57 David Hume, *A Treatise of Human Nature*, ed. by David Fate Norton and Mary Jane Norton (Oxford: Oxford University Press, 2000), 165.

58 Baars claims that 'all unified theories of cognition today are theater models' (*In the Theatre of Consciousness: The Workspace of the Mind* (New York: Oxford University Press, 1997), ix).

59 Daniel Dennett, *Consciousness Explained* (Boston, MA and London: Little Brown, 1991), 107.

60 Susan Blackmore, *Consciousness: An Introduction*, 2nd edn. (London: Routledge, 2010), 54–5.

– that 'it may feel like this'.[61] The experiments of psychologists from Roger Shephard to Stephen Kosslyn have indeed shown that the mind's eye is more than just a 'feeling' or a figure of speech, and that the creation of 'depictive' mental imagery is an intrinsic part of mental processing.[62] As Kosslyn and his colleagues moreover make clear, this imagery is not limited to the visual field:

> Although visual imagery is accompanied by the experience of 'seeing with the mind's eye', auditory mental imagery is accompanied by the experience of 'hearing with the mind's ear,' and tactile imagery is accompanied by the experience of 'feeling with the mind's skin,' and so forth.[63]

As their own work reflects, however, discussions of mental imagery have tended to focus on the visual at the expense of the other senses both in the research conducted by psychologists and neuroscientists and in broader debates about consciousness.

Although the experience of some form of mental imagery is common to almost all readers of fiction, it has never been of much interest to literary critics. In what was until recently the only monograph devoted to the subject, Ellen J. Esrock observes 'the widespread presumption in literary studies that considerations of a reader's visual imaging have no value'.[64] As pioneering as her own study was in addressing this imaging, the absence of any reference to other forms of imagery, such as the auditory or tactile, inevitably creates a rather reductive view of reading as a strictly visual process. While literary critics, inspired by developments in embodied cognition, are only now beginning to explore other forms of mental imagery, philosophers and psychologists have for some time been reflecting on the question of what happens to us when we read. If, as Alan Tonnies Moore and Eric Schwitzgebel point out, 'opinions diverge radically among both philosophers and

---

61 Ibid., 54, 55.
62 See Roger Shephard and J. Metzler, 'Mental rotation of three-dimensional objects', *Science*, (1971), 701–703; and Stephen M. Kosslyn, William L. Thompson and Giorgio Ganis, *The Case for Mental Imagery* (New York: Oxford University Press, 2006).
63 Kosslyn et al., *The Case for Mental Imagery*, 4.
64 Ellen J. Esrock, *The Reader's Eye: Visual Imaging as Reader Response* (Baltimore, MD: Johns Hopkins University Press, 1994), vii.

psychologists',[65] this may be because such opinions have in the past been largely, if not entirely, reliant on introspection. Thus, while Wittgenstein reports, 'I simply read, have impressions, see pictures in my mind's eye, etc. I make the story pass before me like pictures, like a cartoon story',[66] and Calvino describes reading as a 'mental cinema' in which we see scenes 'unfolding before our eyes',[67] Sartre conversely plays down the role of visualization in the act of reading:

> Je lis un roman. Je m'intéresse vivement au sort du héros qui va s'évader de prison, par exemple. J'apprends avec beaucoup de curiosité les moindres détails de ses préparatifs de fuite. Pourtant les auteurs sont d'accord pour faire remarquer la pauvreté des images qui accompagnent ma lecture. De fait, la plupart des sujets en ont fort peu et très incomplètes [...] Bref, les images apparaissent aux arrêts et aux ratés de la lecture. Le reste du temps, quand le lecteur est bien pris, il n'y a pas d'image mentale. Nous avons pu le constater sur nous-mêmes à bien des reprises et plusieurs personnes nous l'ont confirmé.
>
> [I am reading a novel. I take a lively interest in the fate of the hero who is about to escape from prison, for example. I gather the slightest details of his escape preparations with great curiosity. Yet authors concur in pointing out the poverty of images that accompany my reading. In fact, most subjects have few of them and very incomplete ones at that [...] In short, images appear in the interruptions and misfires of reading. The rest of the time, when the reader is caught up in it, there is no mental image. We have been able to try this out on ourselves on several occasions and several others have confirmed this to us.][68]

For Sartre, images only appear when reading stops, when the reader looks back on the events of the novel he is reading. William H. Glass similarly dismisses the idea that it is possible to read and visualize at the same time: 'It also takes concentration, visualization does – takes slowing down, and this alone is enough to rule it out of novels, which are never waiting, always flowing on'.[69] More recently, Peter Kivy

---

65 Alan Tonnies Moore and Eric Schwitzgebel, 'The Experience of Reading', *Consciousness and Cognition*, 62 (2018), 57.
66 Ludwig Wittgenstein, *Zettel*, 2nd edn. (Oxford: Blackwell, 1981), 43.
67 Calvino, *Six Memos for the Next Millenium*, trans. by Geoffrey Brock (London: Penguin, 2016), 102.
68 Jean-Paul Sartre, *L'Imaginaire: Psychologie phénoménologique de l'imagination* (Paris: Gallimard, 1966), 126–7.
69 William H. Glass, *Fiction and the Figures of Life* (Boston: Nonpareil Books, 1979), 42.

dismisses the 'Lockean, Addisonian idea' that 'silent reading produces a kind of theatrical performance before the mind's eye' on the basis that 'simple introspection reveals that a running display of mental "images" is palpably not what the silent reader of novels and other fictional narratives experiences'.[70] For Kivy, the inner sense activated by the reading of fiction is not visual but aural: 'It is not a movie or a play in the mind's eye: it is a story telling in the mind's ear'.[71] If his misplaced confidence in the universality of his own experience reveals the pitfalls of a purely introspective approach, he nonetheless provides a useful reminder that we need to reflect on the aural experience of reading: as J.O. Urmson had earlier claimed, 'in reading a literary work to oneself, one is simultaneously performer and audience, just as when one plays a piece of music to oneself'.[72] Kivy's insistence on the importance of the mind's ear when reading is moreover corroborated by recent scientific research that shows that 'silent reading activates inner speech'.[73] When we read, we perform the text and listen to that performance in our mind's ear.

While Urmson's musical analogy confines the performative aspect of reading to the aural domain, others have imagined this performance in more holistic terms. Wolfgang Iser argues that representation is a 'performative act' which prompts the reader 'to repeat the very same performance out of which it arose'.[74] He represents the reader in simultaneously passive and active terms when he claims,

> the required activity of the recipient resembles that of an actor, who in order to perform his role must use his thoughts, his feelings, and even his body as an analogue for representing something he is not [...] For the duration of the performance we are both ourselves and someone else.[75]

---

70 Peter Kivy, *The Performance of Reading: An Essay in the Philosophy of Literature* (Oxford: Blackwell, 2009), 59.
71 Ibid., 63.
72 J. O. Urmson, 'Literature', in *Aesthetics: A Critical Anthology*, ed. by George Dickie and Richard Sclafani (New York: St Martin's Press, 1977), 337.
73 Marianne Abramson and Stephen D. Goldinger, 'What the Reader's Eye Tells the Mind's Ear: Silent Reading Activates Inner Speech', *Perception & Psychophysics*, 59.7 (1997), 1059–68.
74 Wolfgang Iser, *Prospecting: From Reader Response to Literary Anthropology* (Baltimore, MD: Johns Hopkins University Press, 1993), 236, 243.
75 Ibid., 244.

This tension between the passive and the active is echoed by the psychologist, Richard Gerrig, who draws on the metaphors of 'performing' and 'being transported' in his attempt to capture the reader's experience of fictional worlds. Gerrig, however, is not entirely satisfied by either metaphor, suggesting that 'being transported projects an undue aura of passivity' while 'the performance metaphor appears to presuppose too active an involvement of conscious attention'.[76] Although both metaphors place the reader within the fictional world, Gerrig curiously never considers mental imagery in the course of his study, as if reading were an escape from the senses rather than an escape into them. His is not the only study that invokes reading as immersion while ignoring, or marginalizing, the sensory aspect such immersion implies. Victor Nell, who draws on the equally immersive image of being 'lost in a book', similarly underestimates – at least initially – the role played by mental imagery in the reading process. Rather like Sartre and Glass, Nell at first assumes mental imagery to be a hindrance to readerly immersion. Drawing on his own introspection, he understands reading to be an act of cognition rather than imagination, in which 'propositions liberate the reader from the vagueness of imaginings', and hypothesizes that for other readers 'ludic reading is more likely to be a propositional than an imaginal process'.[77] His hypothesis, however, does not survive first contact with his fellow readers. Discussing the matter with others, he hears accounts of reading that describe seeing the action of a story 'like a movie', and, in the case of horror fiction, a scary movie: 'I get terribly frightened. I see something standing behind me, I feel it, I look around'.[78] Faced with this empirical evidence, Nell concludes to his own surprise that for these readers, 'imagery is an essential aspect of the reading experience for all of them, good and poor imagers alike'.[79]

Having been content to leave the reader's mind in the hands of psychologists and philosophers for several decades, literary critics and theorists, particularly those working in the field of narratology, have in the last two decades joined the conversation about the lived experience

---

76 Richard Gerrig, *Experiencing Narrative Worlds: On the Psychological Activities of Reading* (New Haven, CT: Yale University Press, 1998), 19.
77 Victor Nell, *Lost in a Book: The Psychology of Reading for Pleasure* (New Haven, CT: Yale University Press, 1988), 217, 220.
78 Ibid., 290, 299.
79 Ibid., 246.

of reading. The shift from a classical narratology founded on the text alone to a more cognitive approach has led to increasing interest in the empirical study of literary response – or 'psychonarratology'[80] – and to the kind of 'ludic reading', or reading for pleasure, that literary studies had largely ignored in the past. Building on the work of Nell and Gerrig, theorists such as David Herman and Marie-Laure Ryan have explored the ways in which readers construct and inhabit 'storyworlds', with the latter also drawing on Kendall Walton's theory of reading as a form of 'mental simulation', a process by which readers project themselves into the minds of characters within fictions. Alluding to Walton's claustrophobic evocation of a fictional spelunking expedition,[81] Ryan observes,

> In the spelunking example, mental simulation goes far beyond the attribution of thought to characters; it creates a rich sensory environment, a sense of place, a landscape in the mind. In a reading situation, it executes the incomplete script of the text into an ontologically complete, three-dimensional reality. To the performer of the simulation, the word cave does not simply evoke its lexical definition of 'natural underground chamber' but awakens all its connotations of darkness, dampness, rough texture, earthy smell, silence occasionally interrupted by the noise of dripping water, and whatever else the simulator may associate with the mental image of the cave.[82]

As Ryan suggests here, readers project themselves into the bodies as well as the minds of fictional characters. Anežka Kuzmičová, with evidence adduced from recent work in experimental psychology, has brought further attention to the ways in which narratives trigger 'motor simulation', or 'motor resonance', in readers: 'the actual covert movement that has been unequivocally proven to occur when isolated literal (i.e., non-metaphorical, non-idiomatic) sentences referring to

---

80 A term coined by Marisa Bortolussi and Peter Dixon in their *Psychonarratology: Foundations for the Empirical Study of Literary Response* (Cambridge, UK: Cambridge University Press, 2003).
81 Kendall Walton, 'Spelunking, Simulation, and Slime: On Being Moved by Fiction', in *Emotion and the Arts*, ed. by Mette Hjort and Sue Laver (New York: Oxford University Press, 1997), 37–49.
82 Marie-Laure Ryan, *Narrative as Virtual Reality: Immersion and Interactivity in Literature and Electronic Media* (Baltimore, MD: Johns Hopkins University Press, 2001), 112.

bodily movement are processed'.[83] As she makes clear, readers' somatic experiences of fictional worlds extend far beyond the exteroceptive senses of sight, sound, smell, taste and touch:

> readers, by means of their embodied minds, are physically present in the imaginary world of the story in ways beyond exteroception, with *the motor and proprioceptive modes* (the senses of limb and organ position, velocity, effort, acceleration, balance, etc.) just as exposed to vicarious stimulation as the exteroceptive senses.[84]

If it is still early days for embodied cognition approaches to literature, with the work of Kuzmičová and others such as Guillemette Bolens and Terence Cave still mapping the terrain,[85] the case for such an approach is already a powerful one. So far work in this field has been focussed on setting out approaches and methodologies, but the next stage is evidently to apply the insights gleaned to readings of particular literary texts. Given the force with which Sade's fiction speaks to the body, and the range of affective responses it elicits, it seems an ideal candidate to test the merits of an embodied approach.

The aim in the following chapters is therefore firstly to contextualize the depiction of the senses within Sade's fiction, and secondly to explore the responses of actual readers to those depictions. While the former employs the traditional model of literary criticism, namely a lone researcher and a pile of books, the latter evidently requires outside help. In this regard I was fortunate enough to be able to call upon actual readers in the form of students on the French and Comparative Literature programmes at Queen Mary University of London. But what to ask these readers? And how to ask them? Armed with the requisite institutional ethics approvals for research with human participants, I have over the years asked various groups of students to fill out questionnaires eliciting

---

83 Anežka Kuzmičová, 'The Words and Worlds of Literary Narrative: The Trade-off Between Verbal Presence and Direct Presence in the Activity of Reading', in *Stories and Minds: Cognitive Approaches to the Theory of Narrative*, ed. by Lars Bernaerts, Dirk de Geest, Luc Herman and Bart Vervaeck (Lincoln, NE: University of Nebraska Press, 2013), 114.
84 Ibid., 115.
85 See, for example, Guillemette Bolens, *The Style of Gestures: Embodiment and Cognition in Literary Narrative* (Baltimore, MD: Johns Hopkins University Press, 2012), Terence Cave, *Thinking with Literature: Towards a Cognitive Criticism* (Oxford: Oxford University Press, 2016) and Anežka Kuzmičová, 'Literary Narrative and Mental Imagery: A View from Embodied Cognition', *Style*, 48.3 (2014), 275–93.

their responses to extracts from a range of literary works. It is always on a strictly voluntary basis, and the questionnaires are anonymous. This book draws on the completed questionnaires of two groups of respondents: the first group read an extract from 'Eugénie de Franval', a short story from *Les Crimes de l'amour*, and the second an extract from *Justine, ou les Malheurs de la vertu*. As should already be clear, I do not take the affective force of Sadean fiction lightly, and so students were duly and repeatedly warned of the nature of the episodes they were about to read. After reading the extract, they were asked to reply to a series of questions about the mental imagery they experienced as they read, with a particular focus on what they saw in their mind's eye and heard in their mind's ear. While self-reporting has its limitations,[86] it unquestionably has its insights too, and these will be brought to bear on the first two chapters in particular.

The myth of a statue coming to life at the hands of its creator seems an appropriate place to start a book about the embodied nature of our aesthetic experiences. Chapter 1 thus begins by exploring the myth of Pygmalion in Ovid and eighteenth-century retellings of Ovid before turning to Sade's version of the story in 'Eugénie de Franval'. It pays particular attention to a scene in which young Eugénie performs as a living statue for a libertine, Valmont, who touches himself as he looks at her. This chapter accordingly explores the relationship between the visual and the tactile in Sade's text and beyond, and reveals what the questionnaire respondents saw when they, like Pygmalion, brought a figure of fantasy to life. Chapter 2 examines the aural and kinaesthetic aspects of reading. It begins by showing the somatic power attributed to reading and listening in eighteenth-century fiction, including works by Sade, before concentrating on a scene from *Justine* in which the heroine is raped by the monk, Sévérino. Adducing evidence from the questionnaires once again, this chapter shares what the respondents heard when they read this scene, before investigating the disturbing ways in which the passage invites a kinaesthetic or motor response. Drawing

---

86   Kuzmičová, who stresses both the necessity of introspection and the usefulness of self-reporting questionnaires, acknowledges that 'it may be difficult to determine how much of the verbalized readerly experience really is elicited in the course of reading (online) and how much of it arises during the process of retrieval (offline) used to fill out the questionnaire' (in 'The Words and Worlds of Literary Narrative', 121).

on conceptions of empathy past and present, and recent research in neuroscience, this chapter suggests there is unsettling evidence that readers inhabit scenes of violence as perpetrators and victims rather than as bystanders.

The last two chapters draw on my own experiences as a translator and teacher of Sade respectively. Chapter 3 reflects on the role of the body in both the study and practice of translation, and draws on the embodied experiences of other translators in their encounters with challenging material. After briefly surveying previous attempts to translate Sade into English, it revisits my past experience translating the *120 Journées de Sodome* with my colleague Thomas Wynn. Continuing the tour of the senses, this chapter recalls some of the smells evoked in and by the process of translating the scatological passages in the novel. For the purposes of this book, however, I also wanted to capture afresh some of the mental imagery evoked by the translation of violence; I therefore returned to Sodom to retranslate a passage that I had, in any case, never quite shaken off. Finally, Chapter 4 reflects on the role of the body in learning, and on the pedagogies championed by feminist thinkers such as bell hooks and Jane Gallop. Drawing on the quite different form of embodied pedagogy on display in *La Philosophie dans le boudoir* as a model of how not to teach, this chapter reflects on my own experiences in the university classroom and examines the challenges Sade, and pornography more broadly, pose for instructors and students alike.

The aim in all these chapters is not just to read Sade, but to read readers reading Sade. Such an approach requires doing all the things that literary critics, and Sade scholars in particular, have been loath to do. It requires being subjective, anecdotal, introspective, emotional, but also empirical. While we are taught to be wary of the anecdotal, it would be a mistake for me to ignore the evidence accumulated over years spent listening to students describing their reactions to Sade. Although 'research-informed teaching' has long been a buzzword within the academy, there has been rather less discussion of 'teaching-informed research' – particularly within departments delivering literature programmes. But as Jane Gallop notes in defence of an 'anecdotal theory' that 'honors the uncanny detail of lived experience', it is often the case that 'theorizing arises out of the pedagogical encounter'.[87] As this book makes clear, my own theorizing and thinking not just about Sade but about the roles of teacher, translator and critic have been fundamentally shaped by that encounter. I am aware that my use of empirical methods, and neuroscientific research, may seem ironic given my criticism of the scientific claims made by literary studies in the past. The difference, however, is that I make no such claims in this book. Science, here, is in service of the subjective. This is an unapologetically personal book, and one that I hope feels human rather than clinical in its approach. The 'with' in its title, and in the title of each chapter, is intended to reflect the way this book enlists Sade in its exploration of reading, but also to convey the sense that reading him never feels like a solitary exercise. For the reader, as for the teacher and translator, Sade remains an inescapable presence.

---

87 Jane Gallop, *Anecdotal Theory* (Durham, NC: Duke University Press, 2002), 6.

1. Looking and Touching with Eugénie

Comme un morceau de cire entre mes mains elle est,
Et je lui puis donner la forme qui me plaît.

[Like a piece of wax between my hands she is
And I can give her any form I please.]

Molière, *L'Ecole des femmes*

Introduction

Where better to begin an exploration of embodied reading than a retelling of the story of Pygmalion? Sade's 'Eugénie de Franval', the closing story of *Les Crimes de l'amour*, may not have been original in drawing on Ovid for inspiration: reflecting on Pygmalion's spectacular 'invasion of French arts and letters', Mary Sheriff observes, 'many statues did come to life in eighteenth-century France'[1] both on the stage, from ballet to opera and drama, and on the page, from philosophical treatises to poetry and fiction. Sade's originality, however, resides in his characteristic willingness to expose his readers to what remains implicit or latent in more polite versions of the tale – and, crucially, to invite those readers to play their part in bringing the story and its characters to life. Although the story of Pygmalion has over the centuries been viewed principally as a myth of artistic creation, it is equally a myth of reception, and one which provides a compelling account both of what art can do to us, and what we can do to art. While it may appear, at first,

---

1   Mary D. Sheriff, *Moved by Love: Inspired Artists and Deviant Women in Eighteenth-Century France* (Chicago, IL: University of Chicago Press, 2004), 141.

to be a story with a happy ending, at its heart is a transgression awaiting a punishment: like Eve, Pygmalion touches and tastes forbidden fruit – an object intended for the eye rather than the hand. Over the course of the eighteenth century, this sense of transgression increasingly comes to the fore in retellings of the myth, culminating with Sade's own dark version of the tale. This chapter will thus begin by tracing the roots of 'Eugénie de Franval' in Ovid and eighteenth-century retellings of Ovid before turning to Sade's own reimagining of the myth of Pygmalion as a tale of incest. It will pay particular attention to an extraordinary scene which sheds light – literally – on the embodied nature of our encounters with art: Eugénie's transformation into a living statue for the viewing pleasure of a libertine named Valmont. As well as Valmont's unambiguously embodied reaction to this spectacle, this chapter will examine the responses of twenty-first-century readers as reported in questionnaires, and thus reveal not just what Valmont sees, but what we see as we watch Valmont watching Eugénie. Drawing on eighteenth-century theories and practices of viewing statues, and nineteenth-century concerns about Pygmalionism, or 'statue love', the chapter will turn from looking to touching before addressing more recent anxieties about the uncontrollable urge to touch that pornography aims to inspire in its consumers. Although 'Eugénie de Franval' is a far from pornographic text, it is one that speaks to our susceptibility to pornography as well as art, and to the ways in which the visual may be linked to the tactile in the act of reception. In Sade's hands, the myth of a statue that comes to life serves as a reminder that spectators and readers are themselves made of flesh not stone.

Before Eugénie: Palincests

Transgressive desire is at the very heart of the *Metamorphoses*, which for eighteenth-century French readers constituted the sole source of the myth of Pygmalion, and one transgression or violation almost inevitably begets another in Ovid's poem. Taken in isolation – as it has been in countless depictions and adaptations ever since – the story of Pygmalion might seem to end well, with the sculptor marrying his beloved and being blessed with a daughter, Paphos. Michael Paraskos indeed alludes to 'the happy-ever-after resolution of their tale' and declares 'There is nothing quite like it in *Metamorphoses*'.² Taken within its original context, however, the episode describes an example of deviant masculinity: Pygmalion's love for his statue leads him into folly, as he dresses it in clothes and adorns it with jewellery, but he is saved from ridicule by Venus's intervention. As Charles Segal notes, this good fortune raises the question of whether he is 'a lucky fool or a creative genius'.³ Ovid's Pygmalion is certainly more fortunate than his antecedents in Greek versions of the tale, whose infatuation with a statue leads to their descent into madness; he is also, it transpires, more fortunate than his own descendants. In the *Metamorphoses*, Pygmalion's aberration is both framed by and tied to female criminality: he is driven to celibacy by his horror at the behaviour of the Propoetides, whose defiance of Venus is doubly punished as they are turned first into prostitutes and then into stone. This petrification of women then gives way to its reverse as Pygmalion's statue is transformed from ivory into living flesh, but that is not the end of the story. The tale of Pygmalion is immediately followed by that of Myrrha, his great-granddaughter, who commits incest with her father Cinyras before being transformed into a tree.

The two stories are inextricably, and disturbingly, tied: as J. Hillis Miller observes, 'The narrative of Myrrha's incestuous love for her father is a retrospective reading of the story of Pygmalion'.⁴ According to such a reading, Pygmalion is the father as well as the husband of his transformed statue:

> To sleep with her is to sleep with his own daughter. Pygmalion avoided the painful encounter with the otherness of other persons in ordinary human relations. But a relation in which there is no otherness, in which the same mates with the same, is, precisely, incest. Poor Myrrha pays for the sins of her great-grandfather by repeating his crime in her infatuation with her father.⁵

The story of Myrrha is more than just a reading of the tale of Pygmalion, however: it is a retelling, or reimagining, of that story from the female

---

2   Michael Paraskos, 'Bringing into Being: Vivifying Sculpture through Touch', in *Sculpture and Touch*, ed. by Peter Dent (Farnham: Ashgate, 2014), 65.
3   Charles Segal, 'Ovid's Metamorphic Bodies: Art, Gender, and Violence in the *Metamorphoses*', *Arion: A Journal of Humanities and the Classics*, 5.3 (1998), 18.
4   J. Hillis Miller, *Versions of Pygmalion* (Cambridge, MA: Harvard University Press, 1990), 10.
5   Ibid., 10–11.

perspective of the statue. Myrrha's story moreover brings her nameless and silent great-grandmother to life in a way that Pygmalion cannot – imbuing her with a mind and voice as well as body. In so doing it exposes Pygmalion's fantasy as a nightmare, one which culminates in Myrrha being stripped of her humanity and condemned to an existence that is neither life nor death. In another echo of her ancestor, Myrrha too creates great beauty, as the bark that encases her lignified body splits to give birth to Adonis.

Although it is dwarfed by Myrrha's story in Ovid's poem, it was the tale of Pygmalion that captured the European imagination in the early modern period. In the seventeenth century, as the epigraph to this chapter reflects, the myth was primarily mined in both French and Spanish literature for its comic possibilities. It notably provided the inspiration for a popular plot best described by the title of one of its early manifestations – and the eventual subtitle of Beaumarchais's *Le Barbier de Sévillle* (1773): 'La Précaution inutile' (1655), Paul Scarron's French version of a short story by María de Zayas entitled 'El prevenido engañado' (1637). Christophe Martin identifies five key elements of the storyline: the jealousy of an ageing bourgeois gentleman who regards women as untrustworthy; the buying of a young girl for the express purpose of eventually marrying her; the sequestration of the girl from the outside world; the refusal to educate the girl and, finally, the unsuccessful nature of the enterprise.[6] In this variation of the Pygmalion myth, the young girl replaces the statue as the object to be transformed into the perfect woman – perfect, like the statue, in her innocence and ignorance. For these ageing gentlemen, as for Ovid's sculptor, the impossible dream is thus revealed to be a woman with the mind of a child. Throughout the seventeenth century, from Cervantes's 'El Celoso extremeño' [The Jealous Estremaduran] (1613) to Molière's *L'Ecole des femmes* (1662), these gentlemen are always the butt of the joke, and the failure of their plans their richly deserved humiliation. While the same joke is still being told a century later in *Le Barbier de Séville*, Beaumarchais's play displays some of the ambivalence that increasingly comes to the fore in eighteenth-century retellings of the Pygmalion myth

---

6   Christophe Martin, 'Agnès et ses sœurs : belles captives en enfance, de Molière à Baculard d'Arnaud', *Revue d'Histoire littéraire de la France*, 2 (2004), 343–5.

in prose fiction – an ambivalence that suggests the story of Myrrha has not entirely been forgotten.

As Aurélia Gaillard has shown, the tale of a statue coming to life proved particularly appealing to eighteenth-century philosophers interested in the role played by the senses in the acquisition of knowledge – an interest which this book evidently shares.[7] In one of these retellings, Boureau-Deslandes's 'Pygmalion ou la statue animée' (1741), the divinely inspired sculptor creates a statue so beautiful that it becomes 'le spectacle du jour'.[8] However, he soon withdraws it from the public eye and places it in a 'salon isolé' at the end of his garden, where he spends 'les moments les plus agréables de sa vie, seul, occupé de ses pensées' [the most pleasant moments of his life, alone, occupied with his thoughts].[9] While the statue remains a blank in the text, with no physical description provided, the same cannot be said for the salon in which it is placed:

> Ce salon était peint en vert et or, et des lits de repos, un peu éloignés les uns des autres, offraient des asiles sûrs et commodes qui aidaient à la rêverie. Une lumière douce s'y répandait par quatre fenêtres garnies de feuilles de talc, et l'on diminuait encore le jour par des rideaux faits de peaux d'Espagne, qui se tiraient avec des cordons or et vert.
>
> [This salon was painted in green and gold, and daybeds, each a little apart from the others, offered safe and ready sanctuaries which encouraged reverie. A soft light radiated through four windows covered in sheets of talc, and the daylight was further dimmed by curtains of perfumed leather that could be pulled to and fro with gold and green cords.][10]

In marked contrast to the senseless statue at its centre, the salon provides an intensely sensory setting for the spectator which anticipates the private cabinets of libertine fictions such as *Thérèse philosophe* (1748) and *Point de lendemain* (1777).[11] While there may be no mirrors here, the

---

7   Aurélia Gaillard, *Le Corps des statues: Le vivant et son simulacre à l'âge classique (de Descartes à Diderot)* (Paris: Champion, 2003).
8   André-François Boureau-Deslandes, 'Pygmalion ou la statue animée', in *Pygmalions des Lumières*, ed. by Henri Coulet (Paris: Desjonquères, 1998), 56.
9   Ibid., 57.
10   Ibid.
11   In *Thérèse philosophe*, an old courtier has 'un cabinet environné de glaces de toutes parts, disposées de manière que toutes faisaient face à un lit de repos de velours cramoisi, qui était placé dans le milieu' [a cabinet surrounded on all sides by

daybeds offer a variety of visual perspectives as the 'feuilles de talc' and leather curtains soften the light – the latter perhaps adding an olfactory element to the visual feast. As long as the statue remains a statue, touch is suggestively implied rather than explicitly stated; the moment it comes to life, however, Pygmalion's hands follow the example of his roving eyes:

> Plus Pygmalion regardait attentivement, plus il redoublait d'attention : et moins il savait ce qui convenait le plus d'être regardé. Les mains dociles suivent si aisément ce qui a d'abord plu aux yeux, que Pygmalion ne pouvait se lasser de se rendre propres par le toucher, les beautés qu'il avait saisies par des regards ardents. Grands dieux! quelle fermeté! quel embonpoint! Chaque partie avait les charmes et les attraits qui lui sont destinés. Une gorge soutenue des mains de la nature, et qui repoussait celles qu'on lui opposait, une gorge avant-courrière d'autres beautés plus secrètes, engageait Pygmalion à rechercher ces mêmes beautés. À peine put-il s'en assurer. Quels obstacles ne rencontra-t-il point ? Et quel désir de les vaincre!
>
> [The more attentively Pygmalion looked, the more his attention intensified: and the less he knew what was most deserving of his gaze. Docile hands follow so easily what has already pleased the eye, that Pygmalion could not tire of making the charms his ardent looks beheld his own through touch. Ye Gods! Such firmness! Such plumpness! Each part had the charms and graces they are intended to have. Breasts held up by nature's hands, and which pressed against those that approached them, breasts that heralded other, more secret charms urged Pygmalion to seek these same charms out. It was a struggle to possess them. What obstacles did he not encounter? And what desire to overcome them!]¹²

The statue comes – 'je meure'¹³ – within seconds of coming alive, dying a little death at the same moment as her creator. The impossible dream of possessing a woman with the mind of a child is thus realized here,

---

mirrors, angled in such a way that they all faced a daybed of crimson velvet placed in the middle of the room] (anon., *Thérèse philosophe, ou Mémoires pour server à l'histoire du Père Dirrag et de Mademoiselle Éradice*, ed. by Florence Lotterie (Paris: Flammarion, 2007), 169). In *Point de lendemain*, the young protagonist is led to 'une vaste cage, entièrement de glaces' [a vast cage made entirely of mirrors] (Dominique Vivant Denon, *Point de Lendemain, suivi de* Jean-Francois de Bastide, *La Petite maison*, ed. by Michel Delon (Paris: Gallimard, 1995), 95).
12 Boureau-Deslandes, 'Pygmalion', 63.
13 Ibid., 64.

even if in this retelling the mind of the statue soon becomes more than a match for the mind of her creator.

The nightmarish implications of that dream are increasingly explored in subsequent retellings of the Pygmalion myth. In 'Liebman', a story from the hugely popular *Epreuves du sentiment* (1773), Baculard d'Arnaud marries the seventeenth-century comic tradition of the *précaution inutile* with eighteenth-century sentimentalism. It is, it must be said, an unhappy marriage. The story begins with a spectacle of suffering as the narrator's pity and curiosity are aroused by the sight of a man bent over a tomb in a cemetery:

> Aussitôt la pitié s'empare de moi ; je me dis tout de suite : c'est un père infortuné qui pleure un fils unique, un époux qui s'est vu enlever par un trépas inattendu une jeune épouse adorée, un amant que la douleur va réunir à l'objet de sa tendresse.
>
> [Pity immediately takes hold of me; I tell myself straight away – this is an unfortunate father mourning his only son, a husband who saw his young and much adored wife taken from him by an unexpected demise, a lover who pain will reunite with the object of his devotion.]¹⁴

The impossibility of distinguishing between a father mourning his child and a husband or lover mourning his beloved prefigures the blurring of roles in the story to come. Liebman, as his name suggests, represents male love as if it were all one and the same.

Seeing only fakery in society – 'que des simulacres, et jamais d'objets réels' [only simulacra, and never real objects] (121) – Liebman ironically yearns to create a simulacrum of his own: 'j'aurais souhaité être un autre Pygmalion, et animer une statue qui m'eût consacré son entière existence' [I would have liked to be another Pygmalion, bringing to life a statue that had devoted its entire existence to me] (122). Turning his back on the outside world, he creates a rural idyll filled with 'les fleurs les plus belles et les plus odoriférantes' [the most beautiful and most fragrant flowers] (123). All that is missing from this Eden is an Eve, although Liebman himself alludes to the figure of Armida, who holds Rinaldo captive in her enchanted garden in Tasso's *Gerusalemme liberata*

---

14 François-Thomas-Marie Baculard d'Arnaud, 'Liebman, histoire allemande', in Henri Coulet (ed.), *Pygmalions des Lumières* (Paris: Desjonquères, 1998), 114. Subsequent in-text citations refer to this edition.

(1581). Eve is indeed introduced in the form of Amélie, the newborn daughter of one of Liebman's gardeners. Deviating from the template of the *précaution inutile*, Amélie is not entirely separated from her parents: only her father is banished, as Liebman decrees that 'Amélie ne verra que sa mère et moi' [Amélie will see only her mother and me] (124). Liebman thus creates a perverted family structure in which erotic interests have supplanted paternal ones. Amélie's future husband, not her father, will be the one fortunate enough to hear – and be – the first word she utters: 'Oh! quel plaisir je goûterai à l'entendre former ses premiers sons! Mon nom sera la première parole qui lui échappera' [Oh, the pleasure I shall taste when I hear her make her first sounds! My name will be the first word to escape her lips] (124). When she does indeed babble his name for the first time, the incongruity of his reaction would be comical were it not so disturbing: 'Oui, ma chère, ma divine Amélie, lui disais-je, comme si elle eût pu me comprendre, oui, Liebman est ton amant, ton esclave ; tu es ma maitresse absolue' ['Yes, my dear, my divine Amélie,' I told her as if she could understand me, 'Yes, Liebman is your lover, your slave; you are my absolute mistress'] (125). The same wildly inappropriate romantic language extends to Liebman's paedophilic interactions with four-year old Amélie:

> ses caresses innocentes allumaient dans mon sein un feu qui chaque jour devenait plus dévorant [...] Quand je prenais cette charmante enfant sur mes genoux, c'était alors qu'une langueur délicieuse coulait dans mes veines ; je m'énivrais à longs traits de ma passion ; je brûlais. Un doux frissonnement succédait à cette flamme rapide.
>
> [her innocent caresses lit a fire in my breast that devoured me more each day [...] When I placed this charming child on my knee, a delicious languor flowed through my veins; I became drunk as I imbibed deeply of my passion; I was burning. A sweet trembling succeeded this sudden passion.] (125–6)[15]

As Martin observes, the young girl in seventeenth-century versions of the *précaution inutile* 'n'est pas censée être en elle-même objet de désir mais seulement promesse d'une satisfaction à venir' [is not supposed

---

15 It is difficult to avoid the comparison with the masturbation scene in Nabokov's *Lolita*, in which Humbert attunes his 'masked lust' to the oblivious Dolores's 'guileless limbs' while on the sofa with her (Vladimir Nabokov, *Lolita* (London: Penguin, 1995), 58).

to be an object of desire herself but only a promise of satisfaction to come].[16] Here, however, as the imagery of fire and heat makes clear, Amélie is already an eroticized object.[17] Even if Liebman appears to follow precedent in deferring the consummation of his desire until she is of marriageable age, that semblance of respectability only belies her ongoing subjection to his gaze and touch: 'Ces trésors qui sont sous ma vue, sous mes mains, il viendra un jour où je les posséderai par un engagement légitime' [These treasures which fall under my gaze, beneath my hands, a day will come when I shall possess them by a legitimate commitment] (128).

Liebman's grooming of Amélie is entirely successful in its deceitful manipulation. Raising her in the belief that he is the only man alive, he removes not only any rivals, but the very idea that there could be any rivals until she reaches 'cet âge enchanteur' – the age, we are left to infer from the floral metaphor of a 'belle rose brillante de tout son éclat' [a beautiful rose in all its dazzling splendour] (127), at which she is ready to be plucked. While Amélie's physical transition from child to woman evidently offers a parallel to the metamorphosis of Ovid's statue, it is her mental transition from ignorance to knowledge that provides the *nouvelle* with the dramatic scene of transformation it apparently craves. After much delay as he seeks to be reassured of the steadfastness of Amélie's love, Liebman finally agrees to rouse his princess from her unnatural 'sommeil' [sleep]. Inspired by his friend Rimberg, he concocts a plan designed to allow him the visual pleasure of observing Amélie's awakening. Having drugged her with a sleeping potion, he takes her to a theatre in a nearby town; there, still asleep, she is carried to a box at the opera. Her first response upon opening her eyes and seeing the crowd is to scream, the sensory shock resulting in 'une sorte de révolution' (137) that causes her to slump into Liebman's arms. Much to his relief, Amélie's first sight of another man does not change her feelings towards him: with a reassuring squeeze of the hand, she tells him, 'Ce n'est pas Liebman!'

---

16 Martin, 'Agnès et ses sœurs', 349.
17 On the imagery of fire in erotic discourse see Peter Cryle, *The Telling of the Act: Sexuality as Narrative in Eighteenth- and Nineteenth-Century France* (Newark, DE: University of Delaware Press, 2001), 49–95.

Although Amélie had never seen another man prior to this point, she had been seen by one. Apparently unable to resist showing off his good fortune, Liebman had repeatedly hidden Rimberg in his garden for the latter to observe Amélie in secret. It is when Liebman sees Rimberg 'plongé dans l'extase' [plunged into ecstasy] by the sight of Amélie that he truly feels 'la valeur de mon trésor' [the value of his treasure] (134). For all his solipsism, it is his homosocial desire to see Amélie through the eyes of another man that ultimately renders his precaution *inutile*. Rimberg predictably proves to be the snake in Liebman's Eden, his deceit leading to Amélie's departure and Liebman's despair. When the couple are finally reunited and reconciled, and all obstacles to their marriage have been overcome, Amélie dies on the way to her wedding; Liebman too is allowed to die once he has shared his story with the narrator. While the latter presents this as a tragic ending, and describes himself and Liebman as kindred spirits and fellow 'cœurs sensibles' [sensitive souls] (170), the way in which the marriage is aborted at the last possible moment is striking. Although the narrator offers no criticism or judgement of Liebman, mourning him as 'l'homme le plus malheureux, et le plus digne de ma pitié et de ma tendresse' [the most unfortunate man, and the most worthy of my pity and my tenderness] (170), one is left to infer an author less blind to the transgressiveness of Liebman's desire for Amélie – an author willing to take this transgressiveness to the very brink, but not quite to step over the edge.[18]

Eugénie and Myrrha

In the 'Idée sur les romans', which serves as a preface to *Les Crimes de l'amour*, Sade offers qualified praise of Baculard:

> D'Arnaud, émule de Prévost, peut souvent prétendre à le surpasser ; tous deux trempèrent leurs pinceaux dans le Styx ; mais d'Arnaud, quelquefois, adoucit le sien sur les [fleurs] de l'Élysée ; Prévost, plus énergique, n'altéra jamais les teintes de celui dont il traça *Cleveland*.

---

18   In subsequent editions of the story, a few lines are added in a rather different tone which reinforce the sense of an author distancing himself from his sentimental narrator: they allude to a foolish banker who fails in his own attempt to carry out the same 'projet singulier' [singular project] (170) attempted by Liebman.

[D'Arnaud, a disciple of Prévost, may often lay claim to surpassing him; both dipped their paintbrushes in the Styx; but d'Arnaud, at times, tempered his own with Elysian flowers; the more vigorous Prévost never diluted the colours with which he painted *Cleveland*.] (*Idée* 28)

Sade's indebtedness to 'Liebman' in 'Eugénie de Franval' is evident. Franval raises a newly-born child to be his lover, keeping her away from the world – and one of her parents – for the first seven years of her life, but their ultimately doomed relationship ends in both their deaths. Noting these close similarities in plot, Katherine Astbury argues that 'Eugénie de Franval' is a 'direct parody'[19] of Baculard's tale, and Sade's story certainly does to the sentimental tale what *Justine* had earlier done to the sentimental novel. Once again, Sade uses the tools of sensibility, most notably its scenes of suffering virtue and melodramatic language, to expose its thinly veiled dark eroticism. While Astbury argues that Sade's *nouvelles* reflect his disapproval of the sentimental tale as a genre, I would suggest his parody of Baculard, and of sensibility more generally, should not be reduced to an act of pure hostility. As Margaret Rose notes, parodies are often '*both* critical of *and* sympathetic to their "targets"'[20] and Sade clearly found in the literature of sensibility not just a target but a template to attack other targets beyond the literary excesses of a particular genre.[21]

As striking as the similarities in plot between 'Liebman' and 'Eugénie de Franval' may be, the differences between them reflect Sade's willingness to go further than his contemporaries: in Sade's hands, the *précaution* will no longer be *inutile*. The child Franval raises to be his lover is his own daughter, her mother is the parent excluded from any contact for seven years, and the sexual relationship between father and daughter is consummated long before it is brought to an end by their respective

---

19 Katherine Astbury, 'The Marquis de Sade and the Sentimental Tale: *Les Crimes de l'amour* as a Subversion of Sensibility', *Australian Journal of French Studies*, 39.1 (2002), 57.

20 Margaret A. Rose, *Parody: Ancient, Modern, and Post-Modern* (Cambridge, UK: Cambridge University Press, 1993), 47.

21 Several years later, 'Eugénie de Franval' would serve as a template for Sade's *La Marquise de Gange*, which also tells a story of an abused wife but without the incest plot: the latter similarly features a long-suffering virtuous wife ultimately killed by poisoning, a good priest sent into exile as punishment for his interference, an unsuccessful attempt to make a virtuous wife commit an act of infidelity and the counterfeiting of letters to incriminate her.

acts of suicide. Where 'Liebman' only flirts with incest, 'Eugénie de Franval' commits to it explicitly, and in so doing weaves together the stories of Pygmalion and Myrrha. Whereas Liebman is perversely presented as an almost saintly figure by Baculard's narrator, Franval is very much the libertine. A page after declaring that the sole aim of his story is 'Instruire l'homme et corriger ses mœurs' [To instruct men and correct their mores] (*E* 423), Sade's narrator makes it clear some people are incorrigible: 'Un désordre d'imagination, au-delà de tout ce qu'on peut peindre, était le premier défaut de Franval : on ne se corrige point de celui-là' [A disorder of the imagination beyond anything one could describe was Franval's key flaw: it was not one that can be corrected] (*E* 423–4). As with Ovid, each generation in 'Eugénie de Franval' is seen to influence the next: Franval's abuse of his daughter is tied to his own moral corruption as a boy. His father, described as a 'grand partisan des sophismes à la mode' [a great afficionado of the latest sophisms], had taught him to 'penser *solidement*' [think *solidly*] and given him 'les ouvrages qui pouvaient le corrompre plus vite' [those works which could more quickly corrupt him] (*E* 424).

It is telling that the father is represented here as the sole influence on his son, just as Franval will be the sole influence on his daughter. While 'Liebman' stages an extreme version of Rousseau's 'éducation négative', with Amélie in her early years kept in a state of total ignorance, Franval inverts Rousseau to ensure that virtue, rather than vice, is kept out.[22] Although Eugénie initially gains 'aucune connaissance des principes religieux ou moraux' [no knowledge of religious or moral principles]

---

22 Rousseau lays out the principle behind his 'éducation négative' in a letter to Christophe de Beaumont: 'Si l'homme est bon par sa nature, comme je crois l'avoir démontré, il s'ensuit qu'il demeure tel tant que rien d'étranger à lui ne l'altère ; et si les hommes sont méchants, comme ils ont pris peine à me l'apprendre, il s'ensuit que leur méchanceté leur vient d'ailleurs ; fermez donc l'entrée au vice, et le cœur humain sera toujours bon' [If man is naturally good, as I believe I have demonstrated, it follows that he remains so as long as nothing foreign to him spoils him; and if men are wicked, as they have been at pains to show me, it follows that their wickedness comes from elsewhere; close thus the way to vice, and the human heart will always be good]. Accordingly, a negative education is 'celle qui tend à perfectionner les organes, instruments de nos connaissances, avant de nous donner ces connaissances et qui prépare à la raison par l'exercice des sens' [one which serves to perfect our organs, instruments of our knowledge, before providing us with knowledge, and which paves the way for reason by the exercise of the senses] (*Œuvres complètes*, ed. by Bernard Gagnebin and Marcel Raymond, vol. 4 (Paris: Gallimard, 1969), 945).

(*E* 427), from the age of seven she acquires a team of tutors in subjects including writing, drawing, poetry, natural history, astronomy and anatomy, and languages including Greek, English, German and Italian. Her private 'conférences' with her father, however, are where she is inculcated with his 'maximes sur la morale et sur la religion' (*E* 429). In these formative years for her daughter, Madame de Franval is entirely excluded as Eugénie is kept in an apartment adjoining her father's quarters. Eugénie, however, is not deprived of female company, Franval providing her with a whole retinue of women and girls including 'une gouvernante de beaucoup d'esprit, une sous-gouvernante, une femme-de-chambre et deux petites filles de son âge, uniquement destinées à ses amusements' [a governess of great wit, an under-governess, a chambermaid and two little girls of her own age solely there for her amusement] (*E* 428–9). As this reflects, the misogyny here is directed specifically at the figure of the mother. It is not just that Madame de Franval, and the religious values she represents, are deprived of any part in Eugénie's intellectual formation. Her role in the physical formation of her daughter is also challenged in a manner which seeks to place her on the biological as well as intellectual periphery – challenged not least by her daughter, who in conversation with her father refers contemptuously to 'cette femme que tu appelles la tienne, cette créature qui, selon toi, m'a mise au monde' [that woman you call your own, that creature who, according to you, brought me into the world] (*E* 430). Eugénie dissociates herself from her mother first by associating the latter exclusively with her father ('la tienne'), and second by her apparent scepticism ('selon toi') regarding the circumstances of her own birth. With Franval's encouragement, the ties between mother and daughter are severed so that the two exist in relation to each other only as rivals for male attention. In marked contrast to Ovid's Myrrha, filled with horror at the prospect of becoming her mother's rival, Eugénie embraces her role as antagonist and sees it to its logical, murderous conclusion.

As Sheriff observes, the story of Pygmalion 'invests reproductive power in the male creator'.[23] In Sade's version of the myth, but also in his other works, that investment of power in the father entails an attempt to divest the mother of any significant role in reproduction. It

---

23 Sheriff, *Moved by Love*, 143.

is not just that Sade is 'mother-hating',[24] as several commentators have observed, but mother-erasing. Another Eugénie, the young student of the 'instituteurs immoraux' [immoral teachers] in *La Philosophie dans le boudoir*, finds that her feelings for her parents – hatred of her mother and love for her father – are a reflection of the different parts they played in her conception: as Saint-Ange explains, the 'foutre' [come] secreted by the woman 'ne fait qu'élaborer, il ne crée point, il aide à la création sans en être la cause [...] uniquement formés du sang de nos pères, nous ne devons absolument rien à nos mères' [only elaborates rather than creates, it assists in creation without being the cause of it [...] formed solely from our fathers' blood, we owe absolutely nothing to our mothers] (*PB* 24–5). As Eric Le Grandic has shown, the original manuscript of 'Eugénie de Franval' similarly suggests a biological basis for loving one's father but not one's mother:

> Si donc l'obligation de la vie est un des motifs qui doivent fonder l'amour filial, ce n'est qu'au père que nous devons de la reconnaissance ; lui seul a désiré de donner le jour à l'enfant. Ne sais-je pas assez de physique et d'anatomie pour être bien certaine que l'embryon n'est formé que de la semence du père ; celle de la mère n'y coopère en rien. Elle ne crée rien. Je ne suis donc formée que de toi, cher ami.
>
> [If the imperative of life is one of the motives upon which filial love should be founded, it is only the father who deserves our gratitude; he alone wished the child to see the light of day. Do I not know enough of physics and anatomy to be quite certain that the embryo is formed only from the father's seed; that of the mother contributes in no way to it. She creates nothing. I am thus formed only from you, dear friend.] (*E* 437 n. 30)

As Chiara Gambacorti notes, 'Franval exemplifie parfaitement l'usage manipulateur qui pouvait être fait de l'animalculisme à des fins de prévarication sexiste' [Franval perfectly exemplifies the manipulative use to which animalculism could be put in the service of sexist misconduct].[25] On the final page of the scroll of *Les 120 Journées de Sodome*, in notes for what appears to be another work, Sade goes even further. A list of subjects to be discussed by an unnamed 'comte' in a

---

24 Jane Gallop, 'The Liberated Woman', *Narrative*, 13.2 (2005), 90.
25 Chiara Gambacorti, 'Un Pygmalion des Lumières? Inceste et émancipation féminine dans « Eugénie de Franval »', in *Sade et les femmes*, ed. by Stéphanie Genand (Paris: Itinéraires, 2014), 121.

series of letters includes a 'proof' which imagines not just the erasure of mothers but of all women:

> preuve que les femmes sont inutiles aux grandes vues de la nature, qu'elle a pu faire naître les premiers hommes sans femmes, que les femmes ont été trouvées par les hommes qu'ils en ont joui, et que l'espèce s'est ainsi multipliée, mais qu'elles ne sont qu'un second moyen de la nature qui la prive d'agir par ses premiers moyens et par conséquent l'outrage en quelque manière et qu'elle serait bien servie, si en exterminant toutes les femmes, ou en ne voulant jamais jouir d'elles on obligeait la nature pour reperpétuer l'espèce d'avoir recours à ses premiers moyens.
>
> [proof that women are useless in the great scheme of Nature, who was able to bring about the birth of the first men without women, that women were discovered by men who took their pleasure with them, and that the species thus multiplied in this manner, but that they are only a second means which deprives Nature of her first means and as a result offends her in a way, and that Nature would be well served if, in exterminating all women, or no longer taking our pleasure with them anymore, we made her resort to her first means for the repropagation of the species.][26]

Like the bond between mother and daughter in 'Eugénie de Franval', the bond between mothers and Mother Nature is severed here, and the two cast as antagonists. In these extraordinary lines, women are unwelcome interlopers, usurping Nature by producing children, as Sade imagines an entirely male future. This is Pygmalion on a grand scale, with all women shunned by all men and permanently consigned to history.

'Eugénie de Franval' draws much more directly than its eighteenth-century predecessors on the story of Myrrha, its parody of 'Liebman' often giving way to a parody of the Ovidian original. This is particularly evident in the way that Sade rewrites the conversation between father and daughter regarding potential suitors. When asked by Cinyras which of her suitors she would like to marry, Myrrha is silent at first before replying 'similem tibi' [one like you] – an echo of her ancestor Pygmalion's 'similis mea [...] eburnae' [one like my ivory [girl]].[27] Franval, by

---

26   Sade, 'Liste des différents objets de moral traités dans les lettres du comte', *Les 120 Journées de Sodome*, manuscript, Ms-15877 Réserve, Bibliothèque de l'Arsenal. The reference to letters suggests these could be early notes for *Aline et Valcour*, Sade's only epistolary novel, with the Comte a possible prototype for Blamont.

27   Ovid, *Metamorphoses*, ed. by R. J. Tarrant (New York: Oxford University Press, 2004), X. 364 [p.297], X. 276 [p.293].

contrast, offers himself as suitor to Eugénie but disingenuously leaves her free to choose another if she so wishes. When asked by her mother whether she would like to marry the young and wealthy M. de Colunce, Eugénie follows Myrrha's example in answering equivocally that she desires whatever her father wishes for her. However, while Myrrha cannot bring herself to speak of her feelings either to her father or to her nurse, Eugénie, groomed by Franval, has no such difficulty in declaring her love. Choosing him over other men on the grounds that she is entirely his 'ouvrage' [creation] and therefore belongs to him alone, she also suggests that Franval has 'de doubles raisons pour m'aimer' (*E* 437), and would thus never abandon her as other men would.[28] In this, Eugénie echoes Myrrha seeking to defend incest to herself: lamenting the 'accident' of her birthplace, Myrrha claims,

> [...] there exist
> Peoples, it's said, where sons will marry mothers
> And daughters fathers, and their doubled love
> Increases duty's bond.[29]

Myrrha's appeal to other cultures in her defence of incest also anticipates the moral relativism in which Sadean libertines, including Franval, frequently indulge. When the priest Clervil describes conscience as a book on which Nature inscribes our duties, Franval responds by exchanging this metaphor for one which recalls Arnolphe's lines about Agnès: he describes conscience as 'une cire molle qui prend sous nos doigts toutes les formes' [a soft wax which in our fingers takes on every form] (*E* 453), varying from one human being to the next, and one culture to the next. Franval's words also echo a striking passage from La Mettrie's *L'Homme machine* (1748) in which a mother's imagination is said to have the power to mould her unborn foetus:

---

28 In *Aline et Valcour*, the Bohemian chieftain, Brigandos, makes a similar case for incest: 'il ne blesse en rien le pacte social ; il établit plus d'union dans les familles, il en double et resserre les liens' [it does no harm at all to the social pact; it establishes a greater unity within families, it redoubles and tightens the ties] (*AV* 834–5).

29 'gentes tamen esse feruntur, in quibus et nato genetrix et nata parenti iungitur, ut pietas geminato crescat amore' (Ovid, *Metamorphoses*, X. 331–34 [p.295]). The translation is from Ovid, *Metamorphoses*, trans. by A.D. Melville (Oxford: Oxford University Press, 1986), 235.

> c'est par la même voie que le fétus ressent l'impétuosité de l'imagination maternelle, comme une cire molle reçoit toutes sortes d'impressions ; & que les mêmes traces, ou Envies de la Mère, peuvent s'imprimer sur le fétus
>
> [it is by the same means that the fœtus feels the effect of its mother's impetuous imagination, as soft wax receives all sorts of impressions, and that the same traces or desires of its mother can be imprinted on the foetus][30]

While both Molière and La Mettrie employ the metaphor to describe the fashioning of another human being, Franval uses it to describe an act of self-fashioning, suggesting our conscience is something that we can shape as we wish. Eliding the fact that he has deprived Eugénie of that ability, he thus implies that the act of incest too is an act of self-fashioning – that what he has done to his daughter is the same as what he has done to himself, because he and she are one and the same. In his response to Franval, Clervil is not armed with the strongest of counter-arguments by his author: arguing that even if there is no 'conscience universelle' there is at least one which is 'nationale', Clervil's condemnation of incest manages to downgrade it from a crime to a misdemeanour:

> il n'en reste pas moins démontré que ce délit, qui n'est tel que chez quelques peuples, ne soit certainement dangereux, là où les lois l'interdisent [...] Si vous eussiez épousé votre fille sur les bords du Gange, où ces mariages sont permis, peut-être n'eussiez-vous fait qu'un mal très inférieur.
>
> [it nonetheless remains the case that this offence, which is only one among some peoples, is certainly dangerous where it is forbidden by law [...] Had you married your daughter on the banks of the Ganges, where such marriages are permitted, perhaps you would have committed a much lesser evil.][31] (*E* 454)

---

30 Julien Offray de la Mettrie, *L'Homme machine* (Leiden: Élie Luzac, 1748), 79. The translation is from La Mettrie, *Machine Man and Other Writings*, ed. by Ann Thomson (Cambridge, UK: Cambridge University Press, 1996), 29.

31 Cf. Sade's *Histoire de Juliette*, in which the eponymous (anti-)heroine defends (and commits) incest with the same relativistic logic: 'ce qui est toléré dans les trois quarts de la terre, peut-il faire un crime dans l'autre quart?' [what is tolerated throughout three quarters of the earth, can it be a crime in the other quarter?] (*HJ* 571).

While Myrrha and Sade's libertines (and priests) expound the argument that morality varies from one place or culture to the next, their moral relativism extends beyond the geographical or cultural in distinct ways. Myrrha contrasts the prohibition on human incest with the acceptance of incest between animals, and laments,

> [...] Human nicety
> Makes spiteful laws. What nature will allow
> Their jealous code forbids.[32]

Assertions of the naturalness of incestuous relations are also a commonplace in Sade's fiction, such as Dolmancé's description of them as 'les plus douces unions de la nature [...] celles qu'elle nous prescrit, et nous conseille le mieux' [the sweetest unions in nature [...] those she prescribes and recommends most highly to us] (*PB* 52) in *La Philosophie dans le boudoir*. Although in other matters Dolmancé similarly draws a comparison with animals,[33] on the question of incest he draws one with human history. Evidently presenting a very different account of our origins to the one that opens the *Metamorphoses*, he moreover takes great delight in drawing attention to the part played by incest in the Christian account of our beginnings:

> comment l'espèce humaine, après les grands malheurs qu'éprouva notre globe, put-elle autrement se reproduire que par l'inceste ? n'en trouvons-nous pas l'exemple et la preuve, même dans les livres respectés par le christianisme, les familles d'Adam et de Noé purent-elles autrement se perpétuer que par ce moyen ?
>
> [how could the human species, after the great woes suffered by our globe, have reproduced itself other than by incest? Do we not find an example and proof of this in the very books respected by Christianity – could the families of Adam and Noah have perpetuated themselves in any other way?] (*PB* 52)

---

32 'humana malignas cura dedit leges, et quod natura remittit inuida iura negant' (Ovid, *Metamorphoses*, X. 329–31 [p.295]). Translation by Melville (235).
33 Challenging the idea that children should submit to their parents' will, Dolmancé tells Eugénie, 'écoutons la nature sur un objet aussi intéressant, et que les lois des animaux, bien plus rapprochées d'elle, nous servent un moment d'exemples' [let us listen to Nature on such an interesting matter, and let the laws of animals, much closer to her, serve for a moment as examples] (*PB* 35).

Franval similarly defends incest as part of human history in his conversation with Valmont: 'L'univers n'est-il donc pas rempli de ces faiblesses ? N'a-t-il pas fallu commencer par-là pour peupler le monde ? et ce qui n'était pas un mal, alors, peut-il donc l'être devenu ?' [Is the universe not filled with such weaknesses? Was it not necessary at the beginning in order to populate the world? And if it was not a crime then, could it be one now?] (*E* 439).[34] Echoing Dolmancé in his mockery of Christianity, Franval sarcastically claims that his incestuous relationship has been inspired by the Biblical example of Lot and that he is simply following the example of his 'héros', before exclaiming 'Ah ! mon ami, la folie de Pygmalion ne m'étonne plus' [Oh! My friend, Pygmalion's madness no longer astonishes me!] (*E* 439), thereby explicitly recasting Ovid's tale as a story of incest. Lot, however, resembles Cinyras rather than Franval given that he sleeps with his daughters unwittingly, and is depicted as the victim of his daughters' plotting rather than a plotter himself. In keeping with Sade's claim that incest was once necessary for the propagation of humanity, it is also worth noting that Lot's daughters are not, like Myrrha or Eugénie, motivated by lust but by a desire to maintain their bloodline in the absence of other men – and of a mother turned into a statue of sorts for a transgressive gaze of her own.

Lights, *Camera*, Reaction

Although the story of Lot and his daughters has often been offered as a cautionary tale of the dangers of alcohol, the passage in the Bible uses drunkenness above all to exculpate Lot of knowingly knowing his daughters: on each occasion, 'he perceived not when she lay down, nor

---

34 The pseudo-revolutionary pamphlet in *La Philosophie dans le boudoir* also declares incest to be 'dicté par les premières lois de la nature' [dictated by the first laws of nature] and a part of early human history: 'les premières institutions favorisent l'inceste ; on le trouve dans l'origine des sociétés ; il est consacré dans toutes les religions ; toutes les lois l'ont favorisé' [the first institutions favoured incest; one finds it at the origins of societies; it is consecrated in every religion; every law has favoured it] (*PB 138*). Cf *Aline et Valcour*: 'L'inceste est d'institution humaine et divine. Les premiers hommes durent nécessairement s'allier dans leurs familles' [Incest is an institution both human and divine. The first men by necessity had to conjoin within their families] (*AV 834*).

when she arose'.³⁵ Cinyras – also inebriated – is further protected from knowledge of the incest he is committing with his daughter by 'darkness and black night'.³⁶ This darkness is emphasized at some length, with the moon having fled from the sky, the stars hiding behind black clouds, and Myrrha feeling her way to the bedchamber with one hand while holding onto her nurse with the other. We see nothing of the sex that takes place between them, but we do, possibly, hear something. The only detail given of their encounter is that Cinyras may have called his unknown lover 'daughter' to reassure her, and that she may have called him 'father' – thereby sealing the crime in words and sounds. In a story which Orpheus warns should not be heard by fathers or daughters, incest is thus unseeable but not entirely unsayable: in darkness Myrrha may say what she cannot in daylight.

The same visual restriction applied, at least initially, in 'Eugénie de Franval'. The first edition of *Les Crimes de l'amour* included no description of Eugénie and Franval consummating their relationship, despite the narrative – and Eugénie's entire existence – seemingly building inexorably to that moment. Instead, in an unusually short paragraph, the reader is simply told, 'Cependant Eugénie atteignait sa quatorzième année, telle était l'époque où Franval voulait consommer son crime. Frémissons !... Il le fut' [Meanwhile Eugénie was approaching her fourteenth birthday, the very occasion Franval had chosen to consummate his crime. May we shudder!... It was done] (*E* 430–1). On the surface, the ellipsis here suggests a moment of unspeakable horror – a space for narrator and reader to shudder or tremble together as they contemplate the crime that has been committed. Beneath the surface, however, lurks an invitation to indulge a different kind of trembling – or *frisson* – as readers are left to fill the space with their own visualization. As Peter Cryle has noted, the use of ellipsis to represent – or rather, not to represent – sexual encounters is a commonplace of libertine fiction: a way of 'telling by not

---

35   Genesis 19:33, 35. The protection of Lot's virtue (or what remains of it after his time in Sodom) by rendering him senseless is echoed in the strategy employed by eighteenth-century novelists from Richardson to Sade to ensure their heroines are unconscious during the act of rape through the use of drugs, or fainting, or, as we shall soon see, a blow to the head.

36   'et tenebrae minuunt noxque atra pudorem' [and darkness and the black night diminish shame] (Ovid, *Metamorphoses*, X. 454 [p.300]).

telling'.³⁷ In Sade's more explicit works, ellipses are commonly used to represent fictional characters' arousal, but they also serve as invitations to the reader to share in this arousal. In *La Philosophie dans le boudoir*, for example, the ellipses in Saint-Ange's description of Eugénie de Mistival's body simultaneously suggest her own imagination getting the better of her and an authorial attempt to lure the reader into following suit: 'sa gorge délicieuse... ; ce sont bien les deux plus jolis petits tétons... ; à peine y a-t-il de quoi remplir la main, mais si doux... si frais..., si blancs' [her delectable bosom..., they really are the two prettiest little breasts...; barely enough for a handful, but so soft..., so fresh..., so white] (*PB* 11). Beneath the transparently thin veneer offered by sentimental language, the same dynamic may be discerned in the description of Madame de Franval that immediately follows the ellipsis marking Franval's crime: 'inondée de ses larmes, dans l'abattement de la mélancolie... ses beaux cheveux négligemment épars sur une gorge d'albâtre...' [in floods of tears, beaten down by melancholy... her beautiful hair carelessly strewn over breasts of alabaster] (*E* 431). Sade's narrator, like Saint-Ange, ogles – and invites his reader to ogle – a woman whose suffering he claims only adds to her charms.

There is more than meets the eye, however, in the three little dots marking the moment incest is first committed in the original edition of 'Eugénie de Franval'. The ellipsis is simultaneously rhetorical and literal, marking as it does an omission of several paragraphs from the manuscript version in which the scene of incest is described. If the version of 'Eugénie de Franval' we read today includes those paragraphs, it is not down to Sade but to Maurice Heine, the pioneering twentieth-century editor of Sade's works. Heine transplanted these paragraphs from the manuscript held in the Bibliothèque Nationale, and inserted them into his 1933 edition of *Œuvres choisies et pages magistrales du Marquis de Sade*; virtually every subsequent editor – and translator – has followed his example ever since.³⁸ As he did on a larger scale when he turned *Les Infortunes de la vertu* from a draft into a published work a few years earlier, Heine chooses here to say more than Sade, and in so

---

37 Cryle, *The Telling of the Act*, 166.
38 The only notable exception to this rule is Eric Le Grandic's scholarly edition, which includes the passage in question within the scholarly apparatus rather than in the main body of the text.

doing arguably inverts the traditional subordination of editor to author.[39] The 'Eugénie de Franval' we know today is thus no longer Sade's alone: in a manner that rather echoes the plot of the *précaution inutile*, Sade ultimately fails in his attempt to keep his creation to himself, as it falls into the hands of a younger rival.

There is a particular irony in an author choosing not to share a scene in which his main character is choosing not to share his creation with the world. The restored paragraphs thus tell two tales simultaneously of an author creating a spectacle for himself alone. And in marked contrast to the nocturnal darkness into which Cinyras and Myrrha are plunged, the scene between the incestuous lovers takes place in daylight, in a carefully lit and furnished setting which recalls Boureau-Deslandes's 'salon isolé': 'un salon voluptueux dont les jours étaient adoucis par des gazes, et dont les meubles étaient jonchés de fleurs' [a voluptuous salon, with gauze across the windows to soften the light, and furniture strewn with flowers] with a 'trône de roses' [throne of roses] in the middle (*E* 432). Eugénie, 'comme ces vierges qu'on consacrait jadis au temple de Vénus' [like those virgins once chosen to serve in the temple of Venus], is also dressed to be seen, as she is led to her throne. She is then joined by Franval as the dialogue conveys not just words but touches and looks:

> Quel être dans l'univers peut être plus digne que toi de ces faibles attraits que tu désires… et que déjà tes mains brûlantes parcourent avec ardeur ? Ne vois-tu donc pas, au feu qui m'embrase, que je suis aussi pressée que toi de connaitre le plaisir dont tu me parles ?
>
> [Who in the world could be more worthy than you of these paltry charms you desire… and over which your burning hands are already roaming with such ardour? Do you not see, by the fire blazing within me, that I am as keen as you to know the pleasure you speak of?] (*E* 432)

Like Pygmalion feeling his statue warming to his touch, Franval's hands figuratively transform Eugénie from cool ivory to warm flesh, her exclamations announcing the urgency of her desire. The narrative then turns from her words to his actions, as he overcomes 'tous les obstacles' to take her virginity. Equally suggestively, we are told Eugénie

---

39   For further discussion of Heine's blurring of the roles of author and editor see Will McMorran, 'Intertextuality and Urtextuality: Sade's Justine Palimpsest', *Eighteenth-Century Fiction*, 19.4 (2007), 368–70.

is 'ouverte à toutes sortes d'impressions' and that in the days that follow she is taught all the pleasures of love: 'Franval lui en apprit tous les mystères, il lui en traça toutes les routes [...] elle aurait voulu le recevoir dans mille temples à la fois' [Franval taught her all of love's mysteries, showed her all its paths [...] she would have received him with open arms in a thousand temples at a time] (*E* 432).

The originally published version of 'Eugénie de Franval' thus seems to censor itself at the very moment towards which it had been building, the narrative climax lost along with the sexual climax upon which it relies. The effect is not dissimilar to the ellipsis which marks the repeatedly deferred rape of the virginal heroine in *Justine*, which finally takes place only once she is knocked unconscious, leaving her unable to narrate the pivotal moment in the narrative. While the more explicit *Justine* nonetheless goes on to depict a whole series of graphic scenes after its moment of ellipsis, the original edition of 'Eugénie de Franval' continues to keep sex behind closed doors even as it teases the reader with the promise of the illicit. When Madame de Franval decides to see if her suspicions are true regarding her husband and daughter, she hides in a 'cabinet voisin' [neighbouring cabinet] in the latter's apartment:

> L'instant arrive [...] Eugénie est avec son père ; plusieurs bougies restent allumées sur une encoignure, elles vont éclairer le crime... L'autel est préparé, la victime s'y place, le sacrificateur la suit... Mme de Franval n'a plus pour elle que son désespoir, son amour irrité, son courage... Elle brise les portes qui la retiennent, elle se jette dans l'appartement.
>
> [The moment arrives [...] Eugénie is with her father; several candles remain lit on a corner table, ready to illuminate the crime... The altar is prepared, the victim takes her place upon it, her sacrificer follows her... Mme de Franval is left with nothing but her despair, her outraged love, her courage... She breaks down the doors that hold her back, she bursts into the apartment.] (*E* 444–5)

Ellipsis follows ellipsis as the narrator builds the suspense only for Madame de Franval's entrance to put an end to the titillation. The religious language of sacrifice and immolation from the earlier scene returns, now as a crime committed on an altar. The scene is once again carefully lit, but why? On the surface, one could say this is for the benefit of Madame de Franval, ironically placed here in the position of virtuous voyeur. But it is also for the benefit of the reader: visualizing a scene unfolding in total darkness is as difficult as seeing one, particularly in the absence of any other sensory cues. We see nothing of Cinyras and Myrrha for a reason, even if we hear their possible murmurs of 'father' and 'daughter'.

As the scene of her defloration shows, Eugénie is made to be seen as well as heard.[40] Sade kept his most spectacular use of Eugénie to himself, however, in another scene omitted from the original edition and restored – or intercalated, depending on your point of view – by Heine. When Valmont agrees to seduce Franval's wife, he does so on condition that Franval allow him 'un seul quart d'heure avec Eugénie' [just a quarter of an hour with Eugénie] (E 459). When Franval demurs, Valmont insists on this as an advance payment for his services but reassures him that he will only look and not touch: 'je n'aspire qu'aux charmes de voir Eugénie seule et de l'entretenir une minute' [I aspire only to the delights of seeing Eugénie alone and talking with her for a minute] (E 459). In the original edition, the reader is then told simply,

> Tout était disposé pour satisfaire Valmont ; et son tête-à-tête eut lieu près d'une heure dans l'appartement même d'Eugénie.
> – Eh bien ! es-tu content ? dit Franval, en rejoignant son ami.
>
> [Everything was arranged for Valmont's satisfaction; and his tête-à-tête lasted almost an hour in Eugénie's own apartment.
> 'Well, then! Are you satisfied?' asked Franval, rejoining his friend.]
> (E 462)

Since Heine, however, Sade's story has been published with the following passage inserted between those two paragraphs:

> Là, dans une salle décorée, Eugénie, nue sur un piédestal, représentait une jeune sauvage fatiguée de la chasse, et, s'appuyant sur un tronc de palmier, dont les branches élevées cachaient une infinité de lumières disposées de façon que les reflets, ne portant que sur les charmes de cette belle fille, les faisaient valoir avec le plus d'art. L'espèce de petit théâtre où paraissait cette statue animée se trouvait environné d'un canal plein d'eau et de six pieds de large, qui servait de barrière à la jeune sauvage et l'empêchait d'être approchée de nulle part. Au bord de cette circonvallation, était placé le fauteuil ; un cordon de soie y répondait : en

---

40 Eugénie also makes a spectacle of herself – 'dans le déshabillé le plus coquet et le plus élégant' [in the most flirtatious and elegant négligée] (E 457) – in her failed seduction of Clervil.

manœuvrant ce filet, il faisait tourner le piédestal en telle sorte que l'objet de son culte pouvait être aperçu par lui de tous côtés, et l'attitude était telle, qu'en quelque manière qu'elle fût dirigée, elle se trouvait toujours agréable. Caché derrière une décoration du bosquet, [Franval] pouvait à la fois porter ses yeux sur sa maîtresse et sur son ami, et l'examen, d'après la dernière convention, devait être d'une demi-heure...Valmont se place... il est dans l'ivresse, jamais autant d'attraits ne se sont, dit-il, offerts à sa vue ; il cède aux transports qui l'enflamment. Le cordon, variant sans cesse, lui offre à tout instant des attraits nouveaux : auquel sacrifiera-t-il ? lequel sera préféré ? il l'ignore ; tout est si beau dans Eugénie ! Cependant les minutes s'écoulent ; elles passent vite dans de telles circonstances ; l'heure frappe : le chevalier s'abandonne, et l'encens vole aux pieds du dieu dont le sanctuaire lui est interdit. Une gaze tombe, il faut se retirer.

[There, in a specially decorated room, Eugénie, naked on a pedestal, represented a native girl wearied by the hunt, and, leaning against the trunk of a palm tree whose high fronds concealed an infinity of lanterns, so arranged that their light fell only on the charms of this beautiful girl, showed off their beauty with the utmost art. The kind of small stage on which this living statue stood was surrounded by a channel six feet wide filled with water, which served as a barrier for the native girl and prevented her from being reached from any direction. At the edge of this barrier, Valmont's armchair was placed; it was fitted with a silk cord: by pulling upon it, he could make the pedestal revolve in such a way that the object of his worship could be viewed from every angle, and her pose was such that whichever way she was turned she always remained agreeable to behold. Franval, hidden behind the décor of a grove, could at the same time cast his eyes on his mistress and his friend, and the spectacle, as had finally been agreed, was to last half an hour... Valmont takes his seat... he is giddy – never have so many feminine charms been set before him, he says; he surrenders to the excitement which inflames his senses. The cord, constantly varying the view, offers him at every moment new attractions: to which will he make his sacrifice? Which will he choose? He does not know, for everything about Eugénie is so beautiful! Meanwhile the minutes tick by; they pass by quickly in such circumstances; the hour strikes: the Chevalier can contain himself no longer, and the tribute of his love flies towards the feet of the god whose shrine is forbidden to him. A veil descends, and we must withdraw.] (*E* 460)

So having said that Eugénie is made to be seen, I would like to ask you, dear reader, to take a moment to reflect on what *you* saw as you were reading this passage... Did you form a mental picture of Eugénie? Of

Valmont? Of Franval? How much of them did you see? What did they look like? Where were you looking from? Were you in one place, or did you move from one vantage point to another? Was your response purely visual? Or did you hear anything as you were reading?

These were some of the questions I asked a group of thirty-seven first year literature undergraduates immediately before leading a seminar on the text.[41] The results of their questionnaires made it very clear that visualization was integral to their responses at least to this scene. All but two of the thirty-three students who answered the question, 'Did you see anything in your mind's eye as you were reading this scene?', replied in the affirmative.[42] While almost all the students reported visual imagery, when asked to give details almost a third of them initially responded rather laconically along the lines that they simply saw 'The scene as described in the text'. One could interpret this minimalism in different ways: this was not a question that these literature students were likely to have been asked before, and some may therefore have been uncertain how to respond. A certain reticence given the transgressive sexual content of the scene would also be understandable – not every reader will want to say what they have seen in their mind's eye when that may be a naked sixteen-year-old girl and a man masturbating. It is also possible that these particular readers may simply not have seen that much. The subsequent answers of some suggest their visualization of the scene may not have been particularly detailed: one reported seeing the scene 'from a distance' while another described only forming a 'vague' mental picture of the characters. However, some of the further responses of others who initially replied in this minimalist fashion

---

41   The full list of questions, and the full responses of my students, may be accessed via the Digital Appendix. The questions include some relating to auditory imagery that will be addressed in the following chapter. The questionnaires were based on this translation rather than the original French in order to have a larger sample of responses.

42   One of the two who replied negatively gave as a reason that there was too much noise outside the classroom for her to concentrate properly, implying that she would have done so in other circumstances. The same student, when asked where she was observing the scene from nonetheless gave as an answer 'a changing position' suggesting some rudimentary spatial mapping of the scene at least. The other negative respondent rather contradicted herself by answering affirmatively to the subsequent question, 'Did you form a mental picture of Eugénie and/or the other characters in the scene?' Other surveys I have conducted have been in line with this high rate (94%) of visualization among readers.

suggest these students may have felt there was no need to elaborate on the obvious – that they took it as a given (*à la* Wittgenstein) that what we see as readers is simply whatever texts describe. When given more precise prompts regarding the visualization of the characters within the scene, most of these readers provided more precise responses.[43] Overall, the questionnaires offer invaluable insights into the range of mental imagery experienced by a diverse group of readers.

The responses clearly show that Eugénie serves not merely as a spectacle for Valmont in this scene, but for the reader. Every respondent formed an image of Eugénie, while the same was not true of the two men in the scene. To an even greater extent than previous scenes in the story, great care is evidently taken in the text to make Eugénie as dazzling a sight as possible. Once again, lighting is everything as her body is illuminated by the 'infinite' lanterns hidden discreetly in the palm tree, bathing her in a light described by more than one reader as 'warm'. One respondent described the light of the lanterns on Eugénie's body as the most 'vivid' aspect of the scene, and contrasted it with the 'quite blurred' image of Valmont; another saw Franval as 'a dark sinister man hiding in the shadows'. Others too drew attention to the contrast between light and dark: 'The room is dark with a light on her, it is quite colourful where the light is shining, but the rest is dark'. One (female) reader seemed to speak for many when she made the contrast between the spectacle and the spectator within the scene: 'I could see Eugenie straight away as the story began. It was difficult to see or imagine Valmont. I don't know why?!' It seems that the men, out of the spotlight, are more difficult for readers to see. One male reader speculated his gender and orientation may provide an answer at least to his own erasure of the men in the scene: 'My lack of mental picture of the men could be due to an unconscious effort to augment the eroticism of the scene, as a heterosexual man'. As interesting as such speculation may be, the following chapters will suggest that gender and orientation may play less of a role in mental imagery than one might assume.[44] Some other respondents did form pictures of Valmont and Franval, although

---

43 It is evidently possible that such prompts may trigger some additional mental images, or some fleshing out of the images experienced upon a first reading.
44 See Chapter 2, 'Once more, with Einfühlung', and Chapter 4, 'Sade in the Classroom'.

these were quite varied. One described Valmont as being 'dressed well, not in a modern day suit but something like brocade (but minus the flowers and patterns). He also has a necktie', while others saw him as a 'fat, moustachioed man, greedy eyes, perverted grin' or 'old, large, sweaty' or 'wide-eyed and practically drooling'. In 'Eugénie de Franval', which the students had at least in theory read for that week's class, Valmont is in fact described in the text as a thirty-year old with 'une figure charmante' [a charming countenance] (*E* 438). As we shall see time and again both here and in the next chapter, readers do not necessarily follow the script provided by the author.

In the 'petit théâtre' which Franval has created for this scene, Eugénie is both lit from above and raised from below by the pedestal (an object visualized by several respondents) that serves as a stage. Several respondents referred to her nudity, and her pale skin, made paler for some perhaps by the lights upon her. As exposed as she is, however, it is striking how little of her readers reported seeing. The feature most mentioned in relation to Eugénie by far was her hair: while there seemed to be a consensus that her hair was 'long' and 'loose', its colour was variously reported as blonde or dark (black or brown). The disagreement becomes understandable when one takes into consideration that Eugénie is never described in the text beyond Valmont's allusion to her 'beauté bien plus vive que sa mère' [beauty far more striking than that of her mother] (*E* 440). By leaving her blank, Sade invites readers to play Pygmalion and create their own object of desire – one conjured from their own imagination rather than the words on the page. The reader who accepts that invitation, consciously or not, and is stirred by the spectacle of Eugénie on her pedestal, is thus implicated by the same incestuous logic as Franval.

Eugénie's invisibility in the text, if not the reader's imagination, may also reflect her ties to Myrrha, who, unlike the statue Rousseau christened Galatea, is conspicuous by her absence in the visual arts of the eighteenth century.[45] This is in marked contrast to her mother, whose

---

45 On the rare occasions Myrrha is represented in this period, it tends to be as a tree, in depictions of the birth of Adonis. The same applies to earlier representations of her, such as Titian's *The Birth of Adonis* (1505–10?, see https://commons.wikimedia.org/wiki/File:Tiziano,_nascita_di_adone_01.jpg#/media/File:Tiziano,_nascita_di_adone_01.jpg), Luini's *The Birth of Adonis* (1509–10, see https://commons.wikimedia.org/wiki/File:Birth_of_Adonis_by_B.Luini_from_La_Pelucca.jpg#/

introductory portrait includes details such as 'de beaux cheveux blonds flottant au bas de sa ceinture, de grands yeux bleus où respiraient la tendresse et la modestie, une taille fine, souple et légère, la peau du lis et la fraîcheur des roses' [beautiful blonde hair floating down to her waist, big blue eyes that exuded tenderness and modesty, a slender figure, supple and light, skin white as lilies and the freshness of roses] (E 424). Those readers who imagine Eugénie with long blonde hair may be confusing her with her mother, or perhaps simply seeing her as her mother's daughter. Madame de Franval is indeed a much stronger visual presence throughout the text than her daughter, the aforementioned reference to her decorous weeping echoed later in the scene where she implores her husband to put an end to her suffering with his sword:

> Et elle était à genoux, renversée aux pieds de Franval, ses mains saignantes et blessées du fer nu dont elle s'efforçait de se saisir pour déchirer son sein ; ce beau sein était découvert, ses cheveux en désordre y retombaient, en s'inondant des larmes qu'elle répandait à grands flots.
>
> [And she was on her knees, collapsed at Franval's feet, her hands bleeding and wounded by the naked blade which she was striving to grasp in order to plunge into her breast; that fine breast was uncovered, her dishevelled hair tumbling over it, drenched in the floods of tears she wept.] (E 450)

While Eugénie is cast as a statue, her mother is very much a painting, as the narrator confirms when he likens her to 'ces belles vierges que peignit Michel-Ange au sein de la douleur' [those beautiful virgins that Michelangelo painted in the midst of their suffering] (E 431).[46]

If the absence of any physical description of Eugénie could be interpreted as self-censorship on the part of the author, some of the responses to this extract suggest readers too are capable of self-censorship when it comes to visualization. Eugénie's age in particular is likely to be a factor in the way readers today imagine – or refuse to imagine – her. She is sixteen years old at the time she is presented to Valmont as a statue, although that detail may easily be missed even

---

media/File:Birth_of_Adonis_by_B.Luini_from_La_Pelucca.jpg) and Franceschini's several versions of the same scene at the end of the seventeenth century.

46 This detail may have influenced one respondent's visualization of Eugénie as a figure with 'Curly long blonde hair, fair white skin, like those of Renaissance paintings'.

by attentive readers who may not notice that two years have elapsed since the scene in which she loses her virginity. While the question of potential suitors provides a cue to Sade's contemporary readers that Eugénie has now entered the world of adulthood, the responses to the extract suggest that readers today are less like to follow that cue. More respondents tellingly refer to Eugénie as a girl than a woman, reinforcing the sense of transgressiveness in her representation as a naked statue. Those allusions to her as a woman may moreover reflect an attempt to diminish that transgressiveness by (re)imagining Eugénie as an older, and therefore more permissible, object of desire. One reader indeed reported, 'Eugénie was naked as described, but she appeared to be a fully grown woman in my mind as opposed to a teenager'.[47] Readers imagining Eugénie as a girl rather than woman seem to have employed a variety of self-censoring strategies, from covering Eugénie up 'in some places with leaves' or even a 'dressing gown', to concentrating on the face to the exclusion of the body: one respondent 'saw her hair loose and not the rest of her body' while another reported seeing 'Only the face of Eugénie'. One or two others, by contrast, described Eugénie as 'faceless', a reminder that if we are to see her with a face we have to supply that face ourselves. As these examples suggest, some readers of this scene may play Pygmalion in their evocation of Eugénie only to then find themselves playing censor.

It is impossible to know precisely what readers see, if anything, of Eugénie's body. That several reports describe Eugénie as 'slender' (or words to that effect), and one as her having 'almost a perfect body' suggests, however, that some readers give Eugénie a body conforming to a twenty-first-century ideal rather than an eighteenth-century one.[48] It is telling that the only readers who allude directly to Eugénie's body do so in relation to the light, with one alluding to 'the light of the lanterns constantly changing and creating shadows, the girl's body and the light falling on it' and another to 'The lighting exposing the naked Eugénie's

---

47 In class, more than one (male) student has similarly said that they 'aged' Eugénie in their visualization of her to make the scene less inappropriate.
48 Those who completed the questionnaire may have been unaware of that eighteenth-century ideal. By contrast, an erudite *dix-huitièmiste* who read this scene felt her visualization of Eugénie drew from her own 'cultural stock of Galateas', including an 'engraving for Rousseau's Pygmalion' that very much reflects eighteenth-century beauty standards.

breasts'. If we need the light to see the women in Sade's fiction, Barthes suggests that this is because 'les corps des sujets sadiens sont fades' [the bodies of Sadean subjects are dull].[49] Noting Sade's tendency to assert beauty rather than to describe it, through cultural references (such as the one to Michelangelo) or stock phrases such as 'fait(e) à peindre' [worthy of a painting], Barthes claims that beauty in Sade is best understood in theatrical terms:

> le corps sadien est en fait un corps vu de loin dans la pleine lumière de la scène ; c'est seulement un corps *très bien éclairé*, et dont l'éclairement même, égal, lointain, efface l'individualité (les imperfections de la peau, les couleurs mauvaises du teint), mais laisse passer la pure vénusté.
>
> [the Sadean body is in fact one seen from afar in the full light of the stage; it is just a *very well lit* body, the lighting of which, even, distant, erases the individuality (skin blemishes, unsightly complexion) but lets the pure beauty pass through.][50]

There is something a little dazzling about this light, its intensity effacing even as it illuminates, transforming the real into the ideal. Barthes's insight, which he claims came to him after watching a drag show in a Parisian club, resonates with the staging of Eugénie in Franval's own theatrical *mise-en-scène*.

In the same section on 'Le corps éclairé', Barthes makes another claim that is supported by the responses to the extract: 'pour *faire voir* un corps, il faut ou le déplacer, le réfracter dans la métonymie de son vêtement, ou le réduire à l'une de ses parties' [to *show* a body, one has either to displace or refract it in the metonymy of its dress, or to reduce it to one of its parts].[51] As we have already seen, readers tended to describe seeing a part of Eugénie (hair, eyes, face) rather than all of her; it is also revealing that almost every reader who reported seeing Eugénie on her pedestal saw her rotating upon it. As the following chapter will show, this movement – like the lanterns shining down on her – draws the reader's attention. But Eugénie is not necessarily the only one on the move in this scene. Almost half the respondents stated that their viewing position in relation to the scene changed as it unfolded; in an echo of Eugénie's

---

49   Barthes, *Sade, Fourier, Loyola*, 132.
50   Ibid., 132.
51   Ibid., 131.

movement, one even described their own position as 'revolving' around the room. These mobile readers were fairly evenly split between those whose vantage points were aligned with the characters within the scene and those whose vantage points were not, with two readers starting from a 'third person' or independent position but then shifting to Valmont's point of view. Although one or two of the respondents who observed the scene from a fixed position stated they did so from an 'omniscient' or 'bird's eye' perspective, the rest situated themselves within the scene rather than outside it, and independently of the characters – 'as though I was another person watching her in the room'.

The reason for asking the respondents about the vantage points from which they observed the scene was to investigate the ways in which readers situate themselves in relation to the characters within sexual scenes, and to explore what this might tell us about their experience of these scenes. What strikes me most about the results is that only one reader in the whole group saw the scene from Eugénie's perspective at any point (and that reader then shifted to Valmont's point of view), while several saw it from the positions of Valmont and Franval.[52] As one reader put it, 'I had somehow the perspective first from the point of Valmont and then from Franval, but never from Eugenie (in general while I was reading the story I never understood or "felt" from her point of view)'. Even those who did not see the action from the positions of the male characters followed their example in becoming voyeurs themselves. The linguistic focus on these male acts of seeing ('aperçu par lui de tous côtés'; 'porter ses yeux sur sa maîtresse et sur son ami'; 'offerts à sa vue') doubtless encourages the reader to follow suit. As Esrock has persuasively argued, 'readerly imaging is indeed encouraged when fictional characters are engaged in specifically mentioned acts of visual perception. Verbs like *saw, gazed,* and *looked* all suggest there is something to see. A verb like *behold* practically commands the reader to take a look'.[53] It is, however, worth asking whether seeing Eugénie through the eyes of a Valmont means seeing her *as* he does? The visual lexis of perspective and point of view is conflated in everyday life with intellectual or moral position-taking, but is there any evidence that a

---

52 This may be why some readers did not see the male characters: they were seeing from the perspective of these men, rendering them invisible.
53 Ellen Esrock, *The Reader's Eye*, 183.

specific viewing position either reflects or informs a specific attitude? In the responses to this passage, the correlation between the two is not clear: taken collectively, the descriptions of Eugénie by those seeing her from Valmont's visual perspective do not betray or reveal enough information to identify the predominance of any particular moral attitude. What is clear, however, is firstly that some readers adopting Valmont's position did not emulate his objectification of Eugénie, and secondly that other readers emulated his objectification without adopting his position. One reader observing from the vantage point first of Valmont then of Franval described the scene as 'uncomfortable to read' because 'this young girl was a spectacle, like a piece of meat for perverse men'. Although the same reader did imbue Eugénie with aesthetic appeal, visualizing her as 'beautiful', she added that this was not in any 'developed' sense because she found Eugénie 'extremely dislikeable and therefore did not imagine real beauty'. Approximately a third of all respondents described Eugénie less ambivalently in terms that imply aesthetic appreciation (or objectification, to put it less positively) from imagining her looking 'like a Greek goddess' to various other expressions of her beauty.[54] By contrast, only a tenth of respondents described their visualization of Eugénie in terms that suggested resistance to her objectification, from imagining her as 'uncomfortable on the pedestal' to seeing her as having a 'sad face' or as being 'vulnerable' or 'very pale and thin' (as opposed to the more positive 'slender' or 'lean'). For the most part, it seems that these readers read with rather than against the grain in visualizing Eugénie as an erotic object, encouraged perhaps by the examples offered by the men within the scene.

Although Sade's tale is named after Eugénie, it is never really her story. While the narrative shares the contrasting thoughts and feelings of Franval and his wife throughout, we are given very little direct insight into Eugénie's mind. Closeted away by her father, she is largely kept away from the reader as well as her mother, and rather than hear her thoughts we hear only what she tells Franval in conversation. All we really know of her from the narrator is what is needed for the story to unfold: her love for her father and hatred for her mother. She is a

---

54 There was only a hint of ambivalence in two of these, with one describing Eugénie as a 'beautiful young girl' but 'innocent/fragile-looking', and another as 'lean, graceful and slender' but also 'shy'.

complex rather than a person, a gap in the text in mind as well as body. In this respect she is very different to Ovid's Myrrha, whose anguished psyche is at the heart of her tale, from her internal struggles over her incestuous desires to her eventual flight and transformation. As Segal argues, Orpheus's telling of Myrrha's story begins with 'desperate passion, guilt and incest but ends in a gentler sympathy and pathos', and the reader's sympathy for Myrrha grows as her wandering endures, marked by 'her contrite prayer, her mixture of fear of death and disgust with life, and her feeling of being cut off from all creatures, living and dead'.[55] Unlike Eugénie, Myrrha's voice is audible throughout, from her murmured words overheard by her nurse as she attempts to kill herself, to her final plea to the gods for transformation. The reader may read her story in horror, but not in antipathy, and this contrasts with the kind of responses Eugénie arouses in many readers, including the respondent who revealed that her dislike for Eugénie negatively affected her visualization of her.[56]

While readers may not have any difficulty seeing Eugénie as an object, the way in which she is marginalized as a subject seems to affect their ability – or desire – to see through her eyes. She is the only character who is not described in the act of seeing in the statue scene. Just as the light that illuminates her is reflected and refracted, so is the gaze that falls upon her: within the text, Valmont watches Eugénie, while Franval alternates between watching Eugénie and watching Valmont watching Eugénie – and in so doing recalls Liebman watching Amélie through Rimberg's eyes in Baculard's tale. The sense of *mise-en-abîme* only heightens when one includes readers – and above all those who watch Franval watching Valmont watching Eugénie – in this orgy of spectatorship.

Beyond Eugénie: On Touching Statues

The questionnaire results suggest that Valmont in his chair, like Eugénie on her pedestal, becomes part of the spectacle for most readers. While one respondent describes Eugénie as 'untouchable but not unviewable',

---

55 Segal, 'Ovid's Metamorphic Bodies', 29.
56 The same antipathy towards Eugénie was often expressed by students in class, presenting an opportunity for discussion of the ways in which texts may manipulate their readers into 'victim blaming'.

there is no prohibition on Valmont touching himself, and he is thus able to look with his hand as well as his eyes – in a rather different manner to Goethe's lover, who learned to 'see with a feeling eye, feel with a seeing hand'.[57] Sade's scene thus reveals what La Mettrie addressed in slightly more discreet terms when pondering the relationship between vision (and visualization) and the genital organs:

> Pourquoi la vüe, ou la simple idée d'une belle femme nous cause-t-elle des mouvemens & des désirs singuliers ? Ce qui se passe alors dans certains organes, vient-il de la nature même de ces organes ? Point du tout ; mais du commerce & de l'espèce de sympathie de ces muscles avec l'imagination. Il n'y a ici qu'un premier ressort excité par le *beneplacitum* des Anciens, ou par l'image de la beauté, qui en excite un autre, lequel étoit fort assoupi, quand l'imagination l'a éveillé : & comment cela, si ce n'est par le désordre & le tumulte du sang & des esprits, qui galopent avec une promptitude extraordinaire, & vont gonfler les corps caverneux ?

> [Why does the sight, or the mere idea, of a beautiful woman cause singular movements and desires in us? Does what happens then in certain organs come from the very nature of those organs? Not at all, but from the intercourse and sort of sympathy of those muscles with the imagination. All we have here is one spring, excited by the Ancients' 'beneplacitum' or by the sight of beauty, exciting another one, which was very drowsy when the imagination awoke it. And what can cause this except the riot and tumult of the blood and spirits, which gallop with extraordinary rapidity and swell the hollowed-out organs?][58]

In his attempt to show the power of sight – and inner sight – on the body, La Mettrie elides the ways in which the visual can enlist the tactile. Conversely acknowledging the inhibiting power of being seen, Sade writes in his 'Idée sur les romans' that it is the role of the novelist – as opposed to the historian – to show man as he behaves when he is not being watched.[59] Valmont, apparently oblivious to Franval's presence,

---

57 Johann Wolfgang von Goethe, *Roman Elegies and Venetian Epigrams*, trans. by L. R. Lind (Wichita, KS: University Press of Kansas, 1974), 45.
58 La Mettrie, *L'Homme machine*, 78–9; *Machine Man*, 29.
59 'le roman étant, s'il est possible de s'exprimer ainsi, *le tableau des mœurs séculaires*, est aussi essentiel que l'histoire, au philosophe qui veut connaître l'homme ; car le burin de l'une ne le peint que lorsqu'il se fait voir, et alors ce n'est plus lui ; l'ambition, l'orgueil couvrent son front d'un masque qui ne nous représente que ces deux passions, et non l'homme. Le pinceau du roman, au contraire, le saisit dans son intérieur... le prend quand il quitte ce masque' [the novel being, if it may be so expressed, *the portrait of the manners of every age*, is as essential as history to

offers an example of this hidden truth, albeit one which his author ultimately chose not to reveal in published form. As J. Hillis Miller observes in relation to Ovid, Pygmalion is guilty not only of narcissism and incest but 'a strange kind of onanism'.[60] The masturbatory logic of the sculptor's tale, and its eighteenth-century avatars, is made explicit by Sade in a manner which suggests that Ovid's tale serves as well – if not better – as an allegory of pornographic reception as it does artistic creation. It is even more explicit in the original manuscript of 'Eugénie de Franval', where Franval, prior to the statue scene, gives express permission to Valmont to indulge in 'ces voluptés solitaires qu'un amant goute en animant par ses désirs la statue de celle qu'il adore' [those solitary pleasures a lover tastes in animating the statue of the one he adores with his desires] (E 459 n. 62).

Franval is nonetheless careful to protect Eugénie from Valmont's touch, firstly by placing her on a pedestal and secondly, rather extraordinarily, by creating a kind of moat measuring six feet wide.[61] As Victor Stoichita suggests, 'The plinth is to the statue what the frame is to the painting. It belongs neither entirely to the statue nor entirely to the world'.[62] It serves as a barrier between the fictional and the real but does not in itself offer sufficient protection from desiring hands – hence the need for a further barrier against Valmont. Its absence from Ovid's tale, in which Pygmalion places his statue on a couch and touches it 'saepe'

---

    the philosopher who wishes to know mankind; for the graver of one depicts him only when he shows himself, at which moment it is no longer him; ambition, pride cover his brow with a mask which shows us those two passions only, and not the man. The brushstrokes of the novel, on the contrary, capture what is within him... reveal him when he puts down the mask] (*Idée* 29).

60 Miller, *Versions of Pygmalion*, 10.

61 So extraordinary that few readers seem able to compute or visualize it – including me. When I read the text I (re)imagined the canal as a painted blue line. I suspect this was because my mind was unable to get past the sheer implausibility of what it was being asked to visualize, and so settled for a more plausible if makeshift approximation of the original image. The same implausibility may be what leads David Coward to translate the statue scene from house to garden by mistranslating the French: 'dans l'appartement même d'Eugénie' is rendered as 'in the garden of Eugénie's apartment', and the 'salle décorée' as 'a marquee hung with decorations' (Sade, *The Crimes of Love*, trans. by David Coward (Oxford: Oxford University Press, 2005), 280).

62 Victor Stoichita, *The Pygmalion Effect: From Ovid to Hitchcock* (Chicago, IL: Chicago University Press, 2008), 114.

[often],⁶³ reflects the porousness of the line that separates the sculptor from his creation. To touch, or not to touch, statues was indeed a matter for debate throughout the seventeenth and eighteenth centuries. In his account of Bernini's visit to Paris in 1665, Paul Fréart de Chantelou describes the admiration of the Court for a bust by the Italian sculptor: 'Tout le monde considérant la délicatesse du buste, quelqu'un a dit qu'on ne pourrait jamais s'empêcher d'y toucher, qui est par où l'on commence en France à voir les sculptures' [Everyone contemplated the delicacy of the bust, with someone saying no one would be able to stop themselves from touching it, which is how we are beginning to see sculptures in France].⁶⁴ In 1644, John Evelyn records in his diary a visit to a collector of statues in Rome:

> Hence we went to the house of Hippolito Vitellesco (afterward bibliothecary of the Vatican library), who showed us one of the best collections of statues in Rome, to which he frequently talks as if they were living, pronouncing now and then orations, sentences, and verses, sometimes kissing and embracing them.⁶⁵

Although Constance Classen confidently claims that 'many statues were handled this way in the seventeenth and eighteenth centuries',⁶⁶ the fact that Evelyn recorded the encounter suggests something out of the ordinary – a hint of Pygmalionesque eccentricity at the very least. Nonetheless, Vitellesco was far from the only man moved to embrace statues. Viccy Coltman cites the example of Thomas Orde's encounter with the Medici Venus in the Uffizi: 'The doors of the Tribune opened, and in three steps I had the very Venus de Medicis in my arms... why would she not answer the kisses I could not help printing all over her delicate form?'⁶⁷ Richard Wrigley has shown that touching statues (albeit not embracing or talking to them) was 'not unusual' in the Parisian Salon exhibitions prior to the 1780s, when 'works within arm's reach

---

63 Ovid, *Metamorphoses*, X. 254 [p.292].
64 Paul Fréart de Chantelou, *Journal du voyage du Cavalier Bernin en France*, ed. by Ludovic Lalanne (Paris: Gazette des beaux-arts, 1885), 149.
65 *The Diary of John Evelyn*, ed. by William Bray, 2 vols. (New York and London: Walter Dunne, 1901), I, 130.
66 Constance Classen, 'Museum Manners: The Sensory Life of the Early Museum', *Journal of Social History*, 40.4 (2007), 901.
67 Cited in Viccy Coltman, *Classical Sculpture and the Culture of Collecting in Britain Since 1760* (Oxford: Oxford University Press, 2009), 179–80.

of spectators needed protecting from the crowds' and 'small sculptures were placed behind the barrier'.[68]

Even if touching statues was not necessarily unusual in the early modern period, it does not mean that it met with universal approval. There does indeed appear to have been a gap between the practice of museum visitors and the preaching of art critics. Wrigley notes that 'close physical engagement with sculptures is to a large extent invisible from a reading of sculpture criticism',[69] while Geraldine Johnson has shown that those critics who insisted on the superiority of painting over sculpture, such as Vincenzio Borghini, the sixteenth-century art theorist, saw the tactile appeal of sculpture as part of its coarseness: 'Borghini stresses how vulgar it is to judge a sculpture by touching it, as well as derides women who are obsessively drawn to touching and kissing statues'.[70] Two centuries later, Friedrich Schiller similarly identifies touch as a primitive or 'animal' sense as opposed to the refined senses of sight and sound: 'The object of touch is a force which we endure; the object of the eye and the ear is a form which we create. So long as Man is still a savage he enjoys merely with the senses of feeling'.[71] Touch, according to Schiller, acts upon us, while sight and sound allow us to act. Classen places Schiller's view in opposition to Herder, arguing that the latter upheld 'The importance of touch for the aesthetic appreciation of sculpture' and 'considered sculpture to be the highest form of art precisely because it was perceptible to the sense of touch'.[72] For Herder, however, touch is imagined rather than enacted by the spectator of statues:

> Consider the lover of art sunk deep in contemplation who circles relentlessly around a sculpture. What would he not do to transform his sight into touch, to make his *seeing* into a form of *touching* that feels in the dark? He moves from one spot to another, seeking rest but finding none [...] For this reason, he shifts from place to place: his eye becomes his

---

68 Richard Wrigley, 'Sculpture and the Language of Criticism', in *Augustin Pajou et ses contemporains*, ed. by Guilhem Scherf (Paris: Musée du Louvre, 1999), 78–9.
69 Wrigley, 'Sculpture', 79.
70 Geraldine A. Johnson, 'Touch, Tactility, and the Reception of Sculpture in Early Modern Italy', in *A Companion to Art Theory*, ed. by Paul Smith and Carolyn Wilde (Oxford: Blackwell, 2002), 66.
71 Friedrich Schiller, *On the Aesthetic Education of Man*, ed. and trans. by E. M. Wilkinson and L. A. Willoughby (Oxford: Oxford University Press, 1982), 195.
72 Classen, 'Museum Manners', 902.

hand and the ray of light his finger, or rather, his soul has a finger that is yet finer than his hand or the ray of light. With his soul he seeks to grasp the image that arose from the arm and the soul of the artist. Now he has it! The illusion has worked; the sculpture lives and his soul feels that it lives. His soul speaks to it, not as if his soul sees, but as if it touches, as if it feels.[73]

As Rachel Zuckert notes, according to Herder 'we employ imaginative touch, or, specifically, the sense of sight as "guided" by touch or as a substitute for touch'.[74] For Herder, imagined touch is not a poor substitute for the real thing, but a more refined form of interaction, and one with its own advantages: as Gaiger points out, 'Literal touching of cold marble or bronze would destroy the constitutive illusion of animate life on which figurative sculpture depends'.[75]

Herder's description of the circling spectator, longing to 'transform his sight into touch', is a study of restless sensual yearning, even if he is adamant that the 'pure and beautiful forms of sculpture' could arouse desire 'only in a beast'.[76] Valmont is evidently just such a beast, rotating Eugénie from the comfort of his armchair rather than circling her. No doubt inadvertently, however, Herder's circling spectator recalls a much older story (well known in the eighteenth century) of men admiring a statue from two distinct angles. Lucian's *Erotes* (now attributed to Pseudo-Lucian) relate a debate between Callicratidas, an Athenian, and Charicles, a Corinthian, over the relative attractions of women and boys. When Callicratidas and Charicles visit the Cnidus temple housing Praxiteles' Aphrodite, they find 'a door on both sides for the benefit of those also who wish to have a good view of the goddess from behind'. Charicles, seeing the statue from in front, runs to her and 'started to kiss the goddess with importunate lips', but when the two men go 'round

---

73 Johann Gottfried Herder, *Sculpture: Some Observations on Shape and Form from Pygmalion's Creative Dream*, ed. and trans. by Jason Gaiger (Chicago: University of Chicago Press, 2002), 41. Herder also refers in the same work to 'den Finger seines inner Sinnes' [the fingers of his inner sense] (*Sculpture*, 90).

74 Rachel Zuckert, 'Sculpture and Touch: Herder's Aesthetics of Sculpture', *Journal of Aesthetics and Art Criticism*, 67.3 (2009), 287.

75 Gaiger, 'Introduction', in Herder, *Sculpture*, 18.

76 Herder, *Sculpture*, 52. Herder repeatedly opposes the innocence of sculpture with the seduction of paintings: 'A sculpture always stands there naked, but the beautiful *Danae* by Titian is wisely covered by a curtain: painting is an enchanted panel for a corrupted sense that seduces us, unconstrained by any limits' (*Sculpture*, 52).

to the back of the precinct',[77] it is Callicratidas's turn to embrace her. Callicratidas moreover finds a stain on the inner thigh of the statue, which the reader learns was left there by a young man who spent the night in the temple with her before throwing himself off a cliff – a tragic counterpart to the more fortunate Pygmalion.

Tobias Smollett cites a Latin translation of Callicratidas's rapturous praise of the statue's back and buttocks when describing his own 1764 encounter with the Medici Venus in Florence. Although unimpressed with the statue, he does find that its 'back parts... are executed so happily, as to excite the admiration of the most indifferent spectator. One cannot help thinking it is the very Venus of Cnidos by Praxiteles, which Lucian describes'.[78] As Coltman notes, Smollett 'was one of the few to describe circumambulating the Venus'[79] – in contrast to the majority who describe her from the front and to the side – but there are one or two other notable examples. Sade's Juliette, on her own tour of Italy, was rather more impressed than Smollett, and offers her own passing allusion to Pygmalion:

> la chambre, dite *la tribune*, nous offrit la fameuse *Vénus Médicis*, placée au fond de cette pièce. Il est impossible, en voyant ce superbe morceau, de se défendre de la plus douce émotion. Un Grec, dit-on, s'enflamma pour une statue... je l'avoue, je l'eusse imité près de celle-là ; en examinant les beautés de détail de ce célèbre ouvrage, on croit aisément que l'auteur dut, comme la tradition le rapporte, se servir de cinq cents modèles pour le terminer ; les proportions de cette sublime statue, les grâces de la figure, les contours divins de chaque membre, les arrondissements gracieux de la gorge et des fesses, sont des traits de génie qui pourraient le disputer à la nature

> [the chamber, known as the *tribune*, offered us the famous *Venus de Medici*, placed at the back of this room. It is impossible, upon seeing this superb piece, to resist the sweetest of emotions. A Greek, they say, became inflamed for a statue... I confess, I would have emulated him near this one. When closely examining the beauties of this celebrated work, one could easily believe its creator must, as tradition has it, have

---

77 Lucian, *Soloecista. Lucius or The Ass. Amores. Halcyon. Demosthenes. Podagra. Ocypus. Cyniscus. Philopatris. Charidemus. Nero. Amores*, translated by M. D. Macleod, Loeb Classical Library, 432 (Cambridge, MA: Harvard University Press, 1967), 171.
78 Tobias Smollett, *Travels Through France and Italy*, ed. by Frank Felsenstein (Oxford: Oxford University Press, 1981), 227.
79 Coltman, *Classical Sculpture*, 179.

used five hundred models to complete it: the proportions of this sublime statue, the graces of its features, the divine contours of each limb, the elegant roundness of her breasts and buttocks, are marks of genius to vie with nature] (*HJ* 730–1)

In Zoffany's *Tribuna* (1772–8), six men gather around the Medici Venus.

Fig. 1 Johan Zoffany, *Tribuna of the Uffizi* (1772), Wikimedia Commons, public domain, https://commons.wikimedia.org/wiki/File:Johan_Zoffany_-_Tribuna_ of_the_Uffizi_-_Google_Art_Project.jpg#/media/File:Johan_Zoffany_-_Tribuna_ of_the_Uffizi_-_Google_Art_Project.jpg

There is only one gentleman (James Bruce) in front of her, although his gaze is directed not at her but at the artist painting him (or at us watching him). Five men are behind the Venus: one (Thomas Wilbraham) is examining her with a magnifying glass (perhaps looking for another stain on her thigh) that forms a suggestive 'O', three others (two of them open-mouthed) are staring at her buttocks; the last gentleman (Doughty), however, is staring not at one bottom but two – his gaze distracted by the sculpture of the *Wrestlers*.[80] When Valmont is rotating Eugénie on her pedestal, his eyes devouring her 'charmes', it is because he too must pick a side, so to speak, in the same ancient debate: as the narrator puts it, 'auquel sacrifiera-t-il ? lequel sera préféré ?' [to which will he make his sacrifice? Which will he choose?] (*E* 460). If we are not told which he chooses, we certainly know the customary choice of other Sadean libertines. As Michel Delon puts it in his article on 'L'obsession anale de Sade' (aptly published in the *Annales historiques de la Révolution française*), 'Leur choix du cul et de la sodomie correspond à une option matérialiste et à un cynisme social' [Their choice of the arse and sodomy tallies with a materialist choice and a social cynicism].[81]

Regarding the urge to touch as well as look at statues, Louis XIV is said to have told the anecdote of Mazarin's gentle warning to the Maréchal de Gramont as the latter was examining some of his antiquities: 'Mazarin disait [...] "Monsieur, quand ces choses tombent à bas, elles se cassent" et ne lui disait pas: "N'y touchez pas"' [Mazarin said [...] 'Monsieur, when these objects fall to the ground, they break' and did not say to him 'Don't touch'].[82] As we have already seen, or touched upon, statues offered a tactile as well as visual experience to spectators regardless of setting. However, differences evidently remained between the experience of viewing statues in public as opposed to encountering them in the relative intimacy of a private collection. If the public sphere presented additional hazards for the statues displayed there, the recurring message of eighteenth-century Pygmalion narratives was that the private salon held dangers of its own for the solitary viewer

---

80   Cf. Thomas Patch's *A Gathering of Dilettanti around the Medici Venus* (1760–1; see https://www.nationaltrustcollections.org.uk/object/267120), which depicts Patch with one foot on the pedestal taking measurements, and another admirer behind the statue pointing at her bottom, and Richard Cosway's *Charles Townley with a Group of Connoisseurs* (c.1771–5; see https://artuk.org/discover/artworks/group-of-connoisseurs-151068). Cosway's conversation piece features six gentlemen viewing a group of three marble sculptures that includes a Muse playing a lure and two Venus torsos, one showing her front, the other her rear – once again, offering a choice for the spectators in the room. Two of the gentlemen, as Coltman observes, have 'their hands wedged deep in their pockets', with masturbation thus represented as 'as a sociable pleasure, rather than a solipsistic vice' (*Classical Sculpture*, 180).

81   Michel Delon, 'L'obsession anale de Sade', *Annales historiques de la Révolution française*, 361 (2010), 134.

82   Chantelou, *Journal*, 149.

of statues.⁸³ Valmont's satisfaction soon proves to be only temporary as he is left wanting more – wanting, that is, to touch Eugénie rather than himself. As Coltman notes of the English gentlemen visiting the Medici Venus on the Grand Tour, 'the 18th-century viewer's visual encounter with Venus is quickly superseded by the desire to touch her'.⁸⁴ She cites a T. Assheton who wrote in a letter to Charles Townley, 'I'm greatly afraid that the sight of the Venus in the Florentine Gallery will give you some yammering [...] after a Tuscan whore'.⁸⁵ Female statues – living or otherwise – are thus seen to arouse desires that can ultimately only be satisfied by women of flesh and blood.

Despite Herder's protestations, female, male and hermaphrodite statues evidently offered their male spectators an erotic experience. Being aroused by statues – or, to adapt Rousseau's phrase, looking at statues with one hand – was not in itself an aberration. The aberration was mistaking a statue for a woman – or goddess – and trying to enact rather than merely imagine sex with it. If apparently true stories of individuals making that very mistake read on occasion like the eighteenth-century equivalent of urban myths, there was clearly something about the phenomenon that captured the public imagination. One such case was offered by two 'mousquetaires' who developed a passion for a copy of the Medici Venus in the gardens of Versailles, offering it a novena and taking turns to kiss its buttocks, much to the mirth of the King and Court. Taken from a 1710 collection of comic anecdotes, 'La neuvaine de Versailles' [The Novena of Versailles] may be based on an actual incident but its dialogue is clearly fictionalized and the 'extravagance'⁸⁶ of the musketeers played for laughs – the two go on to become something of a comedic double act in subsequent anecdotes. In a more sentious intervention, Diderot complains rather gloomily in his *Salon de 1767*,

> Ceux qui peuplent nos jardins publics des images de la prostitution ne savent guère ce qu'ils font. Cependant tant d'inscriptions infâmes dont la statue de la Venus aux belles fesses est sans cesse barbouillée dans

---

83   Cf. Lucian's *Erotes*: while Callicratidas and Charicles kiss and caress the statue of Aphrodite in the safety of each other's company, the young man who spent the night with her alone ends up taking his own life.
84   Coltman, *Classical Sculpture*, 179.
85   Ibid., 180.
86   Anon., 'La neuvaine de Versailles', in anon., *L'art de plumer la poule sans crier* ('Cologne: Chez Robert le Turc, au Cocq hardi', 1710), 37.

les bosquets de Versailles ; tant d'actions dissolues, avouées dans ces inscriptions [...] instruisent assez de l'impression pernicieuse de ces sortes d'ouvrages.

[Those who fill our public gardens with images of prostitution know not what they do. Nonetheless all those vile inscriptions endlessly scribbled on the statue of the Venus with the beautiful buttocks in the groves of Versailles; all those dissolute acts, admitted in those inscriptions [...] reveal enough of the pernicious impression made by such works.][87]

A decade later, according to the *Correspondance secrète*, Houdon's *Diane* was allegedly kept out of the Salon 'parce qu'on craint sans doute de renouveller l'aventure de *la Vénus aux belles fesses* du parc de Versailles, qu'un jeune Garde-du-corps a déflorée' [because they fear no doubt a repeat of the episode of *the Venus with the beautiful buttocks* in the park of Versailles, which a young bodyguard deflowered].[88] And in Sade's *Histoire de Juliette*, Noirceuil's world tour of perversions slips from the bestial to the sculptural:

Les Sybarites enculaient des chiens ; les Égyptiennes se prostituaient à des crocodiles, les Américaines à des singes ; on en vint enfin aux statues : tout le monde sait qu'un page de Louis XV fut trouvé déchargeant sur le derrière de la Vénus aux belles fesses. Un Grec arrivant à Delphes, pour y consulter l'oracle, trouva dans le temple deux génies de marbre, et rendit pendant la nuit, son libidineux hommage à celui des deux qu'il avait trouvé le plus beau. Son opération faite, il le couronna de laurier, pour récompense des plaisirs qu'il en avait reçus.

[The Sybarites buggered dogs; Egyptian women prostituted themselves with crocodiles, American women with monkeys; and finally some turned to statues: everyone knows that one of Louis XV's pages was found coming over the behind of the Venus with the beautiful buttocks. A Greek arriving at Delphi to consult the oracle found in her temple two remarkable statues, and offered during the night his libidinous homage to the one he found most beautiful. Once the deed was done, he crowned it with laurel as a recompense for the pleasures it had given him.] (*HJ* 345–6)[89]

---

87 Diderot, *Salon de 1767*, in *Salons III: Ruines et paysages*, ed. by Else Marie Bukdahl, Michel Delon and Annette Lorenceau (Paris: Herman, 1995), 289–90.
88 Alexandre-Balthazar-Laurent Grimod de La Reynière, Guillaume Imbert de Boudeaux, François Métra, *Correspondence secrète, politique et littéraire* (London: John Adamson, 1787), vol. 5, 27 septembre 1777, 177.
89 With the exception of the modern anecdote, this passage draws on Démeunier's *L'esprit des usages et des coutumes* (1785), which in turn draws on Athanaeus's

1. Looking and Touching with Eugénie

In Sade's fiction, sex with a statue is a perversion with a perverse logic all of its own. For the libertine, the female statue has two great advantages over women: firstly, it is not alive, and secondly, it is not a woman. In *Aline et Valcour*, when Sarmiento, courtier of the brutal Ben Mâacoro, claims, 'le plaisir goûté avec l'être inerte ne peut point ne pas être entier, puisqu'il n'y a que l'agent qui l'éprouve' [pleasure tasted with an inert individual cannot be anything other than entire, as it is only the agent who experiences it], Sainville replies that according to such reasoning 'la jouissance d'une statue sera plus douce que celle d'une femme' [pleasure with a statue would be sweeter than with a woman] (*AV* 576, 577). For Ben Mâacoro, pleasure shared is pleasure divided and therefore diminished, and he thus executes any woman 'qui s'avisent de partager ses plaisirs' [who dares to share in his pleasures] (*AV* 576). In both *Justine* and the *Nouvelle Justine*, the monk Clément asks rhetorically, 'N'est-il donc pas visible que la femme ne peut rien partager avec nous sans nous prendre, et que tout ce qu'elle nous dérobe doit nécessairement être à nos dépens ?' [Is it not evident that a woman cannot share with us without taking from us, and that what she steals must necessarily be at our expense?] (*J* 265; cf. *NJ* 677). In a lengthy *dissertation* in which he proclaims 'l'égoïsme est la première loi de la nature' [selfishness is the first law of nature], above all 'dans les plaisirs de la lubricité' [in lubricious pleasures] (*J* 266; cf. *NJ* 678), Clément reduces women to 'les machines de la volupté' [sexual machines],[90] and men who fail to grasp the principles that govern their own sexual behaviour to statues of a different kind:

> Y a-t-il un seul homme raisonnable qui soit envieux de faire partager sa jouissance à des filles de joie ? Et n'y a-t-il pas des millions d'hommes qui prennent pourtant de grands plaisirs avec ces créatures ? Ce sont donc autant d'individus persuadés de ce que j'établis, qui le mettent en pratique, sans s'en douter, et qui blâment ridiculement ceux qui légitiment leurs actions par de bons principes, et cela, parce que l'univers est plein de statues organisées qui vont, qui viennent, qui agissent, qui mangent, qui digèrent, sans jamais se rendre compte de rien.

Deipnosophistae.
90   An echo of Merteuil's dismissal of women such as Cécile de Volanges as 'des machines à plaisir' (Choderlos de Laclos, *Les Liaisons dangereuses* (Paris: Gallimard, 1972), Letter 106, 308.

> [Is there a single reasonable man who would wish to share his pleasure with prostitutes? And are there not millions of men who nonetheless take great pleasure with these creatures? There are therefore as many individuals who are persuaded of what I have established, who put it in into practice, without even suspecting it, and who condemn those who legitimize their actions with sound principles, and do so because the universe is full of living statues who come and go, who act, who eat, who digest, without ever realizing anything.] (J 267; cf. NJ 679)

Clément's appeal to the dehumanizing logic of prostitution is instructive. The prostitute, like the statue, exists only to give pleasure to men, not to take it from them. Eugénie, perched on her pedestal, is in effect transformed into a prostitute as well as a statue – pimped by her father to Valmont. She is thus further tied to Ovid's *Metamorphoses* as a successor not only to Pygmalion's statue, or to Myrrha, but to the women who inspired his disgust for women in the first place: the Propoetides, turned to stone after being the first 'to prostitute their bodies' charms'.[91]

After Valmont: From Fantasy to Perversion

As embedded as Sade's story is in its own time and place, it also looks and speaks to the future, anticipating some of the anxieties provoked by the act of looking in discourses about sex from the nineteenth century to the present day. Although Sade ultimately chose to omit the statue scene from the published version of 'Eugénie de Franval', one very much like it, told by a former Chief of Police, would later find its way into the growing number of treatises about sex, and sexual aberration, in the latter half of the nineteenth century:

> J'entrai dans un cabinet où régnait la plus profonde obscurité ; cette espèce de mystère et les ténèbres qui m'entouraient avaient excité ma curiosité ; S*** me prit par le bras et tira en même temps un rideau qui dissimulait une fissure qu'on avait pratiquée artistement dans une boiserie, et, quoi qu'elle fût imperceptible, elle n'en laissait pas moins voir tout ce qui se passait dans le salon de réception. Lorsque ma conductrice m'eût laissé seul, j'appliquai un œil à cette ouverture en retenant, autant que je le pouvais, ma respiration : sur un piédestal rond, recouvert d'un tapis vert, était placée une statue de femme de grandeur naturelle, le

---

91 Ovid, *Metamorphoses*, X. 240 [p.292]. Translation by Melville (232).

poli du corps était blanc rosé ; un vieillard, un septuagénaire, affublé d'une écharpe verte, un maillet et un ciseau de sculpteur à la main, était en extase au pied de la statue. Après un moment d'examen, il toucha le piédestal qui tourna lentement sur lui-même ; je pus alors et tout à mon aise admirer les formes gracieuses et bien proportionnées de cette statue, qui semblait figurer une des houris promises aux élus de Mahomet. Le vieux barbon arrêta le piédestal, baisa la statue des pieds à la tête, puis se jeta à ses genoux en marmottant quelques mots inintelligibles et d'une voix singulière. Il joignit ensuite les mains en les levant au-dessus de sa tête, et après cette espèce d'invocation, il posa sa main sur la hanche de la statue qui, un moment après, s'anima insensiblement en ouvrant les yeux. Ses bras et ses jambes s'agitèrent comme si un ressort les avait fait mouvoir ; alors le vieillard se débarrassa de son écharpe, du maillet et du ciseau, et, à ma grande surprise, il disparut comme une ombre. R*** qui était de retour vint me chercher, nous partîmes, et chemin faisant il me raconta que ce vieillard était le comte de B*** qui, chaque fois qu'il venait jouer le rôle de Pygmalion avec sa statue, donnait cent francs.[92]

[I entered a chamber where the most profound darkness reigned; this sort of mystery and the blackness enveloping me had piqued my curiosity; S*** took me by the arm and at the same time drew back a curtain concealing a crack that had been skilfully made in a wood panel, and, as imperceptible as it was, it nonetheless allowed us to see everything that was happening in the reception room. Left alone by my conductress, I pressed my eye against this opening, holding my breath as best I could: on a round pedestal, covered with a green rug, was a life-size statue of a woman, her body gleaming a rosy white; an old man, a septuagenarian sporting a green scarf, with a mallet and a sculptor's chisel in his hands, was in ecstasy at the foot of the statue. After a moment's examination, he touched the pedestal, which slowly turned on itself; I was then able to admire at my leisure the graceful and finely proportioned forms of this statue, which seemed to represent one of the houris promised to Mohammed's chosen ones. The old man stopped the pedestal, kissed the statue from head to toe, then hurled himself at her feet, mumbling a few unintelligible words in a singular voice. He then clasped his hands together as he raised them above his head, and after this form of invocation, he placed his hand on the hip of the statue which, a moment later, imperceptibly came to life as it

---

92 Louis Canler, *Mémoires de Canler* (Paris: F. Roy, 1882), vol. 1, 137–8. Canler notes that this was long before 'tableaux vivants' were a phenomenon in Parisian brothels; he also tells of another client at the same brothel who, with the help of three prostitutes and the same rotating pedestal, reenacted Paris's award of the apple to Venus over Juno and Minerva.

opened its eyes. Its arms and legs stirred as if moved by a spring; the old man then got rid of his scarf, mallet and chisel, and, to my great surprise, vanished like a shadow. R***, who had returned, came to fetch me; we set off, and on the way he told me that this old man was the Count of B*** who, each time he came to play the role of Pygmalion with his statue, paid one hundred francs.]

This episode, which Louis Canler claimed took place during the Restoration, and the others mentioned above, might have faded from view entirely were it not for the interest shown in them by the emerging discipline of sexology, which soon turned the Pygmalion myth into a pathology. That Canler's anecdote subsequently found its way into various sexological tracts reflects the early dependence of the discipline on a whole range of sources such as newspapers, memoirs, short stories and novels – including some, like this passage, which seem to sit somewhere between fact and fiction. The story may well be true, but it reads uncannily like a classic scene of voyeurism from an eighteenth-century pornographic novel – or indeed, a risqué short story by Sade.

As the main sources for works of sexology in its early days were other works of sexology, when cases such as those reported by Canler found their way into one study they soon spread virally to the rest.[93] Iwan Bloch, shortly before publishing his inaugural edition of *Les 120 Journées de Sodome* in Berlin, cites the episodes from Canler and *L'art de plumer la poule sans crier* alongside an allusion to Athenaeus from the *Histoire de Juliette* in his *Beiträge zur Aetiologie der Psychopathia sexualis* (1902–3).[94] What seems remarkable today is the confidence sexologists had in the existence of 'statue love' given the evidence was largely drawn from ancient Greek and Latin sources. Heinrich Kaan described the 'satisfaction of lust with statues' as among 'the most common' sexual aberrations in his *Psychopathia sexualis*[95] of 1844, and by the time

---

93   The appearance of Canler's anecdote in Léo Taxil's *La corruption fin de siècle* (1891) is thus swiftly followed by further mentions in Louis Fiaux's *Les maisons de tolerance, leur fermeture* (1892), Albert Eulenburg's *Sexuale Neuropathie* (1895) and Iwan Bloch's *Beiträge zur Aetiologie der Psychopathia sexualis* (1902–3) to name just a few of the more influential studies.

94   Bloch, *Beiträge zur Aetiologie der Psychopathia sexualis*, 2 vols. (Dresden: Dohrn, 1902–3), II, 299. Bloch cites the *Histoire de Juliette* on ten further occasions in the course of this work.

95   Heinrich Kaan, *Psychopathia sexualis*, in *Heinrich Kaan's 'Psychopathia sexualis' (1844): A Classic Text in the History of Sexuality*, ed. by Benjamin Kahan and trans.

Bloch writes about it over half a century later, he can reasonably say, 'The peculiar erotic relation which people can form with statues is well known'.[96] By the early twentieth century there are almost as many terms for the aberration as there are descriptions of it, including three in Bloch's studies alone ('Statuenfetischismus', 'Statuenliebe' and 'Venus statuaria'),[97] and additional coinages such as 'Pygmalionism' and 'Statuophilia'.[98] One further term – 'agalmatophilia' – was proposed in the 1970s, but only in an article which heralds the apparent demise of the disorder it is intended to describe: 'over a few thousand years mankind has dropped at least one pathological condition, agalmatophilia, from its repertoire of pathologies'.[99] As the two authors A. Scobie and A. J. W. Taylor point out, the condition by this point was no longer appearing in contemporary works of sexology or psychiatry, and this has remained the case ever since.[100] They do, however, suggest an alternative possibility when they speculate 'it might merely have changed its form because the burgeoning plastics industry has rendered obsolete the pathological focus on stone statues *per se*'.[101] This rather literal reading

---

by Melissa Haynes (Ithaca, NY and London: Cornell University Press, 2016), 78.

96 'Bekannt ist das eigentümliche erotische Verhältnis, in welches Personen zu Statuen treten können' (Iwan Bloch, *Beiträge zur Aetiologie der Psychopathia sexualis*, I. 211).

97 In *Neue Forschungen über den Marquis de Sade und seine Zeit* (Berlin: Harrwitz, 1904), *Beiträge zur Aetiologie der Psychopathia sexualis* (Dresden: Dohrn, 1902–3) and *Das Sexualleben unserer Zeit in seinen Beziehungen zur modernen Kultur* (Berlin: Louis Marcus, 1907) respectively.

98 'Pygmalionisme', originally coined by Joris-Karl Huysmans in *Là-bas* (1891), was adopted by Eulenburg in *Sexuale Neuropathie* (Leipzig: F. C. W. Vogel, 1895) and Havelock Ellis in *Studies in the Psychology of Sex* (Philadelphia: F. A. Davis, 1905–6) among others, and 'Statuophilie' by Erich Wulffen in *Der Sexualverbrecher* (Berlin: P. Langenscheidt, 1910) and Magnus Hirschfeld in *Sexualpathologie: Ein Lehrbuch für Ärzte und Studierende* (Bonn: A. Marcus & E. Webers, 1920).

99 A. Scobie and A. J. W. Taylor, 'Perversions Ancient and Modern: I. Agalmatophilia, the Statue Syndrome', *The History of the Behavioral Sciences*, 11.1 (1975), 49. The first use of the term in English was by a classicist, Robert Coleman, in an article on Ovid ('Structure and intention in the *Metamorphoses*', *The Classical Quarterly*, 21.2 (1971), 468). The earliest use of the term I could find in another language was by another classicist, Sisto Colombo in 1930: 'Arnobio Afro e I suoi sette libri Adversus nationes', in *Didaskaleion: Studi filologici di Letteratura Cristiana antica*, 8 (1930), 106, 119.

100 There is, for example, no reference to agalmatophilia in any of the American Psychiatry Association 'DSMs' (Diagnostic and Statistical Manuals of Mental Disorders).

101 Scobie and Taylor, 'Perversions Ancient and Modern', 49.

of the paraphilia, more focussed on the material than the figure of the statue, leaves no room for further reflection on the different forms that 'statue love' – understood as a broader phenomenon – might be taking in their own time.[102]

Though not sexologists themselves, Scobie and Taylor follow the early sexologists in blurring if not ignoring the distinction between fictional and factual sources.[103] While they state that 'six cases of agalmatophilia have been documented in the last two centuries', it soon transpires that three of these are 'featured in modern literature':[104] Joyce's *Ulysses* (1922), Durrell's *Justine* (1957) and Grass's *Die Blechtrommel* (1959). As Murray White observed a few years later, of the three so-called 'clinical' cases identified by Scobie and Taylor, 'One had its basis in a note published in the *Classical Review* of 1927'[105] – a note alluding to a newspaper report of a Hungarian who had a wax effigy made of a woman he was not allowed to marry; the other two cases were taken from Havelock Ellis, who in turn had taken them from other sexologists (Tarnovsky, and Krafft-Ebing – the latter via Bloch). Of these two, Tarnovsky's case – that of a young man arrested for 'paying visits by moon-light to the statue of a nymph, situated on the terrace of a country-house'[106] – is unsourced, while Krafft-Ebing's is based on a newspaper report entitled 'La colère du bronze' [The anger of the bronze (statue)] from 1877. The

---

102 More recently, Meghan Laslocky identifies 'doll love' as a form of agalmatophilia in 'Real Dolls: Love in the Age of Silicone', one which is memorably and endearingly depicted in the film *Lars and the Real Girl* (2007) (Laslocky, 'Real Dolls', Salt magazine [online], 17 October 2005 (https://web.archive.org/web/20110927082018/http://www.saltmag.net/display.php?article_id=240&author_id=94). For a contemporary novel that explores a future form of Pygmalionism, in the form of robot love, see Sierra Greer's *Annie Bot* (London: Harper Collins, 2024).
103 Scobie was a classicist while Taylor, a clinical psychologist, had never previously published any articles on sexology, his research publications covering instead 'a wide range from Beatlemania, tattooing, group therapy to social isolation in Antarctica' ('Perversions Ancient and Modern', 49).
104 Ibid., 50. There is no mention of other, more obvious examples, such as Leopold von Sacher-Masoch's *Venus in Furs* (1870) or Henry James's *Last of the Valerii* (1874).
105 Murray White, 'The Statue Syndrome: Perversion? Fantasy? Anecdote?', *The Journal of Sex Research*, 14.4 (1978), 247.
106 Ellis cites the English edition of Veniamin Tarnowksky, *The Sexual Instinct and its Morbid Manifestation*, trans. by W. C. Costello and Alfred Allinson (Paris: Charles Carrington, 1898), 86.

report describes an incident that took place on the Comte de Rouménil's property in Asnières involving a bronze statue of the Venus de Milo:

> Il parait qu'elle inspirait au jardinier du comte, Dourais, des idées folichonnes, car, avant-hier, il eut la singulière idée de la serrer dans les bras...
>
> La déesse fut-elle offensée de cette familiarité ? Toujours est-il que, tout à coup, vacillant sur son piédestal, elle tomba en avant et écrasa sous elle le malheureux jardinier, auquel elle brisa trois côtes – procédé sommaire qui rappelle ceux de la Vénus d'Ille.
>
> [It appears that she inspired in the Count's gardener, Dourais, some rather extravagant ideas, for, the day before yesterday, he had the singular impulse to hold her in his arms...
>
> Was the goddess offended by this familiarity? Whatever the case may be, all of a sudden, tottering on her pedestal, she fell forwards and crushed the unfortunate gardener beneath her, cracking three of his ribs – a summary judgement which recalls those of the Vénus D'Ille.][107]

The literary reference to Mérimée's tale reinforces the sense of a quixotic confusion of fantasy for reality on the part of the gardener, and the impression of an incident that belongs in a work of fiction rather than a newspaper.

Although he does uncover what he believes to be 'the only genuine case of agalmatophilia ever to be reported', that of the so-called 'plaster-of-paris man'[108] reported in a psychoanalytical journal, White is so unimpressed by the evidence adduced by his predecessors that he concludes, 'there is very little evidence supporting its status as a behavioral perversion';[109] he argues that the work of the early sexologists confused fantasy with perversion. This may well be true, but if most of them considered agalmatophilia a fetish or a perversion it was because of the harms they associated with the behaviour – from broken ribs to broken minds. As we have already seen from some of the cases cited in this chapter, agalmatophilia does not fit into a single category, and

---

107 *L'Evènement*, 3rd March 1877, 2 (not 4th March as cited in Krafft-Ebing et al.). The headline alludes to a Victor Hugo poem of the same name published a few days earlier.
108 C. W. Socarides, 'A Psychoanalytic Study of the Desire for Sexual Transformation ('Transsexualism'): The Plaster-of-Paris Man', *International Journal of Psychoanalysis*, 51 (1970), 341–9.
109 Murray White, 'The Statue Syndrome', 249.

could in different contexts be considered fantasy, fetish, paraphilia or symptom of psychosis. There is clearly a difference between a subject who is aroused by statues as fetish objects, one who is aroused by statues as representations of – and perhaps substitutes for – human bodies, and one who is aroused by statues because he, she or they believe them to be human.

For the early sexologists, the concern provoked by reported cases of agalmatophilia was a concern for – rather than about – the unfortunate gentlemen deemed to be suffering from such an affliction. As the twentieth century wore on, and evidence of any such cases failed to materialize, those concerns inevitably dissipated. Just as Scobie and Taylor were announcing the demise of agalmatophilia, however, anxieties about men looking at objects as if they were women were giving way to anxieties about men looking at women as if they were objects – and this time around, the concern was about, rather than for, those men doing the looking. For Andrea Dworkin and her fellow campaigners in the so-called 'sex wars' of the 1970s and 1980s, Sade was very much a paradigmatic figure for the risks posed by pornography, and it is indeed telling that she uses the present tense in hailing him as 'the world's foremost pornographer'.[110] Although Dworkin's chapter devoted to Sade in *Pornography: Men Possessing Women* (1979) does not allude to 'Eugénie de Franval', she would doubtless have seen its statue scene as emblematic of the heterosexual oppression underlying the creation and reception of pornography in its depiction of a young woman turned into an object by one man for the pleasure of another.

For all of Dworkin's condemnations of Sade, she and her fellow campaigners against pornography had more in common with him than may at first meet the eye. The statue scene in 'Eugénie de Franval', for example, suggests a shared belief in the power of pornographic spectacle to unleash uncontrollable desires. For Valmont, as for Robyn Morgan, 'Pornography is the theory, rape is the practice':[111] masturbating over her as a statue is the prelude to his abduction – or *raptus* – of her, with all

---

110 Andrea Dworkin, *Pornography: Men Possessing Women* (New York: Plume, 1989), 70.
111 Robyn Morgan, 'Theory and Practice: Pornography and Rape', in Morgan, *Going Too Far: The Personal Chronicle of a Feminist* (New York: Vintage, 1978), 169.

the threat of sexual violence that implies.[112] Masturbation in 'Eugénie de Franval' indeed becomes a rehearsal for violence in a manner that chimes with some of the claims made by Catharine MacKinnon, Morgan's fellow campaigner: 'Sooner or later, in one way or another, the consumer wants to live out the pornography further in three dimensions. Sooner or later, in one way or another, they do. *It* makes them want to'.[113] This model of pornographic consumption could not be more Sadean in linking reception to enactment: it is a case of 'monkey see, monkey do', even if MacKinnon likens men to a different kind of animal when she claims that showing them pornography is like saying 'kill' to 'a trained attack dog'.[114] The irony of this dehumanizing of men (for dehumanizing women) did not pass unnoticed: as Alan Soble observed, 'Mackinnon does to men what she believes men and pornography do to women, that is, reduce them to the status of their genitals, to the status of pure sex item and object'.[115]

There is nonetheless a key difference between Sade and those modern campaigners against pornography in the 1970s and 1980s which should not be elided. Dworkin and MacKinnon shared a conviction that Sade certainly did not: that pornography had both the ability to instil and compel desire, and to instil and compel the enactment of that desire. Because pornography was all one and the same for them – 'the graphic sexually explicit subordination of women through pictures and/or words'[116] – so too were the desires it produced in men. Sade's fiction conversely suggests that our desires are individual and idiosyncratic,

---

112 As has often been noted, the Roman legal concept of *raptus* (from *rapere*, 'seize, carry off by force, abduct') originally signified the abduction of a woman against the will of her parents or husband, and in the Middle Ages the term covered both rape and abduction. See James A. Brundage, *Law, Sex, and Christian Society in Medieval Europe* (Chicago, IL and London: University of Chicago Press, 1987).
113 Catharine A. MacKinnon, *Only Words* (Cambridge, MA: Harvard University Press, 1993), 19.
114 Ibid., 12.
115 Alan Soble, *Pornography, Sex and Feminism* (Amherst, NY: Prometheus Books, 2002), 17.
116 Taken from the ordinance drafted by Dworkin and MacKinnon and published in Dworkin and MacKinnon, *Pornography and Civil Rights: A New Day for Women's Equality* (Minneapolis, MN: Organizing Against Pornography, 1988), 36. The heteronormative narrowness of the definition is noteworthy, and indeed a common criticism of the ordinance was that it failed to account for other forms of pornography.

and that erotic images or scenarios will only appeal to us if they are aligned to those desires. As the narrator of the *120 Journées* acknowledges,

> Sans doute, beaucoup de tous les écarts que tu vas voir peints te déplairont, on le sait, mais il s'en trouvera quelques-uns qui t'échaufferont au point de te coûter du foutre, et voilà tout ce qu'il nous faut. Si nous n'avions pas tout dit, tout analysé, comment voudrais-tu que nous eussions pu deviner ce qui te convient ? C'est à toi à les prendre et à laisser le reste ; un autre en fera autant ; et petit à petit tout aura trouvé sa place. C'est ici l'histoire d'un magnifique repas où six cents plats divers s'offrent à ton appétit. Les manges-tu tous? Non, sans doute

> [No doubt many of the various excesses you shall see depicted shall displease you, we know, but there shall be others that inflame you to the point of spilling your come, and that is all we require – if we had not said everything, analysed everything, how do you think we could have guessed what appeals to you? It is for you to take what you want and leave the rest – someone else shall do the same and, little by little, everything shall have found its rightful place. This is the story of a magnificent feast where 600 different dishes are offered for your delectation – do you eat them all? Of course not] (*120J* 69; 59)

There is no sense here that the reception of pornography can change us. Some images will be to our taste, and others not, and there is nothing we – or pornography – can do to change that. No one indeed ever plausibly changes in Sade's fiction, as Franval's laughably unconvincing conversion at the end of Sade's story reflects. For Sade, we are what we are, and cannot be anything else, and the same applies to our desires, formed by our earliest experiences.[117] As Clément, one of the monks at the monastery of Sainte-Marie-des-Bois rhetorically asks Justine, 'Mais désirât-on même de changer de goûts, le peut-on ? Est-il en nous de nous refaire ? Pouvons-nous devenir autres que nous ne sommes ?' [Even if we wanted to change our tastes, could we? Is it in us to remake ourselves? Can we become other than what we are?] (*J* 261). Pornography may unleash desires, but it cannot, Sade suggests, impose them.

---

[117] 'C'est dans le sein de la mère que se fabriquent les organes qui doivent nous rendre susceptibles de telle ou telle fantaisie, les premiers objets présentés, les premiers discours entendus achèvent de déterminer le ressort ; les goûts se forment, et rien au monde ne peut plus les détruire' [It is in the mother's womb that the organs that make us susceptible to one fantasy or another are made, the first objects we see, the first words we hear then determining the strength of them; our tastes form, and nothing in the world can destroy them thereafter'] (*J* 263).

Conclusion

In 'Eugénie de Franval', the statue scene is the result of Valmont's desire for Eugénie rather than its cause – as his demand for a tête-à-tête with her makes clear. Eugénie is thus an object to Valmont long before she appears as a statue. The pornographic spectacle created for him works because he is its ideal, as well as its intended, spectator. While he may be the one literally pulling the strings, his susceptibility to his object of desire means he is as much Franval's puppet during the scene as Eugénie is. Like Eugénie, Valmont too has his part to play: to see, to desire, to touch. It is a script he cannot help but follow. But what of the reader? Despite being in a classroom rather than a bedroom or boudoir, the students completing the questionnaires largely succeeded in immersing themselves in a scene which placed them in the same role as Valmont. While, evidently, they were not driven to touch themselves as Valmont is, their responses do show the varying degrees to which we as readers unwittingly follow the dynamics and logic of the Sadean script. Although we tend to talk about texts objectifying characters, this is really shorthand for what we find ourselves doing as we read them. We prefer to implicate the text rather than the reader, but as the questionnaires show, the reader too is implicated, not in some abstract way, but actually, imaginatively, vividly. Only one of thirty-seven readers, as we saw earlier, saw any of the statue scene from Eugénie's perspective; most saw it from a perspective aligned with the men in the room. If the statue scene is very much a scene about looking, the question thus arises, what happens in scenes which are not limited to the visual? While Eugénie is protected by her pedestal and the 'canal' that keeps Valmont at bay, no such protection is afforded the various incarnations of Sade's endlessly suffering Justine. The following chapter will explore the power of the Sadean text to make the reader do more than simply look.

2. Hearing and Feeling with Justine

> *Du mußt [...] Amboß oder Hammer sein.*
> [You must [...] be anvil or hammer.]
> Goethe, 'Zweites Cophtisches Lied'

Introduction

While the focus in the last chapter was on what we see when we read, the aim here is to show that there is much more to reading than meets the eye.[1] As suggested in the Introduction to this book, we are not the mere spectators that Wittgenstein implied when he described his experience as a reader of fiction: 'I simply read, have impressions, see pictures in my mind's eye, etc.'[2] – even if his reference to 'impressions' perhaps opens the door to other modes of reception beyond the visual. The first half of this chapter will thus examine the ways in which stories are staged – and heard – in Sade's fiction before turning its attention to the auditory aspect of our experiences as readers. For most of us, silent reading is not quite as silent as advertised: we hear what we read as well as see it. But there is still more to our reading than sound and vision, or even, as we shall see in the next chapter, smell and taste. An embodied approach to reading that limits itself to Aristotle's five senses cannot tell the whole story. And, in the case of Sade, such an approach would be

---

1 Some of the ideas explored in this chapter were tentatively broached in an article I wrote some time ago ('The Sound of Violence: Listening to Rape in Sade', in *Representing Violence in France, 1760–1820*, ed. by Thomas Wynn, *Studies on Voltaire and the Eighteenth Century*, 2013: 10 (Oxford: Voltaire Foundation, 2013), 229–49.) This chapter is an attempt to answer many of the questions I left hanging there.
2 Wittgenstein, *Zettel*, 43.

omitting arguably the most important – or at least the most unsettling – part of that story. In a recent essay, Jean-Christophe Abramovici reflects the consensus of scholarship on Sade when, with an apparent shrug, he rhetorically asks, 'what can one say about the violence of Sade's texts, other than that one feels it?'[3] As if there were self-evidently nothing more to say on the matter, he limits his analysis to Sade's use of the word 'violence' – a case, I would argue, of not being able to see the wood for the trees. It is clearly no coincidence that an œuvre arguably defined by acts of extreme violence has produced a body of scholarship that continues to be in denial of the body. Whereas an embodied reading of, say, Wordsworth's 'Daffodils' or Cervantes's *Don Quixote* would raise few eyebrows, such an approach still seems risky when it comes to Sade. Although Abramovici avoids going any further himself, his admission that the reader 'feels' the violence of the Sadean text is nonetheless an acknowledgement that it has some somatic power. It may also serve as a useful reminder that as well as thinking of the violence in Sade as something seen and heard, we need to explore it as something felt on our skin, and indeed under it, in our muscles and limbs.

The second half of this chapter will therefore use *Justine* to examine the experience of reading scenes of sexual violence from this more muscular, or kinaesthetic, perspective. As in the last chapter, attention will be paid to one scene in particular, and to the questionnaires completed by my students upon reading that scene. Nancy K. Miller once described Justine as 'the object of a verb',[4] and in so doing suggested that Sade's heroine was doomed to share a similar fate to Eugénie – to remain the textual equivalent of a statue rather than a living and breathing character. This chapter will show, however, that we can do more with these statues made of words than simply look at them. Drawing both on largely forgotten work in aesthetics and psychology and recent developments in neuroscience, the following pages will explore the ways in which we as readers can feel ourselves *into* statues, and indeed fictional characters, and what the implications of this body-swapping may be for our encounters with fictional violence.

---

3   Jean-Christophe Abramovici, '"Avec une telle violence que...": Sade's Use of the Term Violence', 221.
4   Nancy K. Miller, *French Dressing: Women, Men, and Ancien Régime Fiction* (London and New York: Routledge, 1995), 131.

Scenes of Listening

Prior to the nineteenth century, the interpolation of stories was a common feature of the novel, a characteristic inherited from earlier forms of fiction such as classical and chivalric romance. Strangers always had a story to tell: as Tzvetan Todorov observes, 'Tout nouveau personnage signifie une nouvelle intrigue. Nous sommes dans le royaume des hommes-récits' [Every new character signifies a new plot. We are in the realm of men-stories].[5] As narratology has traditionally been more interested in the tellers of tales than their audiences, the role of fictional listeners has arguably not received the attention it deserves. While they may remain silent as a story is told, listeners in novels typically play a more active role than this implies, often eliciting the story, and equally often becoming allies with the storyteller once it has concluded.[6] In early modern comic fiction in particular, stories are moreover often interrupted when sitting silently proves too much of a challenge for an engrossed listener. In Diderot's *Jacques le fataliste*, the eponymous (anti-)hero is obliged to halt his account of an assault at the hands of some bandits:

> JAQUES. – [...] Mon Maitre, qu'avez-vous ? Vous serrez les dents, vous vous agitez comme si vous étiez en présence d'un ennemi.
>
> LE MAITRE. – J'y suis, en effet, j'ai l'épée à la main, je fonds sur tes voleurs et je te venge. [...]
>   En cet endroit le maitre jeta ses bras autour du cou de son valet, en s'écriant : Mon pauvre Jaques, que vas-tu faire ? Que vas-tu devenir ? Ta position m'effraie.
>
> JAQUES. – Mon Maitre, rassurez-vous, me voilà.
>
> [JAQUES. – [...] My Master, what's wrong with you? You're gritting your teeth, you're carrying on as if you were in the presence of an enemy.
>
> THE MASTER. – I am indeed, I have my sword in hand, I'm laying into your robbers and avenging you. [...]
>   At this spot the master threw his arms around his valet's neck, exclaiming: 'My poor Jaques, what are you going to do? What will become of you? Your situation alarms me.'

---

5   Tzvetan Todorov, *Poétique de la prose* (Paris: Seuil, 1971), 82.
6   See Will McMorran, *The Inn and the Traveller: Digressive Topographies in the Early Modern European Novel* (Oxford: Legenda, 2002), 30–4.

JAQUES. – My Master, have no fear – I'm here.]⁷

As much as this is in keeping with the novel's playful mockery of our addiction to fiction, as Jacques's Master quixotically loses himself in the story, it also serves as a reminder of the ability of the spoken word to move us physically as well as emotionally: the Master grits his teeth and grips his sword as he imagines himself coming to the rescue of his beloved servant.

Despite adopting the form of an epistolary novel, Sade's *Aline et Valcour* is less interested in letters exchanged and read than it is in stories told and heard. Among the listeners of the novel's two lengthy interpolations, the stories told by Sainville and Léonore respectively, is a figure who rather resembles Jacques's master: the Comte de Beaulé, a 'brave et honnête militaire' [brave and honourable military man] who is said to embody 'les franches vertus de l'antique chevalerie' [the true virtues of ancient chivalry] (*AV* 423). Now in his middle age, he too cuts a rather quixotic figure, and like Jacques's Master proves susceptible to losing himself in the stories he hears. When Léonore recounts one of her numerous escapes from imminent violation, he interjects, 'Ah! je respire [...] vous m'avez fait une frayeur... moi qui connais si peu ce sentiment-là' [Ah! I breathe again [...] you gave me a fright... me who knows so little of that feeling] (*AV* 771). He is not the only one to tremble as he listens: shocked by a revelation in Sainville's tale, it is Mme de Blamont's turn to interrupt:

> « Oh, Dieu ! vous me faites frissonner, dit la présidente de Blamont, en interrompant Sainville ; quoi, monsieur, c'était Léonore?... Quoi, madame, c'était vous?... Et vous n'avez pas été ... et vous ne fûtes pas mangée? »
>
> Toute la société ne put s'empêcher de rire de la vivacité naïve de la restriction plaisante de madame de Blamont.
>
> ['Oh, God! You make me tremble,' said the Présidente de Blamont, interrupting Sainville. 'What, monsieur, it was Léonore?... What, Madame, it was you?... and you haven't been... and you were not eaten?'
>
> The whole company could not help but laugh at the naïve vivacity of Madame de Blamont's amusing uncertainty.] (*AV* 608–9)

---

7   Denis Diderot, *Jaques le Fataliste et son maitre*, ed. by Simone Lecointre and Jean Le Galliot (Paris: Droz, 1976), 107–8.

As these examples show, we listen not just with our ears but our whole bodies. What we hear can affect how we breathe, or make us tremble with fear, even as our eyes provide us with evidence that we have no reason to be afraid. Sade, however, is predictably more interested in the erotic potential of listening. In a century widely regarded as an age of ocularcentric thinking, the narrator of the *120 Journées* nonetheless declares that the aural has greater sensory, and sensual, impact than the visual:

> Il est reçu, parmi les véritables libertins, que les sensations communiquées par l'organe de l'ouïe sont celles qui flattent davantage et dont les impressions sont les plus vives.
>
> [It is accepted among true libertines that the sensations communicated by the organ of hearing excite more than any others and produce the most vivid impressions.] (*120J* 39; 28)

In one striking scene from the *Nouvelle Justine*, pure sound – unadulterated by other sensory stimuli – is delivered to a libertine audience when Madame de Verneuil is obliged to wear 'un casque à tuyau, organisé de manière que les cris que lui faisaient jeter les douleurs dont on l'accablait ressemblaient aux mugissements d'un bœuf' [a tubed helmet, fashioned in such a manner that the screams prompted by the agonies with which she was assailed resembled the bellowing of an ox] (*NJ* 950) as she is raped and tortured by her son and his accomplices. The sound is transmitted to a neighbouring room where her husband, unaware of his son's involvement, listens in ecstasy to his wife's screams:

> « Oh! foutre, qu'est ceci ? » dit Verneuil en entendant cette musique, et se ruant sur la d'Esterval... « il est impossible de rien entendre de plus délicieux... que diable lui font-ils donc, pour la faire beugler ainsi ? »
>
> ['Oh, fuck! What's this?' said Verneuil on hearing this music, and pouncing on Mme d'Esterval... 'One could not possibly hear anything more delectable... what the devil are they doing to her, to make her moo like that?'] (*NJ* 950)

As Barthes suggests, it is the absence of the visual that heightens the pleasure for the libertine: 'le casque transmet sa douleur aux autres libertins, comme par radio, sans qu'ils voient la scène : ils peuvent, plaisir suprême, l'imaginer, c'est-à-dire la fantasmer' [the helmet transmits the pain to the other libertines, as if by radio, without them seeing the scene: they can, pleasure of pleasures, imagine it, that is to say fantasize it].[8] While the sense of hearing was traditionally regarded alongside that of sight as one of the higher or nobler senses, here it seems closer to the 'base' senses of smell, taste and touch in its visceral transmission of pain direct into the ear – and thus body – of the listener.

It would be oversimplifying to suggest that Sade prizes the aural over the visual. As we saw in the last chapter, Sade delights in creating a spectacle. But he knows, as the Verneuil scene suggests, that the spectacle imagined can be more powerful than the one seen; it is the same logic that leads to those scenes (and screams) heard but not seen by the narrator barred from the private cabinets of the *120 Journées*.[9] Rooted in the materialism of his time, the imagination was for Sade even more powerful than the senses themselves: as Condillac says of the imagination, 'la réaction de cet organe est plus vive que l'action des sens' [the reaction of this organ is more lively than the action of the senses].[10] Sade indeed does his best to demonstrate the truth of Hélvetius's claim that 'L'art d'écrire consiste dans l'art d'exciter des sensations' [the art of writing consists of the art of exciting sensations].[11] He consequently enlists all the senses in his efforts to excite the reader's imagination, and for the most part this means that the aural and the visual go together in his fiction. This is perhaps at its most obvious in the (literal) staging of the storytelling in the *120 Journées*. The four libertines listen to the *historiennes* in the theatrical setting of the *salon d'histoire*: the *historienne*, seated upon a throne raised four feet high, 'se trouvait alors placée comme est l'acteur sur un théâtre, et les auditeurs, placés dans les niches, se trouvaient l'être comme on l'est à l'amphithéâtre' [was placed

---

8   Barthes, *Sade, Fourier, Loyola*, 147.
9   See Will McMorran, 'Behind the Mask? Sade and the *Cent Vingt Journées de Sodome*', *Modern Language Review*, 108 (2013), 1121–34.
10 Etienne Bonnot de Condillac, *Essai sur l'origine des connoissances humaines*, in *Œuvres philosophiques*, ed. by Georges Le Roy, 3 vols. (Paris: Presses universitaires de France, 1947), I, 128.
11 Claude-Adrien Hélvetius, *De l'homme, de ses facultés intellectuelles et de son éducation*, 2 vols. (Paris: Fayard, 1989), II, 707. As Caroline Warman observes, this linking of language to sensation means 'the route towards pornography has been philosophically legitimised' (*Sade: From Materialism to Pornography, Studies on Voltaire and the Eighteenth Century*, 2002: 01 (Oxford: Voltaire Foundation, 2002), 53).

there like an actor on a stage and the listeners in the alcoves looked on as if from the stalls] (*120J* 56; 45). Sade goes into considerable detail regarding the layout and furnishing of the salon, including the gold-fringed black velvet covering the steps to the throne, before describing Duclos's first appearance on stage 'en déshabillé très leger et très élégant, beaucoup de rouge et de diamants' [dressed in a very delicate and elegant negligée, with plenty of rouge and diamonds] (*120J* 80; 71). For all the attention given to the staging of storytelling, however, the spectacle of Duclos fades – at least for the reader – the moment her story begins, as the ageing *historienne* cedes the spotlight to her younger self. While she remains a visual as well as aural presence for her audience in the salon, it is soon clear her role is to be heard rather than seen. Her first evening of storytelling is soon interrupted precisely because her story has not been sufficiently vivid to displace her as a visual presence: as Curval complains,

> 'il faut à vos récits les détails les plus grands et les plus étendus [...] je n'ai nulle idée du vit de votre second récollet, et nulle idée de sa décharge. D'ailleurs, vous branla-t-il le con et y fit-il toucher son vit ? Vous voyez, que de détails négligés !'
>
> ['your tales must include the greatest and most extensive detail [...] I have no sense of your second Recollect's prick, and no sense of his climax – besides, did he frig your cunt, and did he have you touch his prick? You see? Nothing but neglected details!'] (*120J* 84; 75)

Sade is instinctively aware that vision can hinder visualization.[12] If he champions the aural in the *120 Journées* as the most libertine of the senses it is because he understands its capacity to inspire rather than impede visualization. Ultimately, however, the storytelling in Silling is doomed to disruption even when it succeeds in stimulating its audience's imagination: the four libertines listen in order to enact what they hear on those around them, and that enactment requires the *historiennes* to pause 'tant que

---

12 It is easier to visualize an object with one's eyes closed because vision and visualization both use the same part of the brain: the visual cortex. Numerous experiments have shown the ways in which the two may interfere with each other. See, for example, Catherine Craver-Lemley and Adam Reeves, 'How Visual Imagery Interferes with Vision', *Psychological Review*, 99 (1992), 633–49. See the Conclusion of this book for a scene in which Juliette is advised that darkness is helpful to the stimulation of mental imagery.

dureront les plaisirs de celui dont les besoins l'interrompent' ['for as long as it takes to satisfy the friend whose needs interrupt it'] (*120J* 63; 52).

While the *historienne* on her throne, like Eugénie on her pedestal, enjoys a degree of protection from those for whom she performs, the same evidently cannot be said of Sade's most compelling, and compulsive, storyteller: Justine. Of the fourteen occasions the long-suffering heroine tells her story in *Justine*, she is rewarded with the compassionate response she so desperately seeks on only four occasions – and on two of these her listeners are punished for their compassion with lethal poison. In this respect she enjoys none of the luck enjoyed by her predecessors in the sentimental tradition. Marivaux's Marianne, for example, finds beauty and misfortune to be a winning combination: on the one hand, she observes that 'il y a de certaines infortunes qui embellissent la beauté même, qui lui prêtent de la majesté' [there are certain misfortunes that embellish beauty itself, which lend it majesty], and on the other that 'il est bon [...] de plaire un peu aux yeux, ils vous recommandent au cœur...' [it is helpful [...] to please the eyes a little, they commend you to the heart].[13] Justine, however, generally finds that the same combination invites a sexual rather than sentimental response in her listeners. On being orphaned, for example, she turns to her local curate for succour:

> Justine en larmes va trouver son curé ; elle lui peint son état avec l'énergique candeur de son âge... Elle était en petit fourreau blanc ; ses beaux cheveux négligemment repliés sous un grand bonnet ; sa gorge à peine indiquée, cachée sous deux ou trois aunes de gaze ; sa jolie mine un peu pâle à cause des chagrins qui la dévoraient ; quelques larmes roulaient dans ses yeux et leur prêtaient encore plus d'expression. « Vous me voyez, monsieur », dit-elle au saint ecclésiastique... « Oui, vous me voyez dans une position bien affligeante pour une jeune fille
>
> [Justine, in tears, goes to find her priest; she describes her situation to him with the lively innocence of her young age... She was wearing a little white dress; her beautiful hair carelessly tucked under a large bonnet; her barely discernible breasts, hidden beneath two or three ells of gauze; her pretty complexion a little pale from the woes which consumed her; a few tears welled in her eyes and made them even more expressive. 'You see me, Monsieur,' she said to the holy cleric... 'Yes, you see me in a very distressing position indeed for a young girl'] (*J* 135)

---

13   Pierre Carlet de Marivaux, *La Vie de Marianne*, ed. by Frédéric Deloffre (Paris: Garnier, 1957), 80, 146.

Once again, Sade is the master of lecherous ellipsis, the narrator painting a portrait of twelve-year-old Justine as she 'paints' her situation to the priest. Rather than relaying her words, the narrator relays her appearance, emphasizing the visual signs of her distress, from the pallor that matches the whiteness of her dress to the repeated mention of her tears. Justine's eyes are seen rather than seeing here, a spectacle offered by the narrator to the priest. While it may not be clear which of the two is ogling her here (an ambiguity created by an almost Flaubertian use of free indirect discourse), the implication is that it does not really matter: if the two perspectives are indistinct it is because they are perfectly aligned, with both priest and narrator hiding their libertine gaze behind a mask of fake piety. The voracity of this gaze is ironically made more evident by the fact there is little for it to see: her hair tucked under her bonnet, her breasts hidden beneath gauze, Justine's body can barely be glimpsed. Although her repetition of 'Vous me voyez' [You see me] reinforces the sense of the gaze upon her, what the curate sees 'en lorgnant Justine' [ogling Justine] is secondary to what he visualizes with his mind's eye. His mental undressing of Justine ironically leads to him exposing himself, as he is revealed by 'un baiser beaucoup trop mondain pour un homme d'Église' [a kiss far too worldly for a man of the Church] (*J* 135–6).[14]

As this episode reflects, Justine's appeal for the libertines she encounters is that she is the picture – as well as the soul – of innocence. As the crimes against her accumulate, so her story gains in erotic appeal for her predatory listeners. This is most obvious to the reader, if not to Justine, when she tells her tale of woe to Sévérino upon her arrival at Sainte-Marie-des-Bois:

> je ne lui déguise rien. Je lui avoue toutes mes fautes ; je lui fais part de tous mes malheurs ; je lui dévoile jusqu'à la marque honteuse dont m'a flétrie le barbare Rodin. Sévérino écoute tout avec la plus grande attention, il me fait même répéter quelques détails avec l'air de la pitié et de l'intérêt ; mais quelques mouvements, quelques paroles le trahirent pourtant : hélas ! ce ne fut qu'après, que j'y réfléchis mieux ; quand je fus plus calme sur cet événement, il me fut impossible de ne pas me souvenir que le moine s'était plusieurs fois permis sur lui-même plusieurs gestes

---

14 For a translation that reinforces the ogling gaze in this scene, see Chapter 4, 'How Not to Translate Sade'.

qui prouvaient que la passion entrait pour beaucoup dans les demandes
qu'il me faisait, et que ces demandes [...] s'arrêtaient avec complaisance
sur les détails obscènes

[I hide nothing from him. I confess all my sins to him; I share all my
misfortunes with him; I even reveal the shameful mark with which that
barbaric Rodin branded me. Séverino listens to it all with the greatest
attention, he even has me repeat certain details with an air of piety and
concern; but certain gestures, certain words betrayed him nonetheless:
alas! It was only afterwards, when I reflected on it better, when I thought
more calmly about this event, that it was impossible for me not to
remember that the monk had even indulged in several gestures about
his person that proved that the questions he asked of me were largely
inspired by his ardour, and that these questions [...] lingered with
satisfaction on the obscene details] (*J* 227)

Justine here reveals more, and more of her body, than she did to the curate, but, like the libertines of the *120 Journées*, Séverino is more focussed on listening than looking, pressing for ever more detail as he strives to turn her words into mental images. The pleasure for Séverino is aural, visual and tactile, while Justine is conversely unable to process what she sees and hears in time to understand the danger she is in.

Acts of listening in *Justine* generally serve as a prelude to acts of violence. While Justine's 'air de Vierge' [Virginal air] (*J* 133) is evidently part of her appeal, it is the aural reception of her story that inspires her listeners to add their own entry to the list of crimes committed against her. The purity of her voice, described as an 'organe touchant' [a touching voice] (*J* 133),[15] and the depravity of the scenes she is required to describe, appear to offer an irresistible contrast for her libertine listeners – and, indeed, her author. In both *Les Infortunes de la vertu* and *Justine*, the heroine's storytelling reflects Sade's privileging of the female voice, even if she is uncharacteristically silenced in the *Nouvelle Justine* with the switch from first- to third-person narration. From longer works such as the *120 Journées* and the *Histoire de Juliette* to short stories such as 'Florville et Courval' and 'Emilie de Tourville', women in Sadean fiction tell the story of their sexual lives for a male audience. While Justine's storytelling is heard by a woman as well as a man, only the latter has the authority to arrange this and to come to the rescue once it has concluded.

---

15 Note the two senses – tactile and emotional – of 'touchant' [touching].

Taking custody of Justine, Corville tells her 'ce n'est plus que de moi que vous dépendez' [you now depend on no one but me], and Juliette tells her sister to prostrate herself at his feet:

> La voilà, monsieur, la voilà, votre prisonnière : va, Thérèse, va, cours, vole à l'instant te jeter aux pieds de ce protecteur équitable qui ne t'abandonnera pas comme les autres.
>
> [There she is, Monsieur, there she is, your prisoner: go, Thérèse, go, run, fly this instant to hurl yourself at the feet of a just protector who will not abandon you as others did.] (J 386)

A little earlier, a brief pause in Justine's story similarly shows that power in Sadean fiction lies with the listener, when Corville insists she gives as full an account of her sexual experiences as possible:

> nous exigeons de vous ces détails, vous les gazez avec une décence qui en émousse toute l'horreur, il n'en reste que ce qui est utile à qui veut connaître l'homme ; on n'imagine point combien ces tableaux sont utiles au développement de son âme
>
> [we demand all these details of you, you veil them with a decency that blunts them all of all their horror, leaving only what is useful for those who wish to know mankind; one cannot imagine how useful these descriptions are for one's spiritual growth] (J 325)

The echo of Curval's demand for visual detail from Duclos in the *120 Journées* only reinforces the sense of innuendo in the spiritual 'growth' Corville describes.

For the reader, the emphasis on the oral – and aural – imbues the storytelling in *Justine* with an immediacy and urgency that one simply does not find in libertine or pornographic fiction before Sade. Every time Justine opens her mouth to tell her story, the question is posed: what will the listener do? The imminent threat of violence raises the stakes, instilling the scene of storytelling with a sense of jeopardy, and the reader with a sense of dread. For the libertines listening to Justine, the pleasure of hearing the victim's story is rather like the pleasure of hearing her scream or tasting her tears: it is the pleasure of being as physically close to suffering as possible and, of course, the promise of adding to that suffering. As accurate as it is to call Justine's male listeners 'libertines' – a term with which both they and their author identify[16] – there is a risk that this defines them rather too generously. To call them libertines is to explain their behaviour as being philosophically motivated and justified, and to explain (away) the violence they commit as the effect of a philosophical cause. Sade scholars have largely been happy to take the author and his characters at their word in this regard, and less willing to explore the other possibility: that the drive to commit violence is the cause, not the effect, of their philosophy. If, however, we consider Justine's listeners first and foremost as men, and as rapists, rather than as the embodiment of philosophical positions, then recent studies in the field of psychology relating to interpersonal violence may prove instructive.

The intense debate about pornography during the aforementioned sex wars inspired, and was inspired by, a growing body of research by social scientists into the potential harms of sexual, and sexually violent, images. The two groups that most commonly featured in correlational and experimental studies in this period were convicted criminals and college students, as researchers sought to explore whether exposure to pornography might lead to more callous or violent behaviours. Inevitably, such research concentrated almost exclusively on visual pornography, but one study from the early 1990s chose to explore responses to something approximating aural pornography. While previous research had shown, perhaps unsurprisingly, that depictions of rape were more arousing to rapists than non-rapists, what makes this particular study interesting – and pertinent – is that it measured physical arousal (via phallometric response) to a variety of audiotaped first-person narrations of sexual encounters. Some of these encounters were depicted as consenting and some were not, while half of the narrations were voiced by a woman and half by a man. The stories, which the subjects of the study listened to in 'a reclining chair located

---

16   In his *grande lettre* to his wife, Sade repeatedly asserts 'Je suis un libertin, mais...' [I am a libertine, but...] in a paragraph which begins, 'Oui, je suis libertin, je l'avoue ; j'ai conçu tout ce qu'on peut concevoir dans ce genre-là, mais je n'ai sûrement pas fait tout ce que j'ai concu et ne le ferai sûrement jamais. Je suis un libertin, mais je ne suis pas *un criminel* ni *un meurtrier*' [Yes, I am libertine, I admit it; I have imagined everything one could imagine of the sort, but I have certainly not done everything that I have imagined and I certainly never will. I am a libertine, but I am not *a criminal* nor *a murderer*] (Letter of 20 February 1781, in Sade, *Lettres à sa femme*, ed. by Marc Buffat (Arles: Actes Sud, 1997), 229).

in a sound-attenuated and electrically shielded room',[17] were divided into four categories: sexually neutral social interactions, consenting heterosexual interactions, heterosexual rape where the female victim was described as either suffering or enjoying the encounter (the latter a common scenario in pornographic films), and non-sexual violence.[18] Although rapists and non-rapists responded very differently to the stories, what they had in common was that they were both most aroused by a story voiced by a woman. As Figure 2 shows, non-rapists were most aroused by a female-voiced story of consensual sex, while rapists were most aroused by a female-voiced story in which a woman described enjoying a rape.

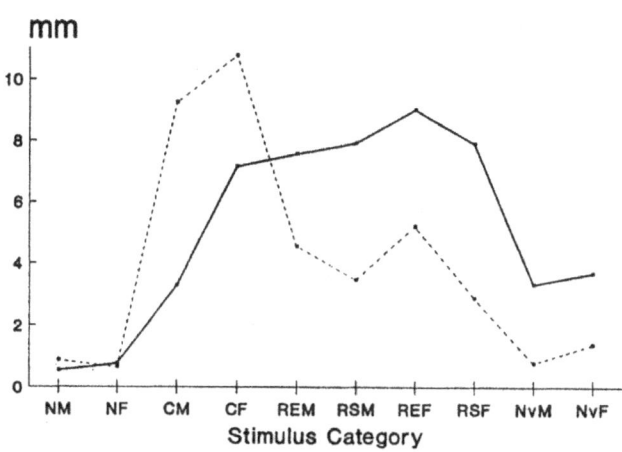

Fig. 2 Mean phallometric response in mm change as a function of stimulus category (N = neutral, C = consenting, R = rape, NV = nonsexual violence; S = victim suffered, E = victim enjoyed; M = stories told from male perspective, F = stories told from female perspective). The dotted line shows the response of non-rapists; the solid line shows the response of rapists. From Marnie E. Rice, Terry C. Chaplin, Grant T. Harris, Joanne Coutts, 'Empathy for the Victim and Sexual Arousal Among Rapists and Nonrapists', *Journal of Interpersonal Violence*, 9.4 (1994), 443

At the other end of the scale, the male-voiced account of consensual sex was the least stimulating sexual story for the rapists, and the

---

17 Marnie E. Rice, Terry C. Chaplin, Grant T. Harris, Joanne Coutts, 'Empathy for the Victim and Sexual Arousal Among Rapists and Nonrapists', *Journal of Interpersonal Violence*, 9.4 (1994), 438.
18 Ibid., 439.

female-voiced account describing suffering was the least stimulating sexual story for non-rapists. These two stories prompted the most marked divergence between the two groups.

For most heterosexual male listeners, the evidence suggests, the female voice is more erotically appealing than the male when describing female enjoyment but less appealing than the male when describing female suffering. This leads the authors of the study to conclude,

> the results are consistent with the view that the sexual arousal of nonrapists is inhibited during stories of rape because they empathize with the victim and experience some of her suffering. Rapists, on the other hand, are not inhibited by the suffering of the victim because they experience little or no empathy for her.[19]

This conclusion rather leaps ahead of the evidence in asserting firstly that empathy is the only possible explanation, secondly that the listeners *experienced* some of the victim's suffering and thirdly that rapists feel little or no such empathy. There will be a fuller discussion of empathy later in this chapter, but for now it is worth noting that there is also such a thing as sympathy. While both these terms have changed in meaning over time,[20] rather than indulge in a semantic discussion here it is perhaps enough to point out that there is a difference – at least in emphasis – between being moved or distressed by someone else's suffering, and experiencing that suffering as if it were happening to oneself. The invoking of empathy in Rice's study, and the use of the word 'experience', suggest the latter, but the study provides no evidence for this and fails to consider the former. The conclusion regarding the lack of empathy experienced by rapists is also an oversimplification: as the graph shows, the rapists enjoyed the female-voiced rape story which described enjoyment more than the one which described suffering. While suffering did not diminish their arousal quite as much as non-rapists, it nonetheless had a marked effect which the authors of the study fail to acknowledge. Their own logic would imply that the rapists too experienced some of the victim's suffering, even if it affected them slightly less; this would undermine their claim that cues of victim distress 'contribute to sexual arousal

---

19 Ibid., 445.
20 See C. Daniel Batson, 'These Things Called Empathy: Eight Related but Distinct Phenomena', in *The Social Neuroscience of Empathy*, ed. by Jean Decety and William Ickes (Cambridge, MA: MIT Press), 3–15.

among rapists'.[21] The study raises a further question about whether the higher arousal for female-voiced stories describing enjoyment follows the same dynamic as those describing suffering: in other words, do male listeners 'experience' – whatever that might mean – some of the female pleasure described in these stories as well as the pain described in others? We shall return to this question below in relation to a scene from *Justine*.

There is a further possible weakness of the study regarding its claims about empathy, although this weakness in a social science context arguably becomes a strength in a literary critical one: the stories used in the study are precisely that – stories. As its title – 'Empathy for the Victim' – reflects, the authors of the study rather elide the fact that these stories are not true, and what they are therefore measuring is empathy for fictional victims. While it is possible that respondents would have reacted in a similar fashion to real first-person accounts, it seems to me at least possible that the fictionality of these stories may have played some part in their responses. A fantasy of violence in which no one is harmed is very different to an account of violence depicting actual harm, and respondents' awareness of this distinction may plausibly have had a disinhibiting effect. As the aim of this chapter is in any case to explore responses to fictional violence, however, this oversight arguably makes the Rice study more rather than less useful for our purposes here. In any case, the study remains intriguing for what it suggests about the impact of voice and perspective on responses to stories of sexual violence. The findings of the study corroborate, for example, Sade's privileging of the female voice within his fiction by confirming its greater erotic appeal for male heterosexual listeners. The study also chimes with the sense one has in Sadean fiction that stories neither corrupt nor change their listeners but merely reveal who they are: a rapist such as Séverino is aroused by Justine's tale of suffering while a non-rapist such as Dubreuil is not.

One cannot help but wonder whether Sade's stories also reveal something of their author: does the endless repetition of what is labelled in the study 'RSF', a female-voiced rape story depicting suffering, imply

---

21   Rice et al., 'Empathy for the Victim', 435. This claim fits the male-voiced rape stories slightly better, although there was only a very marginal preference among rapists for the story depicting suffering over enjoyment.

an author with a rapist's sensibility? As ever with Sade, it is not so simple. Given the study suggests that he would (or should) have focussed more on pleasure than pain had he been solely interested in maximizing erotic response, the fact he chose otherwise could be taken as evidence that this was not his aim. There are, of course, other authors whose novels have featured unremitting depictions of RSF, and whom no one would suspect of having a rapist's sensibility – Andrea Dworkin being perhaps the most obvious example.[22] While no sensible person can read Sade and imagine he was motivated by a desire to expose and protest against the sexual violence suffered by women, it is possible to imagine different sensibilities behind his eroticization of violence ranging from the sadistic to the masochistic – the case for the latter made some time ago by Jean Paulhan.[23] The more pressing question, however, is not what scenes of fictional rape can tell us about the author who wrote them, but what they can reveal about the readers who – like the listeners within Sade's fiction – hear, see and feel their way into them.

Reading as Listening

If I have dwelled on the staging of listening in Sade, and on the experience of listening to stories of sexual violence, it is because the reader too is a listener. Given that even our visual imagery has until recently been largely ignored despite our ingrained ocularcentrism, it should come as no surprise that the aural aspect of reading has been almost entirely neglected within literary studies. While there has been growing interest in literary 'soundscapes' over the last twenty years, the study of these has largely followed the precedent offered by the study of visual imagery in literary criticism: sound is treated as something evoked by a text rather than something experienced by its readers.[24]

---

22 See, for example, Dworkin's *Ice and Fire* (1986) or *Mercy* (1990).
23 See Jean Paulhan, *Le Marquis de Sade et sa complice* (Paris: Editions Complexe, 1987).
24 For recent work on literary soundscapes see Helen Groth, 'Literary Soundscapes', in *Sound and Literature*, ed. by Anna Snaith (Cambridge, UK: Cambridge University Press, 2020), 135–153. Hélène Cussac has led the way in exploring French eighteenth-century sound and soundscapes, with various articles including 'Anthropologie du bruit au siècle des lumières', in *Bruits* (special issue), *L'Autre musique* [online journal], 4 (2016), https://www.lautremusique.net/images/Page/90/56f945375f047.pdf and an edited volume: *Le paysage sonore dans la*

What makes this lack of attention to what readers actually hear when they read rather curious, however, is that narratologists have for decades been discussing the narrator as someone who speaks. Genette was the first to ask the question *'qui parle?'* [who speaks], but only in order to distinguish it from the question *'qui voit?'* [who sees][25] as part of his attempt to untangle narration from focalization. Since Genette, guide after guide to narrative theory has typically included chapters or sections on 'Voice' without ever considering the voice as an aural presence for the reader. As Kuzmičová accurately observes, in works of narratology 'the term *voice* is used as a metaphor, without phenomenal implications'.[26] While poststructuralist theorists sought to eliminate the idea of voice, which they associated with an illusory logocentrism, their efforts were arguably unnecessary given that the voices discussed by narratologists were already silent – textual and readable in conception rather than oral and audible. Ironically this is most obvious in the way these guides to narrative consistently use speech marks to denote a voice that makes no sound, such as when Shlomith Rimmon-Kenan describes the narrator as 'the narrative "voice" or "speaker" of a text', or when H. Porter Abbott explains that 'Voice in narration is a question of who it is we "hear" doing the narrating'.[27] Even recent guides to narrative theory that claim to have a postclassical or cognitive perspective continue to treat voice as a textual rather than aural phenomenon.[28] The only theorist to take

---

littérature d'Ancien Régime, ou du son comme topos de scènes narratives (special issue), *Topiques, études satoriennes* [online journal], 6 (2022), https://www.erudit.org/fr/revues/topiques/2022-v6-topiques07705/. See also Isabelle Bour (ed.), *Noise and Sound in Eighteenth-Century Britain* (special issue), *Études Épistémè : Revue de littérature et de civilisation (XVIe-XVIIIe siècles)* [online journal], 29 (2016), https://journals.openedition.org/episteme/962.

25   Gérard Genette, *Figures III* (Paris: Seuil, 1972), 203.
26   Kuzmičová, 'The Words and Worlds of Literary Narrative', 110.
27   Shlomith Rimmon-Kenan, *Narrative Fiction: Contemporary Poetics* (London: Methuen, 1983), 87; H. Porter Abbott, *The Cambridge Introduction to Narrative* (Cambridge, UK: Cambridge University Press, 2002), 64. See also Mieke Baal, who alludes to 'the "voice" of the narrator' (*Narratology: Introduction to the Theory of Narrative*, 2nd edn. (Toronto: University of Toronto Press, 1997), 21) and Patrick O'Neill, who refers to the 'voice we "hear" telling us the story when we read a novel' (*Fictions of Discourse: Reading Narrative Theory* (Toronto: University of Toronto Press, 1996), 58).
28   See, for example, Richard Walsh, 'Person, Level, Voice: A Rhetorical Reconsideration', in *Postclassical Narratology*, ed. by Jan Alber and Monika Fludernik (Columbus, OH: Ohio State University Press, 2010), 31–57, and Katja Mellmann, 'Voice and Perception: An Evolutionary Approach to the Basic

reading as an auditory experience seriously has been Garrett Stewart, whose *Reading Voices: Literature and the Phonotext* explores 'the combined somatic and cerebral "affect" generated in the reader by the exertion of one syllable or phoneme upon another'.[29] As enlightening as that may be, Stewart's psycholinguistic focus is on what we hear at the level of syllables and phonemes as we read, not on the broader psychological experience of reading.[30] Narrative theory has yet to consider what the voice that we hear as we read sounds like, let alone what difference the sound of it makes, or indeed what other sounds we hear when we read, but that is the aim here.

In the various fictional scenes of storytelling invoked in the previous section, it was evident that the listeners depicted were not just responding to the words but to the voice speaking those words. The Rice study moreover confirms that the gender of a voice has an impact on the aural reception of sexual content. There is a reason, as we have already seen, why Sade's libertines in the *120 Journées* prefer to listen to women. It would seem logical to assume the same reason is behind their author's preference for female narrators – that Sade believed, in other words, that a story narrated by a woman would have more erotic appeal for his male readers than one told by a man. The popularity of novels such as *Fanny Hill* and *Thérèse philosophe* would no doubt have cemented such a belief.[31] The question is, however, to what degree does the process of listening to a person speaking translate to the process of reading a narrator telling a story? The only way to begin to answer

---

Functions of Narrative', in *Towards a Cognitive Theory of Narrative Acts*, ed. by Frederick Luis Aldama (Austin, TX: University of Texas Press, 2010), 119–41. *Psychonarratology*, by Marisa Bortolussi and Peter Dixon, implicitly constitutes an exception to the rule in describing the narrator as 'a representation in the mind of the reader', but does not explore what that representation might sound like (*Psychonarratology*, 95).

29 Garrett Stewart, *Reading Voices: Literature and the Phonotext* (Berkeley, CA: University of California Press, 1990), 23.

30 The same is also true of other examples of the very limited work in this field, such as Richard Aczel, 'Hearing Voices in Narrative Texts', *New Literary History*, 29.3 (1998), 467–500.

31 If, more recently, the extraordinary popularity of the *50 Shades of Grey* trilogy suggests the appeal of the female narrator is far from exclusive to a heterosexual male readership, the subsequent release of male-narrated versions of the trilogy 'as told by Christian' suggests continued belief in the erotic – and perhaps exotic – appeal exerted by a narrator of a different gender to the intended readership (in this case a female one).

this question is to ask actual readers what – or who – they hear when they read. The answers provided by my students when completing their questionnaires offer intriguing insights into the aurality of reading.

The data on which I am relying here is drawn from the results of two sets of questionnaires: the first is the same set of questionnaires used in the previous chapter, relating to the statue scene in 'Eugénie de Franval'; the second is a set of questionnaires relating to a rape scene from *Justine*.[32] While the former is a straightforward third-person narration, the latter is more complex, as Justine addresses her interlocutor in the present before narrating an episode that includes a brief moment of embedded dialogue:

> Vous me permettrez, madame, dit notre belle prisonnière en rougissant, de vous déguiser une partie des détails obscènes de cette odieuse cérémonie ; que votre imagination se représente tout ce que la débauche peut en tel cas dicter à des scélérats [...]
>
> « Allons », dit Séverino dont les désirs prodigieusement exaltés ne peuvent plus se contenir, et qui dans cet affreux état donne l'idée d'un tigre prêt à dévorer sa victime, « que chacun de nous lui fasse éprouver sa jouissance favorite » ; et l'infâme, me plaçant sur un canapé dans l'attitude propice à ses exécrables projets, me faisant tenir par deux de ses moines, essaie de se satisfaire avec moi de cette façon criminelle et perverse qui ne nous fait ressembler au sexe que nous ne possédons pas, qu'en dégradant celui que nous avons ; mais, ou cet impudique est trop fortement proportionné, ou la nature se révolte en moi au seul soupçon de ces plaisirs ; il ne peut vaincre les obstacles ; à peine se présente-t-il, qu'il est aussitôt repoussé... Il écarte, il presse, il déchire, tous ses efforts sont superflus ; la fureur de ce monstre se porte sur l'autel où ne peuvent atteindre ses vœux, il le frappe, il le pince, il le mord ; de nouvelles épreuves naissent du sein de ces brutalités ; les chairs ramollies se prêtent, le sentier s'entrouvre, le bélier pénètre ; je pousse des cris épouvantables ; bientôt la masse entière est engloutie, et la couleuvre lançant aussitôt un venin qui lui ravit ses forces, cède enfin, en pleurant de rage, aux mouvements que je fais pour m'en dégager. Je n'avais de ma vie tant souffert.

> ['You will allow me, Madam,' said our beautiful prisoner as she blushed, 'to cast a veil over the obscene details of this odious ceremony. May your

---

32 The full results of the 'Eugénie' and *Justine* questionnaires may be accessed via the Digital Appendix.

imagination picture for itself the lengths to which debauchery can in such circumstances drive scoundrels [...]

'"Come," said Séverino, whose prodigiously aroused desires can no longer contain themselves, and who in this dreadful state resembles a tiger ready to devour its victim. "Let each of us inflict on her his favourite pleasure." And the villain, placing me on a sofa in the position appropriate to his execrable intentions, with two of his monks holding me down, tries to find satisfaction with me in that criminal and perverted manner which makes us resemble men by hiding what makes us women; but either this rogue is too greatly proportioned, or Nature revolts in me at the merest suspicion of these pleasures; he cannot overcome the obstacles; at the slightest approach he is forced back... He stretches, he pushes, he tears, all his efforts are in vain; this monster's fury is unleashed on the altar his desires cannot reach, he strikes it, he pinches it, he bites it; yet more trials are born of this brutality; the softened flesh offers itself, the path opens up, and the ram penetrates; I cry out awful screams; soon the whole of it is engulfed, and the serpent, spurting a venom that depletes its strength, withdraws at last, weeping tears of rage at my struggles to free myself. Never in my whole life had I experienced such suffering.] (*J* 234)

As in the last chapter, before going further I would like to ask you, dear reader, to take a moment or two to reflect on what you heard, saw and felt when reading this passage... and then to ask yourself the same questions I asked my students:

1. When you were reading this passage did you hear the words in your head?
2. Did you hear the words in the same voice throughout or did it change?
3. Would you identify the voice or voices you heard as belonging to yourself, the narrator, the author, the characters in the scene or a mixture of these?
4. Was the voice you heard male, female, neutral, or changing from one to the other depending on who was speaking?
5. Did you hear other sounds in your head as you were reading?
6. Did you hear Justine scream?
7. Did you see anything in your mind's eye as you were reading this scene?

8. Where would you say you were seeing the scene from? Was it from a fixed point or did your position move?

We shall return to the questions relating to visualization later, and keep for now to the aural aspect of reception explored in the first six of these questions.

Of the forty-three students who completed the *Justine* questionnaires, all but one reported hearing inner speech – a much higher percentage than the 84% who reported inner speech in the 'Eugénie' questionnaires. Why the difference? There is very little in the extract from 'Eugénie de Franval' that draws attention to its own telling, other perhaps than a couple of rhetorical questions, and this may diminish some readers' awareness of their own inner speech. By contrast, the passage from *Justine* immediately announces its own spokenness, with Justine addressing her interlocutor directly in the second person; it then reinforces the orality and aurality of the narration ('dit notre belle prisonnière' [said our beautiful prisoner]) before transitioning to an embedded narrative which also contains direct speech as Séverino addresses his fellow monks. Although inner speech generally occurs 'irrespective of the inferred identity or ontological status of the imaginary voice', and 'No textual markers of overt vocalization are necessary',[33] recent research in psycholinguistics suggests that 'an "inner voice" is particularly pronounced when reading direct speech quotations (and much less so for indirect speech)'.[34] The visual as well as aural staging of storytelling in the *Justine* extract, as the beautiful narrator blushes, doubtless added to the vividness of the direct speech experienced by the respondents.

Kuzmičová has helpfully defined our hearing of inner speech as we read as 'verbal presence': 'the reader's vicarious perception of the voices of narrators and characters'.[35] There is an ambiguity to vicariousness which is worth noting, however: one can vicariously enjoy, for example,

---

33 Kuzmičová, 'The Words and Worlds of Literary Narrative', 111. Marianne Abramson and Stephen D. Goldinger also argue that inner speech is intrinsic to silent reading in 'What the Reader's Eye Tells the Mind's Ear: Silent Reading Activates Inner Speech', *Perception & Psychophysics*, 59.7 (1997), 1059–68.

34 Bo Yao and Christoph Scheepers, 'Inner Voice Experiences During Processing of Direct and Indirect Speech', in *Explicit and Implicit Prosody in Sentence Processing: Studies in Honor of Janet Dean Fodor*, ed. by Lyn Frazier and Edward Gibson, *Studies in Theoretical Psycholinguistics*, 46 (Cham: Springer, 2015), 288.

35 Kuzmičová, 'The Words and Worlds of Literary Narrative', 108.

someone else's performance, or one can vicariously perform a role on behalf of someone else. Which of these is happening in the case of our inner speech while reading? Put another way, who are we hearing? Kuzmičová suggests verbal presence can be 'tinted by individual voicing that is different [to] the reader's own',[36] and it is certainly true that some readers experience these voices as being in some way 'other' than their own. At the same time, however, as Peter Kivy has reminded us, reading is a matter of performance as well as perception, and indeed of our perception of that performance: when we experience these voices as being other than our own, it is because we are concurrently performing them as such, and doing so in a way which is moreover convincing (or convincing enough). Some of this confusion, or complexity at least, is perhaps captured best in one of the respondent's answers to the question of whose voice she was hearing as she read the passage from *Justine*: 'I identify with the voice, but I have no idea to whom it belongs'. This sense of disorientation may reflect what happens when readers are asked to think about a process that normally unfolds unthinkingly: as another respondent said, 'I am not entirely sure about this question since I did not pay attention to it and the voice usually "comes" inevitably and automatically'. Other responses ranged from those stressing the otherness of their inner speech ('I heard the story as if it were being read to me') to those with a clear sense of proprietorship over that speech ('When I read it is my voice that I hear in my head always').

Of those who reported hearing a voice when reading the 'Eugénie' extract, the majority (56%) identified that voice as belonging to the narrator, while 31% identified that voice as their own and a few (3%) identified it as belonging to the author. As for the gendering of that voice, 52% of those who associated that voice with either the narrator or the author heard that voice as neutral, and 48% as male; of those who associated that voice with themselves, 60% heard that voice as neutral, 30% as female and none as male (not even the four male students in the group). Overall, 59% of those who heard a voice experienced it as neutral, 31% as male and only 9% as female. These results suggest both that hearing a voice as one's own does not necessarily mean hearing it as gendered, and that the voice we hear has less to do with

---

36   Ibid., 111.

one's own gender than the gender of the narrator or author to whom we are giving voice. This is confirmed by the findings of the *Justine* questionnaire. Readers of the *Justine* passage were split between those for whom the voice remained the same throughout (36%) and those for whom it changed (55%) (with a few unsure). Of the former, none of the handful of male readers experienced a male voice, and only three (7%) of the female readers who heard a voice experienced it as male. These exceptions are moreover revealing: two of these female readers identified the voice as belonging to the author and attributed this to 'the powerful nature of the author image of Sade' or 'Sade's personality', while the other, in perhaps the most disturbing finding of all, identified the voice as belonging to her lecturer, hearing the passage 'As if it were being read to me in a lecture? I don't know, sorry Will it was your voice!'[37] Of those readers who heard the passage in a female voice throughout, half identified it as the narrator's voice and the other half as their own. Among the latter, two thirds experienced it as female, and one third as neutral – the exact reverse of the 'Eugénie' questionnaire results, suggesting that sharing a gender with a narrator increases the likelihood of identifying the narrator's voice as gendered.

The foregrounding of narration in the *Justine* passage had a measurable impact on the respondents' aural experience of the text. 80% of them experienced the text as if they were listening to someone else, and only 20% as if they were listening to themselves – a pronounced swing to the former when compared with responses to the 'Eugénie' extract. It would seem reasonable to speculate that readers who only hear themselves may be less immersed in a text than those who feel they are hearing others. The questionnaire responses would appear to support such a claim: none of the readers who heard their own voice narrating the text heard any other sounds as they read, whereas half of those who heard other voices also reported hearing other sounds. It is worth noting, however, that hearing the passage in one's own voice did not block visual imagery in the same way that it appears to have blocked auditory images. This finding suggests something analogous to the way in which visualization and vision can interfere with each

---

37 I suspect (hope) that this had something to do with the fact that I was the one who briefed students on the questionnaires before distributing them at the start of a class.

other. Similarly, one form of listening or hearing may drown out another, and one's own voice while reading may become too 'loud' to hear anything else. As this potential conflict is local to the auditory cortex, however, it does not impinge on the ability to generate visual imagery. Conversely, those readers who had given Justine a voice of her own did so because they were more immersed in the story, and thus more able to hear other sounds – and other voices – too. This implies something a little more complex than the direct tension Kuzmičová claims between verbal presence and what she terms 'direct presence': 'the emulated sensorimotor experience of the imaginary worlds that the narrators' and characters' utterances refer to'.[38] She argues that verbal and direct presence vie for our attention when reading fiction and that one always loses: 'where the reader is prone to vicariously hearing the narrative as if read out loud, perception of the world(s) of the story is backgrounded due to the mutually exclusive relationship between verbal presence and direct presence'.[39] As we know from the cinema, however, we are perfectly able to watch a film with a voiceover without there being a clash between our aural and visual experience.[40] Equally, I would suggest, our imagination is able to walk and chew gum at the same time, even if, at times, the pace of our walking – and chewing – may vary.

For those respondents who felt they were listening to Justine, rather than themselves, what did she sound like? For some, rather like themselves: 'a woman['s] voice, which resembled my own voice in my head', as opposed to Séverino's 'manly' voice; 'The voice seems to have a slight resemblance to my own, but it is not exactly the same'; 'It was pitched slightly lower than my voice usually is'. There is something potentially uncanny in this proximity between the voices of narrator and reader, which given the violence described in the scene may develop into something more disturbing. Lucienne Frappier-Mazur describes the Sadean text as 'un texte qui peut agresser le lecteur, et la lectrice encore plus, de façons parfois intolérables' [a text which can assault the

---

38 Kuzmičová, 'The Words and Worlds of Literary Narrative', 108.
39 Ibid., 108.
40 One student reported something like the latter in her experience of the scene: 'It was as if I was in the room watching but at the same time with Justine's voice in my head narrating but I could hear her, no other sound'. In this case, hearing Justine's words blocked out other sound, but not visual imagery.

reader, and the female reader even more, in at times intolerable ways],[41] and, for some readers, sharing a gender with the victims in Sade may indeed inspire anxiety or distress. One respondent reported the disconcerting feeling that Justine was speaking with her (the reader's) voice, and described the experience as 'scary'. Others, however, did not relate Justine's voice to their own, describing it simply as a 'calm and feminine voice', or a 'female and soft one' – again in contrast to Sévérino's, which was 'masculine, harsh'.[42] For one reader, Justine's voice seemed 'Strangely detached?' while another conversely heard the voice of 'A strong-minded yet vulnerable female. Deeply disturbed by what she is encountering [...] combats and defeats her tears'. Responses to the 'Eugénie' extract similarly demonstrate the range of voices readers evoke (or 'evocalize'[43], to use Stewart's term), from one reader describing the narrator as 'Very calm' to another as 'Excited'.

Although the Rice study offers intriguing evidence of the role gender plays in male responses to externally voiced narratives of sexual violence, the situation is not quite the same for readers hearing internally voiced narratives of similar content. Nonetheless, the suggestion in Rice that hearing a female voice describing suffering is likely to decrease arousal and increase empathy for most heterosexual male listeners may well translate to the experience of male readers hearing Justine describe the violence committed against her. For the male reader, hearing a female voice such as Justine's may reflect a greater degree of immersion than hearing one's own voice, a sign perhaps of more vividly imagining the heroine – and the violence against her. But one can equally imagine that a male reader might find hearing his own voice speaking Sade's words unsettling, if not distressing, for rather different reasons to the aforementioned female reader who heard her own voice speaking Justine's words: finding oneself sharing a voice not with the victim but with the author of her suffering may be bad enough, but sharing it with the perpetrator of that suffering is surely even more disquieting. Conversely, hearing the

---

41 Lucienne Frappier-Mazur, *Sade et l'écriture de l'orgie* (Paris: Nathan, 1991), 5.
42 A majority of readers heard Sévérino's voice as well as Justine's (57% of all those readers who consciously experienced inner speech, and 70% of those who heard Justine in a voice distinct from their own).
43 Stewart, *Reading Voices*, 1.

Sadean text in one's own voice may for some readers – male or female – be a sign of circumspection as they attempt to keep the text at arm's length, perhaps to avoid experiencing the kind of anxiety outlined.[44] There would indeed be much to be said for just such an approach to a novel like *Justine*: although Rita Felski has justifiably railed against the suspicion that seems to drive the way literary critics read,[45] if ever there was an author who merited our wariness, it is Sade.

Justine's Scream

As literary theorists and critics have considered 'voice' only as a textual element of narrative rather than an aural phenomenon of reading, little attention has been paid to what else we might hear when we read aside from our inner speech. As mentioned above, those who heard the Justine extract in their own voice heard no other sounds as they read. However, 39% of those who heard Justine in a voice distinct from their own also heard other sounds including a 'struggle', 'rips of clothing', 'echoes and sex', 'manly laughter' and 'The monks shouting as well as prayers and religious related noises'. But by far the sound most reported by almost all (91%) of the readers in this group (and about a quarter of all respondents) was Justine's scream, described in the text as 'des cris épouvantables' [awful screams]. Readers reported hearing 'Bone chilling screams', 'a loud and very high scream', a 'Scream of terror and disgust', Justine 'screaming and crying in pain, and gasping for air', 'screaming her pain' and screaming 'louder and louder'. One reader reported, 'I did not hear a specific scream but more an emphasis on the word scream in my head – like the word scream was screamed', suggesting an entanglement of verbal and direct presence, the sound of the word coloured by what the word represents (rather as one might be more likely to hear the word *whisper* in a whispered voice). It is worth noting here that there is little difference between a scream and a whisper in the mind's ear: auditory images all seem to occur at more

---

44 As we shall see below, these questions of complicity are not limited to the aural reception of the text.
45 See Rita Felski, *The Limits of Critique* (Chicago, IL: University of Chicago Press, 2015).

or less the same volume, despite one respondent's sense of increasingly loud screams.

There is more to a scream than meets the ear, however. Much as I had simplistically thought of the scream as an auditory image – and hence posed the question of whether the respondents had *heard* the scream – some of the responses served as a valuable reminder that images are not necessarily confined to a single sense, or to the sense one might assume. One respondent thus answered no to the question while clarifying 'But I *saw* her scream' (emphasis added), and two others reported both hearing and seeing Justine scream, one stating she could 'picture her screams clearly – like a film scene'. This was not the only response to draw parallels between the process of visualizing and that of watching a film,[46] with one student moreover invoking Stanley Kubrick's *Eyes Wide Shut* (1999) as a reference point for their visualization of an 'obscure scene with pale naked bodies and black hoods'. Cinema may indeed have provided some inspiration – general or specific – for the scream visualized by other respondents, some of whom were students of film as well as literature.[47] No doubt many readers unconsciously draw on what they have seen and heard on television or in the cinema when they visualize literary texts, particularly if they do not have relevant or related lived experiences on which to draw.

The question about Justine's scream was prompted by my struggle to find some kind of answer to the ethical problem posed by reading Sade's scenes of sexual violence, a problem encapsulated for me by Marcel Hénaff's contention that in the case of Sade, 'lire c'est déjà conspirer' [to read is already to conspire].[48] Like the female reader imagined by Rousseau in the preface to *Julie, ou la Nouvelle Héloïse*, Hénaff seems to suggest we are always already damned by the very act of reading. What I was hoping for in posing the question about Justine's scream was to find a way to distinguish between empathetic and prurient readings

---

46 Two students also compared the experience to seeing a play on the stage.
47 Perhaps even the most iconic movie scream of all, from the shower scene in Hitchcock's *Psycho* (1960), a scene as harrowing aurally as it is visually with its discordant score vying with Janet Leigh's screams.
48 Hénaff, *L'Invention du corps libertin* (Paris: Presses universitaires de France, 1978), 77.

of a scene of sexual violence. I had wondered at the time whether Justine's scream might offer the aural equivalent of a litmus test, with those hearing it demonstrating empathy or compassion, and those not hearing it demonstrating either indifference or prurience (or perhaps both). This was doubtless naïve of me, and it soon became clear there were no easy – or reassuring – answers to be had. It may well be the case that the respondents who heard Justine scream were more intensely engaged in their reading of the text than those who did not, particularly given the latter includes those less performative readers who heard the text in their own voice. Hearing Justine scream indeed implies a vivid, and vivifying, reading experience that brings the heroine to life, turning her into a human subject rather than Miller's 'object of a verb'. It does not, however, necessarily imply compassion. It does not preclude, for example, a reading experience that brings Justine to life in order to make her suffer – one which, in other words, replicates what Sade does to Justine. For the sadist, or indeed the masochist, Justine's scream may be a source of pleasure rather than distress; as we have already seen, Sade's libertines are themselves very attentive listeners. Nonetheless, on balance, it does seem to me that hearing Justine scream is more suggestive of a compassionate reading than a prurient one, even if it is also possible the two are not mutually exclusive – that, for example, an initial, perhaps instinctual, prurience when reading this passage may turn into compassion or vice versa, or that the two may, perhaps uneasily, coexist. Although we may think of compassion and prurience as contrasting impulses, both require a reader to make the effort to imagine the pain experienced by a fictional character. It is moreover an effort the text encourages us to make. Even if not all readers may hear Justine scream, they generally will hear her say, 'Je n'avais de ma vie tant souffert' [Never in my whole life had I experienced such suffering]. This sentence comes at the end of the paragraph, the full stop and the blank space after allowing her suffering to linger a little longer in our imagination – a moment of silence that may perhaps engender as much compassion as her scream.

It is of course possible that some of those who hear Justine scream may be indifferent to it, even if the accompanying comments of the questionnaire respondents generally suggest an intense emotional response to the passage. If anyone is capable of hearing a fictional character scream with indifference, it may be the literary critic. Writing on music, Barthes distinguishes between hearing and listening thus: '*Entendre* est un phénomène physiologique, *écouter* est un acte psychologique' [*Hearing* is a physiological phenomenon; *listening* is a psychological act].[49] Judged on his own terms, Barthes seems like a reader who hears but does not listen to the screams of fictional victims such as Justine. In *Sade, Fourier, Loyola* he writes, 'Le cri est la marque de la victime : c'est parce qu'elle choisit de crier, qu'elle se constitue victime' [The scream is the mark of the victim: it is because she chooses to scream that she makes a victim of herself].[50] His transformation of an involuntary expression of pain into a voluntary decision squarely, and callously, blames the victim rather than her torturer. This failure, or refusal, to listen reflects the desensitizing – and desensorializing – impact of the semiotic reading that has been so pervasive in scholarship on Sade in the long wake left by Barthes.

Once More, with *Einfühlung*

We may hear, and see, Justine suffer, but do we *feel* her suffer? The last chapter explored Eugénie's transformation from character into living statue, a transformation eased by the sense that she was an object to her father long before she became a spectacle for his friend (and for the reader). Eugénie exists purely, or impurely, to be seen, and for that seeing to inspire touch. For Herder, as for Pygmalion, the statue is imagined by the spectator as another human being – 'it can become my friend and companion' – even if, in marked contrast to the example of Pygmalion, Herder insists a statue can inspire desire 'only in a beast'.[51] While his lover of art circles a sculpture, later philosophers of art – perhaps, ironically, inspired by Herder – imagine the statue not as another to be seen from the outside but as a self to be felt from the inside. Herder himself describes the importance of

---

49 Barthes, *L'obvie et l'obtus. Essais critiques III* (Paris: Seuil, 1982), 217.
50 Barthes, *Sade, Fourier, Loyola*, 147.
51 Herder, *Sculpture*, 45, 52.

feeling one's way 'into' a text,[52] but a century later Theodor Lipps adopts and adapts Robert Vischer's recent coinage *Einfühlung*, placing it at the heart of what would become a highly influential theory of 'aesthetic satisfaction'. Lipps describes his engagement with a statue very differently to Herder. As well as feeling 'pleased or delighted', Lipps goes on to describe other ways in which he may be affected by a 'beautiful object':

> I feel myself, among other things, striving or willing, bestirring myself, or taking pains and, in such striving or contriving, I feel myself meeting or overcoming obstacles, or perhaps yielding to them. I feel myself attaining a goal, satisfying my striving and my will, I feel my efforts successful. In a word I feel various inner activities. And therein I feel myself strong, light, sure, resilient, perhaps proud and the like.[53]

For Lipps, *Einfühlung* describes the experience of feeling oneself within an object, such that 'the distinction between the self and the object disappears or rather does not yet exist'.[54] This sense of becoming the object of one's attention is reinforced with a moving object (or an object depicting a gesture of movement) such as 'a man making powerful, free light, perhaps courageous motions': 'with my feeling of activity I am absolutely incorporated in the moving body. I am even spatially in its position, so far as the self has a spatial position; I am transported into it'.[55] It is telling that the only figures or objects Lipps invokes in this context are either male or described in masculine terms, from his allusion to Faust's 'trouble and despair' to the phallic columns into which he projects himself when he writes, 'I feel my effort in a column'.[56] As his previous references to strength and effort suggest, the kind of male figure Lipps appears to have in mind is something like the Borghese

---

52 See in particular Herder, *Auch eine Philosophie der Geschichte zur Bilding der Menschheit* (Riga, Hartknoch: 1774), 46.

53 Theodor Lipps, '"Empathy", Inward Imitation, and Sense Feelings', in *Philosophies of Beauty: From Socrates to Robert Bridges, being the Sources of Aesthetic Theory*, ed. by E. F. Carritt (Oxford: Oxford University Press, 1931), 253. Originally published as 'Einfühlung, innere Nachahmung und Organempfindungen', in *Archiv für die gesamte Psychologie*, 1 (1903), 185–204.

54 Lipps, '"Empathy"', 253.

55 Ibid., 253, 254.

56 Ibid., 256, 257.

Gladiator.⁵⁷ The idea of projecting himself within a female figure seems to be as inconceivable to Lipps as it was to Ovid's Pygmalion with his ivory sculpture.

When psychologist Edward Titchener translated the term *Einfühlung* into English in 1909 with the neologism 'empathy',⁵⁸ he placed considerable emphasis on the importance of kinaesthesis – the sense of somatic movement – to this phenomenon. In contrast to the experience described by Lipps, Titchener's empathy does not seem to be bound by gender. Enumerating the visual associations his imagination conjures up from various words, he notes, for example, that the word 'stately' inspires him to visualize a 'stately heroine' with 'a hand holding up a steely grey skirt'. He moreover reports feeling as well as seeing the 'stately heroine' of his imagination: 'Not only do I see gravity and modesty and pride and courtesy and stateliness, but I feel or act them in the mind's muscles'.⁵⁹ Two decades later, the Harvard psychologist, Herbert S. Langfeld, made kinaesthesis central to his work on aesthetic empathy, arguing that 'Empathic response while viewing art could best be understood as embodied perceptions of force, movement, and weight'.⁶⁰ An *Introduction to Psychology*, which Langfeld later wrote with Ewin G. Boring and Harry Porter Weld, extended this view of empathy beyond the realm of art to offer a broader theory of embodied spectatorship wonderfully encapsulated in the following photograph showing a coach's physical response to a (blind) athlete executing a high jump:

---

57   The Borghese Gladiator at the Louvre (ca. 100 AD), https://commons.wikimedia.org/wiki/File:Borghese_Gladiator,_Louvre_Museum,_Paris_2_October_2014.jpg#/media/File:Borghese_Gladiator,_Louvre_Museum,_Paris_2_October_2014.jpg
58   Edward Titchener, *Lectures on the Experimental Psychology of the Thought-Processes* (New York: Macmillan, 1909), 21.
59   Titchener, *Lectures*, 13, 21.
60   Herbert S. Langfeld, *The Aesthetic Attitude* (Port Washington, NY: Kennikat Press, 1920), 76.

Fig. 3 'Empathy' in Edwin G. Boring, Herbert S. Langfeld and Harry Porter Weld, *Introduction to Psychology* (New York: John Wiley and Sons, 1939), 274, public domain.[61] Photo taken by author (2025)

It is difficult to imagine a better illustration of Adam Smith's delineation of kinaesthesis *avant la lettre* in his *Theory of Moral Sentiments* (1759): 'The mob, when they are gazing at a dancer on the slack rope, naturally writhe and twist and balance their own bodies as they see him do, and as they feel that they themselves must do if in his situation'.[62] The dog in the picture, disappointingly for man's so-called best friend, is unmoved.

The muscularity which is so striking in these early conceptions of empathy diminishes, however, as the twentieth century progresses. As Benjamin Morgan observes, 'the aesthetics of empathy underwent a similar and related transition to that which occurred within Anglo-American literary criticism': empathy, as he puts it, lost its 'bodily connotations'[63] to become a psychological rather than physiological

---

61   My brief account of empathy draws on Susan Lanzoni's invaluable *Empathy: A History* (New Haven, CT: Yale University Press, 2018) which alerted me to this photograph.

62   Adam Smith, *The Theory of Moral Sentiments*, 2nd edn. (London: A Millar, 1761), 4.

63   Benjamin Morgan, 'Critical Empathy: Vernon Lee's Aesthetics and the Origins of Close Reading', *Victorian Studies*, 55.1 (2012), 32.

phenomenon. In the twenty-first century, however, this separation of the psychological from the physiological has been increasingly challenged, with advances in neuroscience vindicating much of the work of those early psychologists who had relied quite heavily on their own introspection. Recent developments in embodied cognition, as outlined in the Introduction to this book, have seen kinaesthesis return to the fore with growing interest in the part played by motor resonance[64] in the reading process, and in the last fifteen years literary scholars have increasingly turned to this research for inspiration. Guillemette Bolens, for example, draws on neuroscientific studies that have found that 'the motor and premotor cortex is activated in a somatotopic fashion when a person silently reads action verbs', with verbs such as *lick*, *pick* and *kick* activating 'the brain areas along the motor strip that either is directly adjacent to or overlaps with areas activated by actual movement of the tongue, fingers, or feet'.[65] Terence Cave, drawing on some of the same research, adopts Bolens's notion of 'kinesis':

> the transmission (usually from one body to another) of motor activation which the observer of some salient action or physical sensation feels as a neural readiness to perform the same action. If I see you hammering a nail into the wall, I am likely to feel myself upright, wielding a hammer horizontally [...] If I see you hammering a nail into the floor, the muscular responses will be configured differently: the head and the arm are turned downward.[66]

Cave adds that the same responses are triggered in the reader visualizing such actions as the observer seeing them.

Kuzmičová suggests that when bodily actions are described in a text, 'rather than being visualized from the viewpoint of a passive third-person observer, the actions in question are emulated from an *enactive*, first-person perspective'.[67] I would argue, however, that visualization and

---

64   The 'process by which action observation activates the same neural substrates as those recruited when a perceiver performs an action by themselves' (Sian L. Beilock and Ian M. Lyons, 'Expertise and the Mental Simulation of Action', in *Handbook of Imagination and Mental Simulation*, ed. by Keith D. Markman, William M. P. Klein and Julie A. Suhr (New York: Taylor and Francis, 2009), 21).

65   Guillemette Bolens, *The Style of Gestures: Embodiment and Cognition in Literary Narrative* (Baltimore, MD: Johns Hopkins University Press, 2012), 21.

66   Cave, *Thinking with Literature: Towards a Cognitive Criticism* (Oxford: Oxford University Press, 2016), 36.

67   Kuzmičová, 'The Words and Worlds of Literary Narrative', 114.

enactment are not mutually exclusive but concurrent – just as the coach in the photograph sees the athlete while emulating his movement. It is indeed perfectly possible to visualize from a third-person perspective while enacting actions from a first-person perspective. The pioneering work of the psychologist June Downey, who anticipated my own approach by almost a century in her use of students' reports of reading experiences, contains several examples of readings in which the visual and the kinaesthetic perspectives are unaligned.[68] One of her readers, for example, reports the following response to a poem:

> See self from behind standing on beach, facing west. Has just thrown a shell into the water. Visual and motor consciousness of right arm flexed; tension in back felt. No fusion of visual and motor consciousness. Sometimes an actual oscillation. Self seen about one hundred yards off. Size reduced one-fourth.

The same student also reports 'motor feel of walking behind visual self', while another describes her reading of Keats's 'Hyperion' thus:

> Perfectly clear-cut visual image of the old man in the posture described. Tactual and kinaesthetic feeling of the sodden ground. Feeling of weight and relaxation in right hand. Kinaesthetic feeling of bowed head and of closed eyes. Auditory attention, with strain in ear.

As if this splitting of selves were not disorientating enough, Downey's students also report being in more than one place at a time from a visual perspective alone:

> Visualized and felt self on the shore; optical movement of waves. Saw and felt the sand falling through my fingers; sad relaxed feeling. Saw self distinctly from behind; self wore white dress and big floppy straw hat.[69]

In more ways than one, these reports of reading fundamentally challenge Noel Carroll's influential claim that we respond to fiction 'from the outside', as observers of a situation rather than as participants. Carroll argues, 'When a character is about to be ambushed, we feel

---

68 A key difference, however, is that Downey's students were 'trained' introspectionists, and this training arguably denatures the reading experience to some degree.

69 June Downey, *Creative Imagination: Studies in the Psychology of Literature* (London: Harcourt Brace, 1929), 34, 34, 187, 187.

fear for her; we do not imagine ourselves to be her and then experience "her" fear'.[70] What Downey's readers show, however, is that imagining can take place in many – often contradictory – ways concurrently. Our experience is multisensory or multimodal: we may *see* the character in Carroll's scenario from a third-person perspective, but *feel* her from a first-person perspective, tensing our muscles perhaps as we wait for the ambush to take place.

The more alert reader may sense where I am going with this. Critics adopting a cognitive perspective thus far have taken their examples, like Downey, from canonical literature – Wayne Booth's 'good stuff'[71] – and have presented motor resonance as part of what makes it so good. Kuzmičová claims that 'motor resonance is unique in its potential to make the reader feel physically present in the imaginary world',[72] while Cave presents his kinesic perspective as offering a new and deeper appreciation of the power of literature:

> once one begins to notice such effects in literature and indeed elsewhere, the experience of reading becomes subtly different: kinesic reading brings to the surface something you always already felt when you read the text properly, but somehow ignored for the sake of supposedly 'higher', more intellectual or aesthetic pleasures.[73]

A Yeats poem becomes something 'felt within the muscles of the body and across its skin surfaces'; Jim's leap from a boat in Conrad's *Lord Jim* something 'you feel [...] in your bones, in your muscles'.[74] This all speaks powerfully of the visceral power of literature to move the reader somatically as well as emotionally. But it does raise the question – what happens when we read the 'bad stuff'?[75] To return to Cave's earlier example, what happens when the hammer falls into the wrong hands,

---

70   Noel Carroll, *Beyond Aesthetics: Philosophical Essays* (Cambridge, UK: Cambridge University Press, 2001), 311–12.
71   Booth, *The Company We Keep*, 294.
72   Kuzmičová, 'The Words and Worlds of Literary Narrative', 108.
73   Terence Cave, *Thinking with Literature*, 29.
74   Ibid., 36, 124.
75   Booth indeed cites 'the sadomasochistic novels of the Marquis de Sade and Georges Bataille' as examples of the 'bad stuff', or works that 'will for most people in most cultures provide a highly dubious diet'. He strikingly exempts, however, the 'professional critics who have argued for the value of writers like Sade or Bataille' from those readers who may be harmed by such material (*The Company We Keep*, 59).

such as in the 106th criminal passion of the *120 Journées*, which simply reads 'He vigorously flattens a foot with a hammer'? Several of that novel's tortures, after all, are little more than the description of one or more motor actions. With these questions in mind, and with apologies for inflicting it upon my reader a second time, it is worth rereading the depiction of Justine's rape in the passage cited earlier:

> et l'infâme, me plaçant sur un canapé dans l'attitude propice à ses exécrables projets, me faisant tenir par deux de ses moines, essaie de se satisfaire avec moi de cette façon criminelle et perverse qui ne nous fait ressembler au sexe que nous ne possédons pas, qu'en dégradant celui que nous avons ; mais, ou cet impudique est trop fortement proportionné, ou la nature se révolte en moi au seul soupçon de ces plaisirs ; il ne peut vaincre les obstacles ; à peine se présente-t-il, qu'il est aussitôt repoussé... Il écarte, il presse, il déchire, tous ses efforts sont superflus ; la fureur de ce monstre se porte sur l'autel où ne peuvent atteindre ses vœux, il le frappe, il le pince, il le mord ; de nouvelles épreuves naissent du sein de ces brutalités ; les chairs ramollies se prêtent, le sentier s'entrouvre, le bélier pénètre ; je pousse des cris épouvantables ; bientôt la masse entière est engloutie, et la couleuvre lançant aussitôt un venin qui lui ravit ses forces, cède enfin, en pleurant de rage, aux mouvements que je fais pour m'en dégager. Je n'avais de ma vie tant souffert.
>
> [and the villain, placing me on a sofa in the position appropriate to his execrable intentions, with two of his monks holding me down, tries to find satisfaction with me in that criminal and perverted manner which makes us resemble men by hiding what makes us women. But either this rogue is too greatly proportioned, or Nature revolts in me at the merest suspicion of these pleasures – he cannot not overcome the obstacles: at the slightest approach he is forced back... He stretches, he pushes, he tears, all his efforts are in vain. This monster's fury is unleashed on the altar his desires cannot reach; he strikes it, he pinches it, he bites it. Yet more trials are born of this brutality: the softened flesh offers itself, the path opens up, and the ram penetrates. I cry out awful screams. Soon the whole of it is engulfed, and the serpent, spurting a venom that depletes its strength, withdraws at last, weeping tears of rage at my struggles to free myself. Never in my whole life had I experienced such suffering.]

It may well be, as Frappier-Mazur suggests, that the Sadean text assaults the reader. But we also have to consider the possibility that it may position and implicate the reader as a perpetrator of assault. When viewed in the context of Sévérino's striving to 'vaincre les obstacles' [overcome the obstacles] in his rape of Justine, Lipps's almost climactic depiction of kinaesthetic communion suddenly takes on a much more sinister air:

> I feel a sense of effort. I may carry this out in real imitative movements. If so, I feel myself active, I do not merely imagine but feel the endeavour, the resistance of obstacles, the overcoming, the achievement.[76]

Bolens's evidentially supported claim that 'kinesic' verbs such as *to drag* trigger 'a perceptual simulation of what it sensorily and perceptually entails to perform such an action'[77] also raises some very uncomfortable questions about our reading of this passage from *Justine*. What, for example, is the effect on the reader of the kinesic verbs used to depict Sévérino's assault – verbs like 'écarter' [to stretch], 'presser' [to push], 'déchirer' [to tear], 'frapper' [to strike], 'pincer' [to pinch], 'mordre' [to bite]? If we experience these too 'within the muscles of our bodies', are we not enacting the rape of Justine ourselves?

A growing disquiet about the way the Sadean text implicates the reader prompted the questions I posed my students regarding both what and whence they saw in their reading of the passage from *Justine*. The number of respondents reporting a fixed viewpoint is slightly higher than the equivalent figure among respondents to the 'Eugénie' passage (69% as opposed to 57%), perhaps because the *Justine* passage does not feature the same switches in gaze from one character to another. Of those who gave details, the majority (54%) reported seeing the scene from the perspective of an observer, although this position ranged from being 'Quite close' to 'from a distance', and from seeing it from 'a bird's eye view', 'a fixed point to the side', 'like a fly on the wall' to 'from the front as if it were happening on a stage'. In contrast to the solitary student who reported seeing from Eugénie's perspective, six of the thirty-three who read the *Justine* passage (18%) reported seeing most of the scene if not all from Justine's point of view. This difference suggests that Justine is less of an object to the reader than Eugénie, the first-person narration potentially encouraging the reader to see from her perspective, and possibly also to project themselves into her body. However, some of these

---

76   Lipps, '"Empathy"', 254.
77   Bolens, 'Relevance Theory and Kinesic Analysis in *Don Quixote* and *Madame Bovary*', in *Reading Beyond the Code: Literature and Relevance Theory*, ed. by Terence Cave and Deirdre Wilson (Oxford: Oxford University Press, 2018), 57.

respondents did not seem to see that much: two of them reported no visual imagery and another 'figures of characters – vague. No identities'. Although one student saw a little more – more indeed than was in the text ('an obscure scene with pale naked bodies and black hoods. Sort of *Eyes Wide Shut* scenario') – the other two reported simply 'the rape' and 'A serpent'. Not seeing much would make sense, given that Justine, with her back to the action, is unable to see what is happening to her and can only feel the pain it causes. Those respondents stating they can see 'the rape' and 'A serpent' from Justine's perspective are thus in contradiction with the logic of the scene as they are seeing what Justine cannot. It may be that what they are describing is what they emotionally or somatically feel rather than what they see; it may also be, however, that their positioning within the scene is not as tied to Justine as they imagine.

It will perhaps not come as a surprise that in marked contrast to the passage from 'Eugénie', no respondents reported viewing the scene from Sévérino's point of view. One student, however, did report her perspective moving from 'watching Justine to as if standing behind her' and another as moving from the sofa to 'around the mon[k]/altar', which may suggest alignment with Sévérino's visual perspective. This could be taken as reassuring confirmation that the great majority of respondents did not experience the rape from the perspective of the rapist. As I have already suggested, however, it would be unwise to assume visual responses are necessarily an accurate guide to motor responses. Furthermore, one cannot ignore the fact that for most conceivable respondents (other than convicted rapists perhaps) to report the perspective of the rapist in this scene would be to say the unsayable – perhaps even to themselves, let alone anyone else – no matter how anonymous the process. This is moreover even assuming consciousness of a response that for many may be subconscious. When designing the questionnaire, I thus decided that a question asking the respondents where they were 'feeling' from was almost certainly pointless, and potentially inappropriate. For all these reasons, the extract from Justine arguably demonstrates the limits of what can be asked and therefore learned through questionnaires. It is possible that fMRI scans could play a role here in showing what self-reporting cannot by revealing activity in the pre-motor or motor cortex triggered by those action verbs in the passage; it is worth noting, however, that such activity could just as easily be triggered by subjects imagining themselves bracing or struggling against the violence as opposed to inflicting it.

Part of the complexity here is that kinesic or kinaesthetic images, including action verbs, may also be exteroceptive images, and thus simultaneously stimulate other senses alongside that of movement. In light of this complexity, and in the absence of fMRI, there may therefore still be a place for some old-fashioned close reading of the passage in question. Justine's account of her rape begins with Sévérino 'me plaçant sur un canapé' [placing me on a sofa] and 'me faisant tenir par deux de ses moines' [with two of his monks holding me down]. While Justine is acted upon rather than acting here, and so one might imagine the reader enacting the first verb at least from Sévérino's perspective, his passiveness in relation to the second makes it more likely that readers may feel themselves being held down rather than holding someone down – particularly if they are hearing Justine's voice describing the experience. The passage then describes in more abstract terms both Sévérino's struggle ('essaie' [tries]) and Justine's resistance ('se révolte en moi' [revolts in me]); this abstractness continues with 'il ne peut vaincre les obstacles' [he cannot overcome the obstacles] before returning to verbs which are proprioceptive, kinaesthetic and visual: 'à peine se présente-t-il, qu'il est aussitôt repoussé' ['no sooner does he approach than he is forced back'[78]]. While it is possible that some readers may experience these images of attempted penetration from Justine's proprioceptive and kinaesthetic perspectives, the visual and spatial emphasis here is on Sévérino's actions as he approaches and is then pushed back. Had Justine employed the active 'je le repousse' [I force him back], this would have made somatic identification with her more likely; the passive 'il est repoussé' [he is forced back], however, keeps the visual, proprioceptive and kinaesthetic focus on Sévérino. It also allows the text to maintain an unbroken chain of third-person pronouns, asserting his agency as Justine is linguistically as well as physically objectified as 'l'autel' [the altar]. At times, she is barely even an object – linguistically absent from the first trio of action verbs ('il écarte, il presse, il déchire' [he stretches,

---

78   The English translation used for the questionnaires replaces the first verb with a noun and thus slightly diminishes the kinaesthetic potential of this phrase for the reader.

he pushes, he tears]) and present in the subsequent trio only as a body-part represented by a masculine pronoun ('il le frappe, il le pince, il le mord' [he strikes it, he pinches it, he bites it]). With all the attention on Sévérino, it is difficult to see how the reader can do anything other than enact these motor images, consciously or unconsciously. This kinaesthetic element persists into the next trio of verbal phrases with the depiction of penetration ('les chairs ramollies se prêtent, le sentier s'entrouvre, le bélier pénètre' [the softened flesh offers itself, the path opens up, and the ram penetrates]), as Sévérino is himself reduced to a body-part, but the emphasis here has shifted to the visual, as the reader sees what Sévérino sees, and what Justine cannot. Justine returns as subject in order to express her suffering, the scream aural and visual, as the respondents confirm, but also, I suspect, kinaesthetic, with the emphasis on the physical effort of pushing out ('je pousse'). However, Justine then immediately disappears once more as the image of being engulfed rather than engulfing implies a return to Sévérino's sensorimotor perspective. The ram has now turned into a serpent, and those respondents who reported visualizing a snake provide ample evidence that figurative language may prompt literal imagery. The focus of the passage finally switches back to Justine kinaesthetically with her 'mouvements' as she struggles to free herself, and the episode is brought to a close with her reiteration of her suffering.

From start to finish, the kinaesthetic perspective shifts five times between Justine and Sévérino in this scene, implicating the reader not just as rapist and victim, but as their own rapist and their own victim.[79] There is, however, no guarantee that all readers will necessarily follow all the motor or visual cues the passage provides, and it is difficult to know – because it is difficult, as we have seen, for readers to say – how conscious readers may in any case be of their responses to such cues. It is moreover worth bearing in mind that a close reading is also necessarily a slow reading, and certainly slower than the respondents are likely to have practised. They were indeed specifically told to read the passage at their usual speed because I was hoping as far as possible to capture the kind of imagery that the natural reading process produces. Although some of them reported experiencing the scene much as if they were watching a

---

79 The Conclusion of this book briefly explores a filmic approximation of this scenario.

film, our mental imagery, like our perception of the outside world, is more fragmentary by its very nature than most of us realize.[80] I suspect those respondents reading at normal speed will have experienced snapshots rather than a continuous flow of images; one indeed observed, 'Everything that occurs was like flashing images in my head, not precise and exact but visible in an unorganised way'. Another also suggested that her 'pace of reading' and the aural presence of the narrator's voice had precluded anything other than 'a vague image of a young woman being raped'. A third, who perceived the text from a single position throughout, stated it would have taken 'too much of an effort' on his part to adopt other positions while progressing through the passage. I also suspect that some readers may read material they find challenging more hurriedly precisely in order to avoid potentially distressing mental imagery. Reading Sade is difficult enough – reading it slowly can be even more torturous. General readers, as opposed to literary critics or students, are thus unlikely to read Sadean fiction slowly unless they are able to enjoy, on some level, the mental imagery it stimulates – perhaps like the respondent who said she found the passage 'shocking' but 'interesting to play with'. This student, who incidentally was one of those to hear Justine scream, may possibly have felt differently had she been subjected to the whole of *Justine* rather than simply a few lines. Her comment, however, is striking for the way it evokes both a text acting upon a reader and a reader acting upon a text: this reader felt the power of the text to shock, but also her own power to turn the text into a form of imaginative play – into something she could manipulate or control.

Bad Vibrations

There is another aspect of our somatic responses to scenes of violence that needs to be addressed. We have explored the disturbing ways in which the action verbs in *Justine* may position the reader as both rapist and victim by stimulating motor resonance, and noted the imagery that might allow us to hear, see, and even feel in our chest the heroine's scream. But what of the pain that provokes the scream? Is it possible for

---

80 'Images are fragmentary. We recall glimpses of parts, arrange them in a mental tableau, and then do a juggling act to refresh each part as it fades' (Steven Pinker, *How the Mind Works* (London: Penguin, 1998), 294).

the reader not just to see and hear Justine's pain but to feel it? Although the very existence of pornography is predicated on the power of the word or image to produce physical pleasure, and a study such as Rice's provides evidence of what we already knew in that respect, there has until recently been little scientific evidence that what we see or read could vicariously cause us physical pain. There has, however, been anecdotal evidence for some time of our ability to feel pain vicariously. As well as anticipating kinaesthesis in *The Theory of Moral Sentiments*, Smith also suggested that observed pain might trigger its own form of resonance when we see 'our brother is upon the rack':

> By the imagination, we place ourselves in his situation, we conceive ourselves enduring all the same torments, we enter as it were into his body, and become in some measure the same person with him, and thence form some idea of his sensations, and even feel something which, though weaker in degree, is not altogether unlike them.[81]

In order to feel our brother's pain, Smith suggests, we must first feel ourselves into his body, like the mob he describes watching the rope-dancer. Social psychologist Daniel Batson doubtless had the latter anecdote in mind when he observed, 'To find oneself tensing and twisting when watching someone balance on a tightrope is a familiar experience; it is hard to resist. Yet we may watch someone file papers with little inclination to mimic the action'.[82] Batson does not, however, elucidate why motor mimicry should happen in the former case and not the latter; the answer is offered not in Smith, but in Smith's unstated source for his anecdote, the Abbé Dubos's *Réflexions critiques*:

> Plus les tours qu'un Voltigeur temeraire fait sur corde sont perilleux, plus le commun des Spectateurs s'y rend attentif. Quand il fait un saut entre deux épées prestes à le percer, si dans la chaleur du mouvement son corps s'écartoit d'un point de la ligne qu'il doit décrire, il devient un objet digne de toute nôtre curiosité. Qu'on mette deux bâtons à la place des épées, que le Voltigeur fasse tendre sa corde à deux pieds de hauteur sur une prairie, il fera en vain les mêmes sauts & les mêmes tours : on ne daignera plus le regarder, l'attention du Spectateur cesseroit avec le danger.

---

81 Smith, *Theory of Moral Sentiments*, 4.
82 Batson, 'These Things Called Empathy', 5. One could conversely hypothesize that the same motor resonance occurs when observing someone filing papers but in a less intense and therefore less noticeable manner.

[The more dangerous the turns a fearless Acrobat takes on the rope, the more the typical Spectator pays attention. When he takes a leap between two swords ready to pierce him, if in the flush of movement his body deviates an inch from the line he is to follow, he becomes on object worthy of all our curiosity. With two sticks there instead of the swords, or with the rope stretched two-feet high over a field, the Acrobat would make the same leaps & the same turns in vain: no one would deign to watch, the Spectator's attention would cease with the danger.][83]

As Dubos suggests, it is the threat or fear of pain which triggers a motor response, and in Smith's version causes the spectators to 'writhe and twist'.

Sade's fiction, which is evidently suffused with the threat of pain, unsurprisingly offers myriad examples which speak to Batson's claim and illustrate Dubos's argument. While he makes no use of rope-dancers, Sade on more than one occasion creates his own version of Dubos's scenario by placing women at a similar risk of falling, including one of Justine's fellow victims in Sainte-Marie-des-Bois:

> La femme de trente-six ans, grosse de six mois, ainsi que je vous l'ai dit, est huchée par eux, sur un piédestal de huit pieds de haut ; ne pouvant y poser qu'une jambe, elle est obligée d'avoir l'autre en l'air ; autour d'elle sont des matelas garnis de ronces, de houx, d'épines, à trois pieds d'épaisseur, une gaule flexible lui est donnée pour la soutenir : il est aisé de voir, d'un côté l'intérêt qu'elle a de ne point choir, de l'autre l'impossibilité de garder l'équilibre ; c'est cette alternative qui divertit les moines ; rangés tous les quatre autour d'elle, ils ont chacun une ou deux femmes qui les excitent diversement pendant ce spectacle ; toute grosse qu'elle est, la malheureuse reste en attitude près d'un quart d'heure ; les forces lui manquent enfin, elle tombe sur les épines, et nos scélérats enivrés de luxure, vont offrir pour la dernière fois sur son corps l'abominable hommage de leur férocité…[84]

---

83   Dubos, *Réflexions critiques sur la poésie et sur la peinture*, 2 vols. (Paris: Jean Mariette, 1719), I, 13.

84   A more extreme version of the same scenario occurs in the *120 Journées*: 'Un second campait une femme grosse de sept mois sur un piédestal isolé à plus de quinze pieds de hauteur. Elle était obligée de s'y tenir droite et sans perdre la tête, car si malheureusement elle lui eût tourné, elle et son fruit étaient à jamais écrasés. Le libertin dont je vous parle, très peu touché de la situation de cette malheureuse, qu'il payait pour cela, l'y retenait jusqu'à ce qu'il eût déchargé, et il se branlait devant elle en s'écriant : « Ah ! la belle statue, le bel ornement, la belle impératrice! » ' [A second man would plant a woman who was 7 months pregnant on a free-standing pedestal over 15 feet high: she had to stand straight and keep her head, because if she were unfortunate enough to lose it, she and her unborn

[The thirty-six-year-old woman, six months pregnant, as I said to you, is perched by them on a pedestal eight feet high; allowed to stand on one leg only, she is obliged to keep the other aloft; around her are mattresses stuffed three feet thick with brambles, holly, and thorns; a flexible pole is given to support her: it is clear to see, on the one hand that it is in her interest not to fall, and on the other the impossibility of maintaining her balance; it is this outcome that entertains the monks; placed all four of them around her, they each have one or two women to arouse them in various ways during this show; as pregnant as she is, the unfortunate woman maintains her pose for almost a quarter of an hour; her strength fails her at last, she falls on the thorns, and our scoundrels, drunk with lechery, shower her body for the last time with the abominable tribute of their brutality...] (J 238).

Whereas Eugénie, standing still on her pedestal, is designed for visual objectification rather than kinaesthetic projection, with virtually no sensory cues to prompt the mind's muscles, the victim here is a very different proposition. Although Sade's monks respond in the same masturbatory fashion as Valmont, the emphasis is nonetheless very much on the muscles, as the woman stands on one leg, struggles to maintain her balance, and then falls. The stakes have moreover been raised to add to the sense of jeopardy and physical vulnerability, firstly with the victim's pregnancy, and secondly with the mattresses of thorns that lie in wait rather like the swords in Dubos's anecdote. While the rope-dancer is likely to succeed, the woman here is doomed to fail, and the suspense as we wait for her to do so heightens our sense both of the strain on her body and of the pain that awaits her – and this sense, it is equally clear, heightens the pleasure for the monks.

Sade's libertines inflict violence not because they are indifferent to their victims' suffering but precisely because they are sensitive to it.[85] The pain of others is something to be consumed through the senses, from Verneuil's listening to the 'musique' of his wife's screams to Séverino's

---

fruit would be crushed for ever. This libertine I'm describing, caring very little for the plight of this poor woman (whom he'd pay for this), would keep her up there until he had come and would frig himself in front of her as he shouted, "Oh, the beautiful statue, the fine ornament, the beautiful empress!"] (120J 290; 295).

85 A point made by Warman (*Sade: From Materialism to Pornography*, 77). Warman persuasively demonstrates the particular debt Sade's physiology of pain owes to the sensationist materialism of Helvétius, d'Holbach and Robinet (*Sade: From Materialism to Pornography*, 27–9).

tasting and even inhaling of Justine's agonies as he flogs her: 'osant mêler l'amour à ces moments cruels, sa bouche se colle sur la mienne et veut respirer les soupirs que les douleurs m'arrachent... Mes larmes coulent, il les dévore' [having the audacity to mix these cruel moments with love, his mouth glues itself to mine and wishes to breathe in the sighs these agonies wrest from me] (J 234).[86] No matter how close the Sadean libertine comes to the pain of others, it is somehow never quite close enough. Sévérino's greedy consumption of Justine's tears and sighs suggests a yearning for an experience that extends beyond the exteroceptive, that translates the pain felt by another into something felt within. As Noirceuil explains in the *Histoire de Juliette*, attempting to please 'les objets qui servent à la jouissance' [the objects which we use to come] is a common mistake:

> ce ne sont pas des plaisirs qu'il faut faire goûter à cet objet, ce sont des impressions qu'il faut produire en lui ; et celle de la douleur étant beaucoup plus vive que celle du plaisir, il est incontestable, qu'il vaut mieux que la commotion produite sur nos nerfs, par ce spectacle étranger, y parvienne par la douleur, plutôt que par le plaisir

> [it is not pleasures that this object is required to taste, it is a matter of producing impressions within the object; and that of pain being much sharper than that of pleasure, it is indisputably better for the commotion produced on our nerves by this strange spectacle to reach it by pain, rather than by pleasure] (HJ 414)

Pain offers an intensity that pleasure cannot match, and as Dolmancé tells Eugénie in *La Philosophie dans le boudoir*, only this added intensity is capable of triggering the 'vibrations' that libertines need to satisfy their desires:

> il s'agit seulement d'ébranler la masse de nos nerfs par le choc le plus violent possible ; or il n'est pas douteux que la douleur affectant bien plus vivement que le plaisir, les chocs résultatifs sur nous de cette sensation, produite sur les autres, seront essentiellement d'une vibration plus vigoureuse, retentiront plus énergiquement dans nous, mettront dans une circulation plus violente les esprits animaux qui [...] embraseront aussitôt les organes de la volupté, et les disposeront au plaisir

---

86 Later, Cardoville also seeks to breathe in Justine's pain: 'mon bourreau jouit, sa bouche imprimée sur la mienne, semble respirer ma douleur pour en accroître ses plaisirs' [my executioner comes, his mouth imprinted on mine, seems to breathe in my pain to heighten his pleasures] (J 380).

[all that is required is to rattle the bulk of our nerves with the most violent shock possible; now there is no doubt that as pain affects us much more intensely than pleasure, the resulting shocks of this sensation, inflicted on others, upon ourselves will essentially offer a more vigorous vibration, will reverberate more energetically within us, will let flow with greater violence the animal spirits that [...] will set the sensual organs ablaze, and ready them for pleasure] (*PB* 67)

In contrast with the mirroring of pain that we see in Smith's image of compassion or 'fellow-feeling', in Sade's account the physiological shock of the pain rather than the pain itself is mirrored, and that shock resonates in the nerves of the libertine's body as pure pleasure. This transformation is linked to the sensorimotor in the most vicious of circles, the libertine feeling his own body as it inflicts suffering on his victim, and feeling himself into his victim's body as it reacts to that suffering. It is a nightmarish form of *Einfühlung* or empathy, one in which feeling someone's pain has become a pleasure, and one in which, as we have already seen with the rape of Justine, the reader is moreover invited to partake.

Recent research in neuroscience has provided fresh evidence of the ways in which pain and the sensorimotor are neurally intertwined, and revealed the capacity of images of pain to resonate in much the same way as images of movement.[87] Chris Frith's studies of pain, for example, have confirmed the insights of Smith and Condillac[88] regarding the power of the imagination to create or recreate the feeling of pain, demonstrating that 'when we see someone else in pain [...] the same

---

[87] See Alessia Avenanti, Ilaria Minio-Pauello, Ilaria Bufalari and Salvatore M. Aglioti, 'Stimulus-Driven Modulation of Motor-Evoked Potentials During Observation of Others' Pain', *Neuroimage*, 32.1 (2006), 316–24, and Alessia Avenanti, Domenica Bueti, Gaspare Galati and Salvatore M. Aglioti, 'Transcranial Magnetic Stimulation Highlights the Sensorimotor Side of Empathy for Pain', *Nature Neuroscience*, 8.7 (2005), 955–60.

[88] Condillac, for example, had suggested that imagined pain might even pose a risk to the body: 'La perception d'une douleur réveille dans mon imagination toutes les idées avec lesquelles elle a une liaison étroite. Je vois le danger, la frayeur me saisit, j'en suis abattu, mon corps résiste à peine, ma douleur est plus vive, mon accablement augmente, & il se peut que, pour avoir eu l'imagination frappée, une maladie légère dans ses commencemens me conduise au tombeau' [The perception of pain awakens in my imagination all those ideas with which it is closely connected. I see danger, fear takes hold of me, I am struck down, my body barely resists, my pain is more intense, my exhaustion increases, & it is possible that, by having had my imagination struck, an illness mild at the start, will lead me to the grave] (Condillac, *Essai*, I. 129).

brain areas become active as when we experience pain ourselves'. Frith makes a distinction, however, between the physical aspect of pain, and the subjective experience of pain. Noting that the two are not 'directly coupled' – 'A hot rod feels less painful if you are distracted, even though the temperature of the rod has not changed'[89] – he suggests that vicarious pain only activates those areas in the brain linked to the subjective experience. Subsequent research by Osborn and Derbyshire has found, however, that a 'significant minority' of normal subjects 'can share not just the emotional component of an observed injury but also the sensory component'.[90] Presenting healthy volunteers with a series of images and video clips, they found that almost a third 'felt pain in response to at least one of the 10 images' and 'felt their pain in the same location as the observed injury'.[91] Another study has moreover shown that vicarious pain is not limited to those looking at photographs of actual injuries but also applies to those responding to 'artistic pain representations'.[92]

This is evidently not to say that vicarious pain has the same intensity as direct, or first-hand, pain. Other studies have confirmed what common sense tells us, that both observed and imagined pain 'partially overlap with, but are nevertheless qualitatively different from, first-hand experiences of pain'.[93] The vicarious pain that some readers may experience when encountering images of pain is perhaps best understood as equivalent to the 'ghost echo of movement'[94] prompted by kinesic images according to Cave. It may only be an echo of pain,[95] but even an echo can be enough

---

89 Chris Frith, *Making Up the Mind: How the Brain Creates Our Mental World* (Oxford: Blackwell, 2007), 150. Frith is drawing here on the findings of a study published in 2004: Tania Singer, Ben Seymour, John O'Doherty, Holger Kaube, Raymond J. Dolan and Chris D. Frith, 'Empathy for Pain Involves the Affective but not Sensory Components of Pain', *Science*, 303 (2004), 1157–62.
90 Jody Osborn and Stewart W. G. Derbyshire, 'Pain Sensation Evoked by Observing Injury in Others', *Pain*, 148 (2010), 271.
91 Osborn and Derbyshire, 'Pain Sensation', 270.
92 Martina Ardizzi, Francesca Ferroni, Maria Alessandra Umiltà, Chiara Pinardi, Antonino Errante, Francesca Ferri, Elisabetta Fadda and Vittorio Gallese, 'Visceromotor Roots of Aesthetic Evaluation of Pain in Art: An fMRI study', *Social Cognitive and Affective Neuroscience*, 16.11 (2021), 1113–22.
93 Claus Lamm, C. Daniel Batson and Jean Decety, 'The Neural Substrate of Human Empathy: Effects of Perspective-Taking and Cognitive Appraisal', *Journal of Cognitive Neuroscience*, 19.1 (2007), 54.
94 Cave, *Thinking with Literature*, 37.
95 The same may be said of the discomfort commonly felt when one sees – or reads of – an accident such as someone falling from a bicycle: a 'flinching feeling in the

to affect a reader's experience of a text – a little jolt that may, in the case of Justine's rape, accompany the sudden switches in perspective from Sévérino to Justine, and thereby somatically reinforce the bond between reader and heroine. Recent research has also revealed contextual factors that may exacerbate the subjective pain experienced by observers of images. In one study by Lamm, Batson and Decety, participants were shown video clips of 'patients' (played by actors) undergoing a painful sound therapy for a neurological disease. They were further told that the health of some of these patients improved after the therapy, and that the health of others did not. It was found that participants exhibited 'higher pain intensity and unpleasantness ratings'[96] when reacting to the suffering of those patients whom they were told had not been helped by the treatment. The unhappy outcome imagined for these patients thus made the experience of observing their suffering more painful.[97] I suspect that this may well translate to our experiences of fictional suffering: seeing an action hero we know will prevail subjected to torture is very different to seeing a character we believe to be doomed submitted to the same treatment. And in Sade's fiction that sense of doom hangs over every scene of violence: part of what makes reading the *120 Journées* so oppressive is the sense of inevitability given the impossibility of escape, the awareness that every day, like the day before, will bring suffering until the last day, which will bring death. For many readers of *Justine*, their increasing awareness as they progress through the novel that the heroine is trapped in a cycle of violence that can end only with her demise may well have a sensitizing, rather than desensitizing, effect. If this becomes too distressing, however, some readers are likely to adopt strategies to diminish their discomfort, such as consciously taking 'a detached observer position'[98] to distance themselves from Justine and

---

groin area' as Jamie Ward, a leading authority on vicarious pain, described it to me in an email. See also Thomas Grice-Jackson, Hugo D. Critchley, Michael J. Banissy and Jamie Ward, 'Common and Distinct Neural Mechanisms Associated with the Conscious Experience of Vicarious Pain', *Cortex*, 94 (2017), 152–63.

96 Lamm, Batson and Decety, 'The Neural Substrate of Human Empathy', 55.
97 As it may in a Sadean context, with the unhappy ending awaiting the pregnant victim in *Justine*.
98 A strategy which we know can be effective: other studies have found that 'a cognitive strategy of detachment attenuates subjective and physiological measures of anticipatory anxiety for pain and reduces reactivity to receipt of pain itself' (Raffael Kalisch, Katja Wiech, Hugo D. Critchley, Ben Seymour, John P. O'Doherty, David A. Oakley, Philip Allen and Raymond J. Dolan, 'Anxiety Reduction Through

thus her pain. Something like this strategy may be behind the way in which attitudes towards Justine among students reading the novel (as opposed to a short extract) often seem to shift from initial compassion to frustration and even victim-blaming animosity as they progress through the text.

As the variety of responses to Justine's suffering reflects, the perspectives readers adopt, either instinctively or consciously, determine the intensity of their response to depictions of suffering, and vice versa. The Lamm, Batson and Decety study showing video clips of patients in apparent pain indeed explores the impact of what psychologists refer to as 'perspective-taking', namely adopting either an 'other-perspective' (imagining how another person feels) or a 'self-perspective' (imagining how one would feel in another person's situation). The participants in their study were each given an instruction either to imagine the feelings of the patient in the video clip, or to imagine themselves in the patient's situation. Those instructed to 'imagine other' showed stronger empathic concern (compassion), whereas those instructed to 'imagine self' experienced heightened personal distress.[99] The students on my course who read *Justine* are given no such instruction, however, and nor are any other readers of the novel outside the academy. Nor indeed am I sure what an appropriate instruction would be. In any case, I suspect that any such direction would not linger very long in any reader's consciousness: reading a novel over a period of hours or weeks is very different to watching a short video clip, and, as we have already seen, texts are continually offering the reader perspective-taking instructions of their own in the form of sensory cues. As the example of those students expressing hostility to Justine shows, however, there are times when students need to be reminded that too much detachment can lead to the kind of callousness that Sade scholars have historically shown. Conversely, at the other end of the spectrum, there is evidently a risk that too self-orientated a perspective in relation to scenes of sexual violence may lead to very real distress to no real end or benefit.[100] That said, even an other-orientated reading of a novel like *Justine* can – and, I would argue, should – cause some degree of distress to the reader. *Justine*, after all, is an

---

Detachment: Subjective, Physiological, and Neural Effects', *Journal of Cognitive Neuroscience*, 17 (2005), 874).

99 Lamm, Batson and Decety, 'The Neural Substrate of Human Empathy', 53.

100 A risk that all sensitive readers face, but evidently a more acute one for readers who have experienced sexual violence in their own lives.

upsetting novel. And while shedding tears over fictional suffering in and of itself does no one any good, if those tears prompt ethical reflection or action, then they begin to be a price worth paying.

Conclusion

This chapter has aimed to show that there is far more to reading than the stimulation of visual mental images. The same may be said of our spectatorship of the visual arts. R. K. Elliot cites Matthias Grünewald's *The Mocking of Christ* (1503–5) as an example of a painting that 'induces the spectator to identify with the only powerfully active character in the picture, a soldier whose fist is raised in the act of striking Christ'.[101]

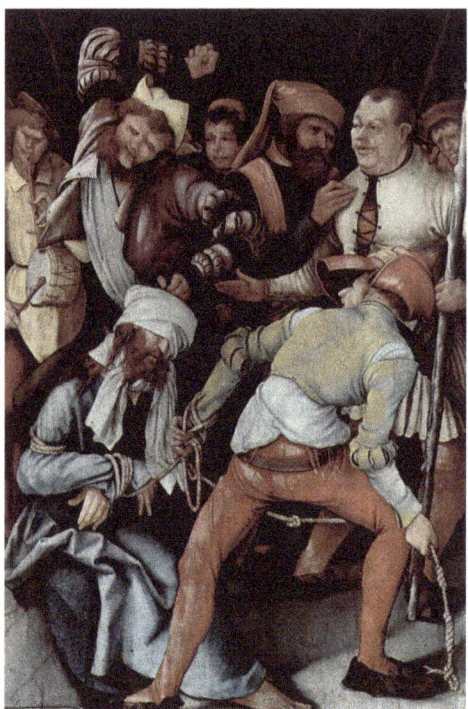

Fig. 4 Matthias Grünewald, *The Mocking of Christ* (1503–5), Wikimedia Commons, public domain, https://commons.wikimedia.org/wiki/File:Mathis_Gothart_Gr%C3%BCnewald_062.jpg#/media/File:Mathis_Gothart_Gr%C3%BCnewald_062.jpg

---

101 R. K. Elliot, 'Imagination in the Experience of Art', *Royal Institute of Philosophy Supplement*, 6 (1972), 89.

As well as observing the scene visually, Elliot suggests, the spectator enters 'the world of the work' to feel the scene kinaesthetically, 'experiencing the movement from within' and thus consummating the blow. Elliot then switches to the first person to implicate himself in this act of violence:

> I do not merely imagine myself striking at nobody in particular, nor do I seem to aim a blow from where I am standing in front of the picture. It is as if I were in the world of the picture, in the place of the striking soldier, delivering a blow at the Christ, whom I see from my ordinary spectatorial standpoint. But although in the place of the soldier, I am not performing the action on his behalf. The satisfaction I feel is not his but my own.[102]

There is an evident echo of Lipps's account of *Einfühling* here, but the aesthetic satisfaction that Lipps evoked has now taken on a darker hue: although Elliot describes the experience as 'exhilarating' and a *'tour de force'*, he observes rather dolefully that it 'seems a pity that it should result in uncomfortable self-knowledge, and a sort of implication in the Crucifixion'.[103] Jason Gaiger, returning to the same painting more recently, seems more reluctant than Elliot to accept that the spectator may be implicated in this act of violence, and consequently suggests an alternative view:

> It can be argued, with equal plausibility, that the painting prompts us to project ourselves into the position of the person receiving the blow rather than delivering it and thus to identify empathetically with Christ's sufferings. On this modified account, the viewer can imaginatively adopt different standpoints within the depicted scene, including that of the onlookers.[104]

Gaiger then turns to another painting depicting a suspended act of violence: Artemisia Gentileschi's *Jael and Sisera* (1620).

---

102 Ibid., 89, 90.
103 Ibid., 90.
104 Jason Gaiger, 'Projective and Ampliative Imagining', in *Philosophy of Sculpture*, ed. by Kristin Gjesdal, Fred Rush and Ingvild Torsen (New York: Routledge, 2020), 20.

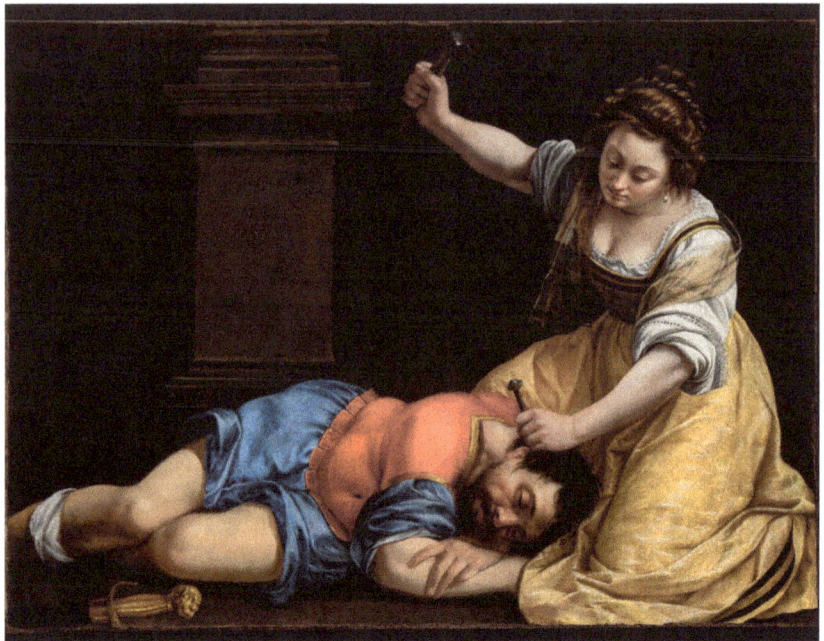

Fig. 5 Artemisia Gentileschi, *Jael and Sisera* (1620) © Szépművészeti Múzeum / Museum of Fine Arts, Budapest, 2025

Not for the first time in this chapter, we find ourselves contemplating a hammer blow. In contrast to the previous painting, there is little here to give the spectator any clear sense of whether the blow is righteous or criminal, or the holder of the hammer virtuous or vicious. Noting this 'deliberate indeterminacy', Gaiger concedes that it may be 'more natural to project ourselves into the position of the person carrying out the blow' but again leaves open the possibility of taking up another position to 'imaginatively identify'[105] with the sleeping body.

Gaiger's eagerness to seek alternative positions for the spectator to that of the wielder of violence suggests a certain queasiness about the moral position in which our projective imagination may place us in our responses to art. One senses that he would – understandably – prefer to believe he was identifying with the victim of violence than the perpetrator, because that is clearly a more morally comfortable position to be in: as Angela Carter observes in *The Sadeian Woman*, 'the victim is always morally superior to the

---

105 Gaiger, 'Projective and Ampliative Imagining', 20.

master; that is the victim's ambivalent triumph'.[106] Elliot's phenomenological description of sensorimotor projection, however, describes a 'momentary' act of the 'involuntary imagination' – an act which he claims the 'voluntary imagination' can only achieve 'more sluggishly and with some shoring up of detail'.[107] Gaiger's alternative subject positions read (at least to me) less like instinctive sensorimotor responses than defensive reactions to – and against – those responses, the result perhaps of a troubled conscience. That said, as with the scene of Justine's rape, such defensive reactions may also take place in those initial moments of spectatorship, and thus may themselves be sensorimotor as well as emotional. In both paintings, as the direction of a blow guides our eye towards the victim, so our attention turns to the victim's body and the anticipation of pain. Once again, it seems, scenes of violence leave the spectator experiencing the worst of both worlds: the guilt of the perpetrator and the pain of the victim.

As disturbing as depictions of violence may be for the engaged reader or spectator, it is also important to retain a sense of proportion. At a recent Artemisia Gentileschi exhibition, I did not see any visitors assaulting each other or writhing on the floor in agony. I did, however, see and hear visitors moved by what they saw, some literally taken aback by the violence of paintings such as *Judith Beheading Holofernes* (1612–13),[108] and discreetly murmuring expressions of shock and awe – external signs, in other words, of the ghostly echoes of sensation felt within. Although our immersion in most novels unfolds over hours or days rather than the minutes we typically spend with paintings or sculptures, the individual episodes of violence within them will generally be similarly fleeting. Some sensory cues may be missed, or repressed, along the way – particularly for those who read the scenes in haste in order to blunt their effect. One senses nonetheless in Sade's fiction, as in any work of pornography, a desire to make those ghostly echoes loud and clear. Figured within the scenes of violence as the libertine's desire to vibrate with his victim's sensations is an authorial fantasy of a reader feeling what the characters depicted feel, and thereby becoming part of a chain reaction: the reader's body resonating with the libertine's body resonating with the victim's body.

---

106 Angela Carter, *The Sadeian Woman: An Exercise in Cultural History* (London: Virago, 2000), 58.
107 Elliot, 'Imagination in the Experience of Art', 90.
108 See https://commons.wikimedia.org/wiki/File:Artemisia_Gentileschi_-_Judith_Beheading_Holofernes_-_WGA8563.jpg#

3. Translating with Sade

translation is the most intimate act of reading, a prayer to be haunted.
Gayatri Spivak, 'Translation as Culture'

Introduction

This chapter will build on the embodied approach of the previous chapters by exploring that very particular form of reception – and (re)production – that is known as translation. While previous chapters have drawn on the responses of other readers, this chapter and the next will draw more explicitly on my own experiences as a translator and teacher of Sade respectively – and, inevitably, as a reader. Those experiences have been intertwined from the beginning: as the next chapter will show, I read Sade for the first time in order to teach him, and the same motivation played a part in my translations of two of his works: *Les 120 Journées de Sodome*, which I translated with Thomas Wynn,[1] and *La Marquise de Gange*. I was keen to make these works – the first badly translated and the latter not translated at all – available to students on our Comparative Literature undergraduate programme, as well as to students in other institutions. This chapter will begin by exploring the curious disconnect that continues to exist in translation studies between a disembodied view of translation as an activity, and the embodied – even visceral – rhetoric that has for centuries been used to describe that activity. A review of previous attempts to translate Sade into English will then provide the context for some of the challenges my co-translator and I faced as we set about our translation of the *120 Journées*. Drawing on

---

1   For my co-translator's perspective on the practice and ethics of translating Sade, see Thomas Wynn, 'Translation, Ethics and Obscenity', in *Erotic Literature in Adaptation and Translation*, ed. by Johannes D. Kaminski (London: Legenda, 2018), 13–32.

my own experiences from that time, and on my experience retranslating an episode for the purposes of this book, it will focus on the sensory, emotional and ethical challenges posed by the task of translating a work of extreme and misogynistic violence.

The Translator's Body

At the conference to celebrate the bicentenary of Sade's death mentioned in the Introduction to this book, one of the two days was devoted to the subject of Sade in translation. In the lively discussions that day, the translator was heralded more than once as a model reader. It is not difficult to understand why one might make such a claim: a translator evidently has to read and reread a text very closely, and in doing so enjoys – or endures – a sustained intimacy with that text that matches if not surpasses that of the literary critic. Perhaps it was my own natural inability to accept a compliment graciously, but it confirmed my sense that Sade scholarship, and literary studies more broadly, was prizing the wrong kind of reading. If translators were being hailed as ideal readers it was because they were being seen as linguistic technicians, focussed purely on words and not content. It implied a model not just of translation but of reading as a purely cognitive process, uncontaminated by the senses or the imagination, a model which, as we have already seen, and shall further see – and smell – below, bears little relation to the realities of either reading or translating. This model has nonetheless remained as influential in the context of translation studies as it has in literary studies. As Kathleen Shields and Michael Clarke observe, translation as a practice is generally 'considered to be a transfer of cognitive content as opposed to, for example, a performance or an act'.[2] While some practitioners – particularly within a feminist tradition of translation studies – have reflected on the emotional costs of translating psychologically or ethically challenging material, very few scholars have engaged with the idea that we translate, as we read, with our bodies. As a translator of Sade, it moreover often seemed to me that my body was doing as much if not more work than my brain – or, to put it as

---

2   Kathleen Shield and Michael Clarke, *Translating Emotion: Studies in Transformation and Renewal Between Languages* (Bern: Peter Lang, 2011), 4.

Douglas Robinson does, that 'translation is largely an intuitive process'.³ For many years, Robinson was a lone voice in decrying the disembodied approach prevalent in translation studies, and in calling for what he described as a 'somatics of translation':

> Good translators choose words and phrases by reference not to some abstract system of intellectualized rules, which most of us have never internalized in the first place, but rather to 'messages' or impulses sent by the body: a given word or phrase feels right. Intuitively, not just for the translator but for all language users, sense is not cognition but sensation.⁴

Robinson rather simplistically defines 'good' translation as instinctive and 'bad' translation as intellectual. I would suspect, however, that there are as many bad intuitive translations as there are good ones, and instinct alone can only get you so far. The binary opposition moreover risks obscuring the ways in which cognition and emotion suffuse and shape each other: what Robinson describes as intuition, for example, is often only arrived at after a period of methodological reflection: if a word 'feels right' it is generally because it is a good fit for the strategy the translator has formulated for that particular text – a strategy that, over time, has become second nature.

Despite Robinson's best efforts, translation studies as a discipline has largely ignored his pleas for further exploration of the embodied aspects of translation. Although Translation Process Research has emerged as a new branch of study this century, it has been narrowly cognitive in its approach, tracking eye movements and logging keystrokes rather than exploring the emotional or affective aspects of translation.⁵ As Séverine Hubscher-Davidson notes, the question of the role played by emotion in translation 'has attracted surprisingly little interest from translation researchers' despite the occasional 'musings of professional translators'⁶

---

3 Douglas Robinson, *The Translator's Turn* (Baltimore, MD: Johns Hopkins University Press, 1991), xii.
4 Ibid., xii.
5 This may, however, be starting to change with the recent work of Séverine Hubscher-Davidson and Kaisa Koskinen: see, in particular, Séverine Hubscher-Davidson, *Translation and Emotion: A Psychological Perspective* (New York and Abingdon: Routledge, 2018), and Séverine Hubscher-Davidson and Caroline Lehr (eds.), *The Psychology of Translation: Interdisciplinary Approaches* (Abingdon: Routledge, 2022), and Kaisa Koskinen, *Translation and Affect: Essays on Sticky Affects and Translational Affective Labour* (Amsterdam: John Benjamins, 2020).
6 Hubscher-Davidson, *Translation and Emotion*, 80.

on this subject – a reflection perhaps that the 'widespread hostility'[7] that Robinson identified between theorists and practitioners of translation decades before has not entirely dissipated. The reluctance of translation studies to contemplate the somatic aspect of translation is all the more surprising given that the discourse of translation has for centuries been littered with metaphorical minds and bodies. The Earl of Roscommon's frequently invoked advice to the translator is worth citing here:

> Examine how your *Humour* is inclin'd,
> And which the *Ruling Passion* of your Mind;
> Then, seek a *Poet* who *your* way do's bend,
> And chuse an *Author* as you chuse a *Friend*.
> United by this *Sympathetick Bond*,
> You grow *Familiar*, *Intimate*, and *Fond*;
> Your *Thoughts*, your *Words*, your *Stiles*, your *Souls* agree,
> No longer his *Interpreter*, but *He*.[8]

While the previous chapter explored some of the ways in which readers may project themselves into fictional characters, here translation is imagined as an act of empathy, a 'Sympathetick Bond' leading not just to a meeting of minds but a form of communion verging on possession.[9] It is not entirely clear, however, who is possessing who – is the translator becoming the author, or the author becoming the translator? Who of the two is erased in the process, or do two translator-authors emerge? Either way, what is striking is that the translator's choice is a personal one in more than one sense: a choice of friend – and kindred soul – rather than a choice of text.

Similar questions about the relationship between author and translator arise in a more recent evocation of the pleasures of translation. Among these, Lydia Davis includes 'company versus solitude':

---

7   Robinson, *The Translator's Turn*, xiii.
8   Wentworth Dillon, Earl of Roscommon, *An Essay on Translated Verse* (London: Jacob Tonson, 1684), 7.
9   Roscommon's image anticipates by several centuries Georges Poulet's phenomenological conception of reading as a form of communion between author and reader: 'I am aware of a rational being, of a consciousness; the consciousness of another, no different from the one I automatically assume in every human being I encounter, except that in this case, the consciousness is open to me, welcomes me, lets me look deep inside itself... to think what it thinks and feel what it feels' ('Phenomenology of Reading', *New Literary History*, 1.1 (1969), 54).

when you are translating, you are working in partnership with the author; you are not as alone as you are when writing your own work. You sense the author's hovering presence, you feel an alliance with him, and a loyalty to him, with all his good and his less good character traits[10]

As these remarks reflect, on the rare occasions when translators describe their lived experiences of translating, it is evident that the authors of their source texts are far from dead to them (*pace* Barthes) even when they are very much dead. If Davis here conjures the image of a shadowy or ghostly presence hovering over the translator as she works at her desk, another of the pleasures she describes is that of 'entering another person—you are speaking in his or her words, a ventriloquist; you are writing what he or she wrote. You become a sort of shadow person, for a time, insubstantial. But this is restful'.[11] As in Roscommon's poem, there is a promise, rather than a threat, of erasure here, as the translator becomes a shadow of herself in order to embody the author's words. Davis also echoes Roscommon in imagining translation as a process that makes new selves possible as well as new texts: 'You develop the ability, if you did not have this before, to be both yourself and another, or multiple others, at the same time'.[12] Her translator shares an affinity with the one Willard Trask likens to an actor:

> I realized that the translator and the actor had to have the same kind of talent. What they both do is to take something of somebody else's and put it over as if it were their own [...] So in addition to the technical stunt, there is a psychological workout, which translation involves: something like being on stage.[13]

While Lawrence Venuti cites Trask's comments as an example of the 'weird self-annihilation'[14] that finds translators seeking their own invisibility, he rather underplays the performative aspect to which Trask

---

10 Lydia Davis, 'Eleven Pleasures of Translating', *The New York Review*, 8 December 2016, https://www.nybooks.com/articles/2016/12/08/eleven-pleasures-of-translating/?lp_txn_id=1531994.
11 Ibid.
12 Ibid.
13 Willard Trask, cited in Edwin Honig, *The Poet's Other Voice: Conversations on Literary Translation* (Amherst, MA: University of Massachusetts Press, 1985), 13–14.
14 Lawrence Venuti, *The Translator's Invisibility: A History of Translation* (London: Routledge, 1995), 7.

is drawing attention: Trask's translator, after all, is the one on stage playing to an audience.[15]

The depictions Roscommon and Davis offer of the author-translator relationship give little sense of a power imbalance at work, let alone one informed by gender. Author and translator are represented as equals, with Roscommon's translator free to 'choose a friend' who suits him, and Davis describing the relationship between the two as a 'partnership' and an 'alliance'. Carlos Batista, however, adds a gendered element in his own tale of translators metamorphosing into authors:

> Une traductrice amoureuse de son auteur vint frapper à sa porte. Il demanda derrière la porte "Qui est là?" Elle répondit: "C'est moi!" Il dit "Il n'y a point de place pour toi et moi dans cette maison." Alors la traductrice s'en fut méditer dans des bibliothèques et des bars de nuit et, quelques mois plus tard, elle revint toquer à la porte de son auteur bien-aimé. Celui-ci questionna: "Qui est là?" La traductrice répondit: "C'est toi..." Alors seulement la porte s'entrouvrit.
>
> [A translator in love with her author came knocking at his door. Behind the door he asked, 'Who's there?' She replied: 'It's me!' He said, 'There's no room for both you and me in his house.' So the translator went off to ruminate in the libraries and late-night bars and, a few months later, she returned to knock at the door of her beloved author. He asked: 'Who is there?' The translator replied: 'It's you...' And only then did the door open a little.][16]

If translators can be likened to actors, Batista's is certainly of the method variety, haunting the bars and books that presumably shaped her author. There is something queer about this evocative fable, which presents the author as narcissist, only willing to see his translator when she can offer him a perfect reflection of himself – a suggestion, perhaps, that the translator may have to change gender in order to grow 'intimate and fond', as Roscommon suggestively puts it, with the author. As Jean Anderson observes, the power dynamic of this passage is anything but

---

15 Cf. the parallel (quoted in the Introduction) Iser draws between the 'recipient' or reader and the actor: 'For the duration of the performance we are both ourselves and someone else' (*Prospecting*, 244).

16 Carlos Batista, *Bréviaire d'un traducteur* (Paris: Arléa, 2003), 13. Cited in Jean Anderson, 'The Double Agent: Aspects of Literary Translator Affect As Revealed in Fictional Work by Translators', *Linguistica Antverpiensia, New Series – Themes in Translation Studies*, 4 (2021), 179.

egalitarian: 'Here the translator must subjugate herself to the author, and to his work: in other words, must occupy no space'.[17]

While Batista, like Roscommon and Davis, imagines the encounter between author and translator as a meeting of minds, he adds a sexual element that suggests this will be a prelude to a meeting of bodies. In so doing, consciously or not, he evokes a long lineage of sexualized and sexist discourse on translation brought powerfully into focus by feminist theorists and practitioners such as Lori Chamberlain in the 1980s.[18] Ever since, the figure of the *belle infidèle* has been endlessly invoked as emblematic of the gendering of translation as handmaiden to male creativity. However, Chamberlain also notes an aggressive strand of discourse on translation that identifies — and endorses — the translator as an agent of male violence and the text (and often author) as his feminized victim. The four-stage model of translation delineated by George Steiner in *After Babel* offers a striking example of this phenomenon: the translator must first approach the text ('initiative trust'), penetrate and capture it ('aggressive penetration'), incorporate or embody it, and then compensate for what has been taken away.[19] As if Steiner's articulation of rape as a model for translation were not bad enough, Serge Gavronsky draws from him to go even further, arguing that translators should be 'cannibalistic' and aggressive rather than 'pious' and submissive. In Gavronsky's oedipal scenario, the author is father, the translator son and rival, and the text mother and object of desire. Although he presents cannibalistic translation as a form of liberation from 'cultural and ideological restrictions', needless to say it does not end well for the mother in a scene with rather Sadean undertones: 'The original has been captured, raped, and incest performed. Here, once again, the

---

17 Anderson, 'The Double Agent', 179.
18 See Lori Chamberlain, 'The Metaphorics of Translation', *Signs*, 13.3 (1988), 454–72.
19 George Steiner, *After Babel: Aspects of Language and Translation* (Oxford: Oxford University Press, 1975), 312–455. For some authors, such as Primo Levi, this is also apparently how it feels to be translated: 'When the author comes across a passage of his work translated into a language he knows, the author feels — one at a time or all at once — flattered, betrayed, ennobled, x-rayed, castrated, flattened, raped, adorned, killed' (Primo Levi, 'Translating and Being Translated', trans. by Harry Thomas and Marco Sonzogni, *Berfrois*, 26 July 2017, https://www.berfrois.com/2017/07/primo-levi-translating-and-being-translated/).

son is father of the man. The original is mutilated beyond recognition'.[20] According to this logic, my model as a translator of the *120 Journées* was staring me in the face the whole time.

The visceral nature of this discourse on translation makes the lack of attention paid to the visceral nature of translation itself all the more curious. It is no coincidence that one of the few theorists to explore translation from a somatic perspective is also a practitioner. When translating journal entries by the Chilean educator and feminist Amanda Labarca, Carol Maier did not feel intellectually engaged by her source text, but began to notice that 'work on the project had begun to affect me physically. I had no trouble locating words or references, but each time I returned to the translation I felt tired and dispirited, my head and shoulders ached, my legs felt heavy'.[21] Maier suggests these symptoms were a somatic manifestation of the 'physical turmoil' she found in Labarca's journal. As Hubscher-Davidson observes, 'One of the most striking aspects of Maier's recounted experiences of translating is the power, violence, and impact of the emotions involved'.[22] In marked contrast to the masculine rhetoric of translators penetrating or raping source texts, Maier has described feeling 'insulted and ridiculed' and even 'battered'[23] by one source text, and feeling metaphorically penetrated by another: 'This summer, punctuation has been penetration into my palms, a sliding back of skin, the separation of its subcutaneous layers'.[24] While Peter Cole describes translation as 'the power of assuming someone else's skin, for a moment, or a month, or a year',[25] Maier's experience conversely describes the power authors have to get

---

20 Serge Gavronsky, 'The Translator: From Piety to Cannibalism', *SubStance* 6/7.16 (1977), 60.
21 Carol Maier, 'Translating as a Body: Meditations on Mediation (Excerpts 1994–2004)', in *The Translator as Writer*, ed. by Susan Bassnett and Peter Bush (London and New York: Continuum, 2006), 140.
22 Hubscher-Davidson, *Translation and Emotion*, 81.
23 Carol Maier, 'Translation, *Dépaysement*, and their Figuration', in *Translation and Power*, ed. by Maria Tymoczko and Edwin Gentzler (Amherst, MA: University of Massachussetts Press, 2002), 188.
24 Maier, 'Translating as a Body', 144. Maier adds, 'ever since I began to translate literature I have sensed that many of the texts [on] which I worked found their way into my blood and became a part of my organism' (ibid., 144).
25 Peter Cole, 'Making Sense in Translation: Towards an Ethics of the Art', in *In Translation: Translators on their Work and What it Means*, ed. by Esther Allen and Susan Bernofsky (New York, Columbia University Press, 2013), 8.

under the skin of their translators. In so doing she offers a reminder that translation is as much about being acted upon by a text as it is about acting upon one – that it is, after all, as much an act of reception as it is an act of production. As both Hubscher-Davidson and Kaisa Koskinen make clear, translation is a task that makes emotional demands of the translator; the latter, drawing on Sara Ahmed's work on 'sticky affect',[26] claims,

> affect affects translating and interpreting in multiple ways. Some of these are sticky and immediately recognizable, and they bear witness to the notion of translating and interpreting as affective labour, as activities that are fundamentally inscribed with managing emotions.[27]

As these remarks reflect, Koskinen – like Hubscher-Davidson – focusses on some of the emotional challenges translation poses the practitioner, and the ways in which these challenges can be met. While she recognizes that 'affective states often include an embodied element',[28] her emphasis is on emotion rather than sensation. Although translation studies first showed an interest in the pedagogic potential of visualization techniques for translators as far back as the 1960s, Celia Martín de León observes that 'very few studies have addressed the actual role, if any, played by mental images in translation and interpreting processes'.[29] In this regard, translation studies has perhaps unsurprisingly followed the example of the overlapping discipline of literary studies.

How Not to Translate Sade

Sade's afterlife in English provides plentiful evidence of the active, and at times overactive, imagination of his translators. In the previous chapter, I referred to a scene from *Justine* in which the newly orphaned heroine appeals to her local priest – in more ways than one:

---

26 'Affect is what sticks, or what sustains or preserves the connection between ideas, values, and objects' (Sara Ahmed, 'Happy Objects', in *The Affect Theory Reader*, ed. by Melissa Gregg and Gregory J. Seigworth (Durham, NC: Duke University Press, 2010), 29).
27 Koskinen, *Translation and Affect*, 46.
28 Ibid., 14.
29 Celia Martín de León, 'Mental Imagery in Translation Processes', *HERMES - Journal of Language and Communication in Business* (2017), 201–20.

« Vous me voyez, monsieur », dit-elle au saint ecclésiastique... « Oui, vous me voyez dans une position bien affligeante pour une jeune fille [...] Le charitable prêtre répondit en lorgnant Justine, que la paroisse était bien chargée ; qu'il était difficile qu'elle pût embrasser de nouvelles aumônes, mais que si Justine voulait le servir, que si elle voulait faire le gros ouvrage, il y aurait toujours dans sa cuisine un morceau de pain pour elle. Et, comme en disant cela, l'interprète des Dieux lui avait passé la main sous le menton, en lui donnant un baiser beaucoup trop mondain pour un homme d'Église, Justine qui ne l'avait que trop compris, le repoussa

['You see me, Monsieur,' she said to the holy cleric... 'Yes, you see me in a very distressing position indeed for a young girl' [...] The charitable priest replied, ogling Justine, that the parish was greatly burdened; that it would be difficult for it to take on fresh requests for alms, but that if Justine were willing to serve him, that if she were willing to do the hard work, there would always be a crust of bread for her in his kitchen. And, as God's spokesman had slipped his hand beneath her chin as he said this, giving her a kiss that was far too worldly for a man of the Church, Justine, who had understood him all too well, pushed him away] (J 135)

When translators add imagery of their own to a source text, it does not necessarily tell us what they were visualizing upon reading it. It does, however, strongly suggest what they were visualizing upon writing their target text, and, indeed, what they were intending their readers to visualize. As noted earlier, this scene from *Justine* is striking for the leering gaze to which the heroine is subjected by the narrator as well as the priest. In more than one English version of this passage, the translator seems to implicate himself as well as the ogling priest. In Harold Berman's 1931 translation of *Justine*, for example, the single word 'lorgnant' [ogling] is considerably fleshed out: 'Having carefully feasted his greedy eyes all along the graceful budding outlines of her fragile little person, the charitable priest replied that the parish was burdened enough'.[30] John Phillips's more recent version of *Justine* for Oxford World's Classics renders 'l'interprète des dieux lui avait passé la main sous le menton' [God's spokesman had slipped his hand beneath her chin] as 'God's spokesman slipped his hand into her cleavage'[31] – the

---

30 Sade, *Justine, or the Misfortunes of Virtue*, trans. by Harold Berman (New York: Risus Press, 1931), 6–7.
31 Sade, *Justine, or the Misfortunes of Virtue*, trans. by John Phillips (Oxford: Oxford University Press, 2012), 9.

mind's eye, and perhaps hand, of the translator also seemingly slipping from chin to chest. That this almost immediately follows a description of the twelve-year-old heroine as having a 'gorge à peine indiquée, cachée sous deux ou trois aunes de gaze' [barely discernible breasts, hidden beneath two or three ells of gauze] (*J* 135) reminds us once again of the ways in which readers may stray from the scripts their authors provide.

For English readers curious about Sade, one of the major difficulties has indeed been finding reliable editions of his works. The liberties taken above pale in comparison to some of the others taken by Berman and his successors both in Britain and the United States. Berman's translation, for example, removes Justine as the narrator of her story, turning it into the third-person narrative it would become in the *Nouvelle Justine* – a move that moreover necessitates drastic structural changes. It is also worth noting that the circulation of Berman's translation was not limited to its print run of 1500: in 1964 it was reprinted by the Lancer Press as a 95 cent paperback, and in 2006 it became the basis for an Arabic translation of *Justine*[32] – or rather translation of a translation of *Justine*. Other editions of *Justine* in English have failed even to be the text their titles promise: a Corgi edition that appeared in 1964 (and was invoked as an inspiration for the Moors Murders) was actually based on *Les Infortunes de la vertu*, and is still circulating today as a 'Harper Forbidden Classic'. Perhaps the most egregious example of Sadean mis-selling is also still in print: Dr Paul J. Gillette's far from complete *The Complete Marquis de Sade* (1966), which features only heavily abridged and free versions of *Justine*, the *Histoire de Juliette* and the *120 Journées* alongside a few shorter texts. While *Justine* is once again turned into a third person narrative, the *120 Journées* is even more radically transformed: of the first part of the novel, Gillette only includes the first day – which he renames 'A Day in the School of Libertinage'.[33] The rest of the first part is turned into a list of perversions in order to resemble the second to fourth parts which Sade had left in note form.

The editors of the Gillette edition distance themselves from the methods adopted by the 'so-called "complete" editions' appearing on

---

32 Sade, *Jûstîn*, trans. by Mohamed Eid Ibrahim (Libya [city unspecified]: Ishraqat Publishing, 2006).

33 Sade, *The Complete Marquis de Sade*, trans. by Paul J. Gillette (San Francisco, CA: Holloway House, 1966), 193.

the market, and from the 'literal translation into English of Sade's exact language' in particular. Staying faithful to Sade, they claim, would mean staying faithful to all of 'Sade's repetitions and redundancies, his dreary polemics and his use of a syntactically complex Eighteenth Century idiom which is all but unreadable today'.[34] The translations they no doubt had in mind were the Grove Press editions of Sade's fiction (based on Austryn Wainhouse's translations for the Olympia Press in Paris a decade earlier) which were selling in the hundreds of thousands in counterculture America.[35] Leaving aside Gillette's efforts, the Wainhouse version of the *120 Journées*[36] was the only one available to Anglophone readers prior to the translation Thomas Wynn and I published with Penguin Classics in 2016. While we took a markedly different approach, reading the Wainhouse translation was certainly instrumental to us landing on that approach, in part because it crystallized what we did – and did not – want our translation to be. The criticism of Sade's idiom levelled by the Gillette editors was probably inspired by their reading of the Wainhouse translations, which do indeed take an idiosyncratic approach to the translation of eighteenth-century French. Two examples from the Grove Press translation of the *120 Journées* alongside the original should suffice:

> This schedule affirms that unto the Duc shall fall nine pucelages: the first encuntments of Fanny, Sophie, Zelmire, Augustine, the original embuggeries of Hébé, Michette, Giton, Rosette, and Zéphyr.
>
> [Par ce tableau, on voit que le duc aura eu les pucelages des cons de Fanny, Sophie, Zelmire, Augustine, et ceux des culs d'Hébé, Michette, Giton, Rosette et Zéphire.][37] (*120J* 111)
>
> Upon that day, Messieurs celebrate the festival of the fourteenth week, and, in the guise of a woman, Curval becomes Bum-Cleaver's wife, and, as a man, takes Adonis to be his helpmeet; 'tis not till then that child is

---

34 Ibid., 11.
35 Sales for the first volume of Grove's edition of Sade's works reached 240,000 copies by 1967. See Loren Glass, *Counterculture Colophon: Grove Press, the Evergreen Review and the Incorporation of the Avant-Garde* (Stanford, CA: Stanford University Press, 2013), 138.
36 Although the Grove Press translation adds Richard Seaver as a co-translator, this was very much Wainhouse's version, with Seaver's role essentially editorial.
37 Sade, *The 120 Days of Sodom and other Writings*, trans. by Austryn Wainhouse and Richard Seaver (New York: Grove Press, 1966), 305.

depucelated, and the event occurs very publicly, while Bum-Cleaver is fucking the Président.

[On célèbre, ce jour-là, la fête de la quatorzième semaine, et Curval épouse, lui comme femme, Brise-cul en qualité de mari, et lui comme homme, Adonis en qualité de femme. Cet enfant n'est dépucelé que ce jour-là, devant tout le monde, pendant que Brise-cul fout Curval.]³⁸ (*120J* 352)

Wainhouse's thinking is clear: to translate eighteenth-century French one should use eighteenth-century English. What he creates instead, however, might best be described as a linguistic form of mock-Tudor that would have seemed archaic even to eighteenth-century readers. His translation is simultaneously domesticating and foreignizing, transforming the source text into a target text so English that it seems foreign to a modern reader. The result is a linguistic flamboyance that detracts – and distracts – from the brutal violence of the original, a distraction compounded by the comic tone and lexis Wainhouse adopts. Words such as 'encuntments', 'embuggeries' and 'depucelated' – inspired by the efforts of seventeenth-century translators of French pornography³⁹ – risk making child-rape sound somehow comical rather than horrifying. So indeed do Wainhouse's translations of the names of the 'fouteurs', such as 'Bum-Cleaver' for 'Brise-cul'. In this respect, our own translation could justifiably be accused of suppressing some of the humour of Sade's text by retaining the French names of these characters. This may be a fair criticism, but it seemed to us a price worth paying in order to avoid turning our text into the kind of comic novel that Wainhouse had produced.

If some of Sade's English translators could be charged with tempering Sade, the same could equally be said of his French editors. The last edition of the *120 Journées* to scrupulously follow the original scroll was Maurice Heine's private edition published in the 1930s. Heine's edition

---

38 Ibid., 633.
39 *The School of Venus* (1680), an English translation of the pornographic *L'Ecole des filles* (1655), features the first (and until Wainhouse the last) use of verbs such as 'encunt' and 'discunt' (for 'enconner' and 'déconner'), while a 1693 translation of Rabelais was among the first to use 'depucelate' as a verb (Rabelais, *The Third Book*, trans. by Thomas Urquhart and Peter Anthony Motteux (London: Richard Baldwin, 1693–4), 58) although to 'depucel' features in earlier translations from Latin and French.

is essentially a transcript of the scroll, steadfastly revealing the text for the incomplete and unrevised draft that it is – complete with all the mistakes, repetitions, and notes to self one would expect to find in a draft. It also adheres to the scroll's minimal paragraphing and minimalistic punctuation, with very long sentences broken up by commas alone, no speech marks, question marks or colons and only the very occasional semicolon or exclamation mark. By contrast, every editor since Heine has offered far more polished and refined versions of the text in which the punctuation is elegant, the paragraphing consistent, abbreviations given in full, mistakes corrected, and missing words added. The result is an editorially tamed text that also in its own way obscures the rawness of the original manuscript. For this reason, we decided to base our translation on Heine's transcript and to keep corrections to a bare minimum. Our aim, as editors and as translators, was to make our text, and the reader's experience of our text, as raw as humanly possible.

The rawness of Sade's language in the *120 Journées* is inseparable from the rawness of the violence it conveys. As stated in the Introduction to this book, the tradition of Sade scholarship that insists the violence in Sade is purely linguistic continues to be in denial of the representational power of language over readers' minds and bodies. As translators, we were under no such illusions, and therefore had ethical questions to confront before we could settle on a strategy – including, of course, whether or not it was ethical to translate arguably Sade's most extreme text at all, given its seemingly endless scenes of rape, torture and paedophilia. More pertinent for this discussion, however, was the question of what our approach should be when it came to translating such scenes. Should we simply do what the Sadean text dictated? Or should we refuse to be dictated to by the Sadean text? What would such a refusal even look like?

Feminist critics, as we have already seen, drew attention to the misogyny informing much of the discourse around translation as an act of male aggression against, but within, a male literary tradition. The same critics evidently also had to address the question – what happens when the translator of this tradition is a woman? How, in other words, should female translators deal with misogynistic male authors? The answer, it seemed, was to subvert them. Suzanne Jill Levine led the way in her approach to translating Guillermo Cabrera Infante's *La Habana para un infante difunto* (1979), a work which 'mocks women and their words' and 'whose content is oppressively male'.[40] Levine elegantly expresses the dilemma she faced: 'Where does this leave a woman as translator of such a book? Is she not a double betrayer, to play Echo to this Narcissus, by repeating the archetype again?'[41] Her claim to have evaded this trap rests on a few examples of what might be described as small acts of subversion, such as when she chooses the (literally) belittling 'no wee man can rape a woman' over the more literal 'no one man can rape a woman'.[42] If 'micro-aggressions' might be a better description for these interventions, some within the field of feminist translation studies seem disappointed by the small scale of Levine's rebellion. Luise Von Flotow finds that Levine ultimately does little more than 'undermine the text here and there'.[43] She writes much more admiringly of the 'anti-traditional, aggressive and creative approach to translation'[44] taken by a small number of Canadian translators who identified their practice as feminist, and – in marked contrast to Levine – only translated texts they considered to be feminist. This more aggressive practice is marked by a more aggressive rhetoric, which Von Flotow approvingly cites, around the 'hijacking' of source texts, and 'womanhandling' of paratexts (such as footnotes and prefaces).[45] For some, such as Rosemary Arrojo, this does not seem like much of an improvement on the sexually violent rhetoric these translators had themselves condemned. Arrojo asks, 'on what grounds can one justify that "womanhandling" texts is objectively positive while "manhandling" them is to be despised?'[46] Although Arrojo underplays the local context in which these terms were used, and in particular the fact they were adopted by feminist translators translating the work of feminist authors (with their permission), the

---

40 Suzanne Jill Levine, 'Translation As (Sub) Version: On Translating Infante's *Inferno*', *SubStance*, 13.1 (1984), 92, 94.
41 Ibid., 92.
42 Ibid., 92.
43 Luise Von Flotow, *Translation and Gender: Translating in the 'Era of Feminism'* (Ottowa: University of Ottowa Press, 1997), 27. Von Flotow expresses the same misgivings about Carol Maier's approach.
44 Luise Von Flotow, 'Feminist Translation: Contexts, Practices and Theories', *TTR: Traduction, terminologie, rédaction*, 4.2 (1991), 70.
45 Ibid., 74.
46 Rosemary Arrojo, 'Fidelity and the Gendered Translation', *TTR : Traduction, terminologie, rédaction*, 7.2 (1994), 157.

broader point about the potential pitfalls of adopting an aggressive rhetoric to describe feminist practice is a reasonable one.

It is telling that Von Flotow cites Peter Newmark in support of her interventionist approach to translation. Newmark advocates that the role of the translator is to 'correct' various types of 'defect' in source texts, ranging from misprints, scientific, material and 'moral facts', 'bad writing' and 'Statements infringing human rights'.[47] Rather than point out the very obviously problematic nature of such a stance when applied to literary translation, Von Flotow glosses 'moral facts' as 'truths', and declares that 'feminist translators "correct" texts that they translate in the name of feminist "truths"'.[48] There is, however, a clear difference between correcting a text by rewriting it in some way, as Von Flotow seems to advocate, and providing critical commentary in the scholarly apparatus of that text (an option that Newmark allows). A case often cited as an example of the former strategy is Sharon Bell's translation of Madame de Staël's 'Appel aux souverains, réunis à Paris, pour en obtenir l'abolition de la traite des nègres' [An Appeal to the Sovereigns Convened in Paris to Grant the Abolition of the Slave Trade][49] (1814). Bell, a woman of colour, states in an interview to her fellow-translator of Staël, Françoise Massardier-Kenney,

> There was a place where I very deliberately changed the sentence because she said something I found shocking; she called blacks 'savages,' or something like that [...] I deliberately softened that one sentence [...] I remember that the statement offended me so much I could not put down what the sentence actually said.[50]

To be fair to Bell, her 'change' relates to a single word in Staël's text: 'sauvages', which she translates as 'primitives'.[51] Nonetheless, it is clear

---

47 Peter Newmark, *About Translation* (Clevedon: Multilinguial Matters, 1991), 46.
48 Von Flotow, *Translation and Gender*, 24.
49 Sharon Bell's translation of the title.
50 Sharon Bell and Françoise Massardier-Kenney, 'Black on White: Translation, Race, Class and Power', in *Translating Slavery: Gender and Race in French Women's Writing, 1783–1823*, ed. by Doris Y. Kadish and Françoise Massardier-Kenney (Kent, OH: Kent State University Press, 1994), 174–5. In the same interview, but for different reasons, Massardier-Kenny also admits of her own translation, 'I tried to soften the excesses and wanted to valorize her [Mirza's] speech' (ibid., 175).
51 The full sentence in the original is 'Souvent, sous le ridicule prétexte de la sorcellerie, ces infortunés sont pour jamais exilés des bords qui les ont vus naître, loin de cette patrie plus chère encore aux sauvages qu'aux hommes civilisés'; Bell

which position she has taken in answer to the translatorial dilemma she articulates in the same interview: 'Do we soften ideas offensive to modern sensibilities in an otherwise sympathetic writer, or do we let them speak freely, for better or worse?'[52] The obvious problem with the former approach, however, is that it creates a false impression of such material, and of the culture in which that material is embedded. As Brian James Baer notes in relation to misogynistic works,

> While intervening in the translation to erase or downplay patriarchal or misogynistic aspects of a source text might have the salutary effect of removing such discourse from circulation, it might also have the more ambivalent effect of whitewashing an author's work or reputation and obscuring the reality of gender bias.[53]

While correcting or 'softening' a problematic text may make it more palatable to modern readers, this comes at the expense – ironically, given Von Flotow's framing – of historical 'truths'.[54]

Correcting a work like the *120 Journées* in the main body of a translation, as opposed to its paratext, was never a plausible option: it is difficult to imagine a more incorrigible text. Without the misogyny, violence and obscenity, not much remains. To soften that violence would be to denature the original and, ironically, to commit the kind of violence against it that we have seen evoked in the aggressive rhetoric around translation rightly decried by feminist critics. As disappointed as Von Flotow seems to be by Maier's decision to limit her own translatorial interventions to paratextual commentary, the latter's position seems to

---

renders this as 'Often, under the ridiculous pretext of sorcery, these unfortunates are exiled forever from the shores where they were born, far from that land even dearer to primitive than to civilized men' (ibid., 158).

52   Ibid., 175.
53   Brian James Baer, 'Translation, Gender and Sexuality', in *The Cambridge Handbook of Translation*, ed. by Kirsten Malmkjær (Cambridge, UK: Cambridge University Press, 2022), 280. As Baer's allusion to whitewashing reflects, the debate within translation studies is reflective of a much broader one ongoing in the public sphere regarding the ways in which we curate and commemorate the past in museums and monuments.
54   The recent commotion around the 'corrected' versions of Roald Dahl's children's stories provides a useful illustration of the problem: a case can be made for removing some of the fatphobic and other politically incorrect language so that young children do not encounter it, but the removal of this language creates a misleading impression of those stories (and their author).

me the only tenable one, and indeed to apply to all translators regardless of gender:

> the translator's quest is not to silence but to give voice, to make available texts that raise difficult questions and open perspectives. It is essential that as translators women get under the skin of both antagonistic and sympathetic works. They must become independent, 'resisting' interpreters who not only let antagonistic works speak in English but also speak with them and place them in a larger context by discussing them and the process of their translation.[55]

Hence, in part, this very discussion. Maier's suggestion that translators should allow the works they translate to speak, in all their ugliness, before speaking in their own voices to frame them, seems to me more constructive – and progressive – than the other option Von Flotow suggests for works of intolerable misogyny: 'Censorship, if only for reasons of the translator's mental health, is definitely an option'.[56] As I shall touch on below, however, she is right to warn that getting 'under the skin', as Maier puts it, of 'antagonistic' material has its risks for the translator.

Our aim in translating the *120 Journées* was thus not to protect our readers in the way that Bell protected hers from the shock and offence she experienced when reading Madame de Staël. As far as possible, I wanted our readers to have the same visceral experience as anyone reading the text in French today: I wanted them to be just as shocked and offended as I was when I first read it. Softening the language seemed ultimately more dangerous to me than presenting Sade's text warts and all (in the spirit of Heine's French edition). Airbrushing out those warts risked making the text less rebarbative, and this was the last thing I wanted: throughout the process my underlying anxiety was that we might inadvertently produce an appealing text. (Aware of the dubious ways in which Sade had been linked to serial killers such as Ian Brady and Ted Bundy in the past, it was impossible not to be concerned about the prospect of some reader 'out there' being inspired by the text to emulate its violence in the real world.) This was the reason I stated at the time of the translation's release that we felt 'We had a duty to be just as

---

55 Carol Maier, 'A Woman in Translation, Reflecting', *Translation Review*, 17 (1985), 4.
56 Luise Von Flotow, *Translation and Gender*, 28.

rude, crude, and revolting as Sade'.⁵⁷ What reassured me to some extent was the sense that the *120 Journées* was a less dangerous text for being so extreme – it is a work that assaults, rather than seduces, its readers. As long as we could match its extremeness, we and our readers would be on safe, if unpleasant, ground. In this regard, Emily Wilson's enunciation of the 'Feminist Translation Strategy' she adopted for her translation of Homer's *Odyssey* resonates very much with the approach we took to the *120 Journées*. Wilson states, 'I worked, wherever possible, to make vivid the voices of Odysseus's opponents and victims, and to treat them with as much narrative respect as I could – while still remaining within the parameters of the original';⁵⁸ this included the plight of the enslaved women hanged for sleeping with Penelope's suitors:

> In my version, I wanted the reader to feel the women's pain as much as possible – not as a source of vicarious thrills, but as something genuinely painful, suffered by people who are truly people.⁵⁹

As sadistic as it may seem, I too wanted the readers of our translation to feel the victims' suffering viscerally. In the case of a work as long and as endlessly violent as the *120 Journées*, it moreover seemed particularly important to present that suffering as vividly as possible to mitigate against the risk of readers becoming desensitized to the violence.

It is obviously one thing to formulate a 'no-holds-barred' translation strategy, but quite another to overcome a lifetime of socially learned behaviours and taboos around the use of obscene language and the depiction of extreme violence. The Bell case serves as a useful reminder that self-censorship may play as significant a role in the translation of material that challenges or offends our modern values as censorship itself – and perhaps in this century a greater one. As that case reflects, part of the power of self-censorship is that it works by stealth: the monolingual readership of a target text, which often includes the very

---

57 McMorran, 'We Translated the Marquis de Sade's Most Obscene Work – Here's How', *The Independent*, 2 November 2016, https://www.independent.co.uk/arts-entertainment/books/we-translated-the-marquis-de-sade-s-most-obscene-work-here-s-how-a7393066.html.

58 Emily Wilson, 'Epilogue: Translating Homer as a Woman', in *Homer's Daughters: Women's Responses to Homer in the Twentieth Century and Beyond*, ed. by Fiona Cox and Elena Theodorakopoulos (Oxford: Oxford University Press, 2019), 285.

59 Ibid., 290.

editors who commission and publish that text, will for the most part remain in ignorant bliss of any softening or moderating of the source text by the translator. As José Santaemilia has moreover noted, source texts that depict sex and use sexual language are particularly vulnerable to translatorial acts of self-censorship. He identifies

> a more or less general axiom at work that prescribes that translation of sex, more than any other aspect, is likely to be 'defensive' or 'conservative', tends to soften or downplay sexual references, and also tends to make translations more 'formal' than their originals, in a sort of 'hypercorrection' strategy.[60]

Sure enough, as we embarked on our translation of the *120 Journées*, my own instinctive tendency to soften obscenity soon manifested itself in my continual baulking at the coarseness of the English options available to me. As immersed as I have always been in French culture, the obscenities I was translating into English seemed to gain rather than lose force in translation, triggering the urge to modulate them. As I stated at the time, translating rude words into one's first language 'brings the obscenity home in more ways than one'.[61] There was something physically jarring about hearing these ugly words (*dick, cock, cunt* etc.) in my own inner voice as I tried them out. As an exception to Robinson's claim that translators know in their gut when a word or phrase 'feels right', it was often in these early stages only when it felt wrong that I knew it was the right one. The process of translating obscenity only became easier when, for the sake of consistency, we compiled what we called our 'Sadean lexicon' of agreed translations for those words that recurred most frequently in the source text. In order to translate Sade I had to become someone I am not, someone who could use words that I could or would not use in my own life: pre-emptively taking the decision-making out of the process with our lexicon allowed me to become the obscene translator the text required. Making the decision about a particular obscenity once, rather than on every occasion it appeared,

---

60 José Santaemilia, 'The Translation of Sex, The Sex of Translation: *Fanny Hill* in Spanish', in *Gender, Sex and Translation: The Manipulation of Identities*, ed. by Santaemilia (Manchester: St Jerome, 2005), 121.
61 McMorran, 'We Translated the Marquis de Sade's Most Obscene work – Here's How'.

introduced a level of automatism that eased some of the affective load of the translation process.

Smelling Silling

While using rude words in the process of translation became second nature to me over time, other aspects of translating the *120 Journées* proved more difficult. As this book has attempted to show throughout, the reading process is not limited to a single exteroceptive sense, so it was not simply a matter of becoming used to the sound of obscene or offensive words. Translating and editing Sade's work, with all the reading and rereading that entailed, engaged all the traditional five senses and more, and triggered a range of affective and emotional responses. The next two sections will focus on the two aspects of the text that provoked the strongest reactions from a somatic perspective: the shit and the violence.

It is perhaps testimony to Barthes's singularly semiological focus that he was able to persuade himself that 'écrite, la merde ne sent pas' [written down, shit does not smell]. He would evidently have had no patience for Steiner's claim that 'poets can even smell words'[62] and would doubtless have been irked by the exceptionalism implied therein. While it is dangerous to generalize for all readers, Robinson is broadly right to correct Steiner by stating that 'We smell words, all of us, as well as see them; taste words as well as hear them', and to add that 'We also feel words in the tactile sense – we can feel assaulted or bludgeoned by words'.[63] Recent neuroscience has indeed confirmed that metaphors involving texture (such as 'The singer had a velvet voice' and 'He had leathery hands') activate the somatosensory cortex,[64] while words with strong olfactory associations – such as 'cinnamon' or 'perfume' or 'coffee' – activate the primary olfactory cortex.[65] Unfortunately, it became

---

62 Steiner, *After Babel*, 293.
63 Robinson, *The Translator's Task*, 5.
64 Simon Lacey, Randall Stilla and K. Sathian, 'Metaphorically Feeling: Comprehending Textural Metaphors Activates Somatosensory Cortex', Brain and Language 120.3 (2012), 416–21.
65 Julio González, Alfonso Barros-Loscertales, Friedemann Pulvermüller, Vanessa Meseguer, Ana Sanjuán, Vicente Belloch and César Ávila, 'Reading Cinnamon Activates Olfactory Brain Regions', NeuroImage, 32.2 (2006), 906–12.

increasingly clear when translating the *120 Journées* that the same applies to words with less pleasant olfactory associations. I'm afraid I have to ask you to read the following as immersively as it is possible to read two extracts taken out of context. The *historienne*, Duclos, is describing the coprophagic exploits of d'Aucourt and his friend Desprès:

> « Allons, dit-il, mon enfant, mettons-nous à l'œuvre ; la merde est prête, je l'ai sentie, souvenez-vous de chier peu à peu et d'attendre toujours que j'ai dévoré un morceau avant de pousser l'autre. Mon opération est longue, mais ne la pressez pas. Un petit coup sur les fesses vous avertira de pousser, mais que ce soit toujours en détail. » S'étant alors placé le plus à l'aise possible relativement à l'objet de son culte, il colle sa bouche, et je lui dépose presque tout de suite un morceau d'étron gros comme un petit œuf. Il le suce, il le tourne et retourne mille fois dans sa bouche, il le mâche, il le savoure, et, au bout de deux ou trois minutes, je le lui vois distinctement avaler. Je repousse : même cérémonie, et comme mon envie était prodigieuse, dix fois de suite sa bouche se remplit et se vide sans qu'il ait l'air d'être rassasié.
>
> [...] le voyant prêt à faire lui-même l'opération, je lui demandai quelle nécessité il y avait à ce que je baisasse le cul. « La plus grande, mon cœur, me répondit-il, car mon cul, le plus capricieux de tous les culs, ne chie jamais que quand on le baise. » J'obéis, mais sans me hasarder, et lui s'en apercevant : « Plus près, morbleu ! plus près, mademoiselle, me dit-il impérieusement. Avez-vous donc peur d'un peu de merde ? » Enfin, par condescendance, je portai mes lèvres jusqu'aux environs du trou ; mais à peine les a-t-il senties qu'il débonde, et l'irruption fut si violente qu'une de mes joues s'en trouva toute bariolée. Il n'eut besoin que d'un seul jet pour combler le plat ; de ma vie, je n'avais vu un tel étron : il remplissait à lui tout seul un très profond saladier. Notre homme s'en empare, se couche avec sur le bord du lit, me présente son cul tout merdeux et m'ordonne de le lui branler fortement pendant qu'il va faire subitement repasser dans ses entrailles ce qu'il vient de dégorger. Quelque sale que fût ce derrière, il fallut obéir.

> ["Come, my child," he said, "let's get to work. The shit is ready – I have felt it. Remember to shit little by little and always to wait until I've devoured one morsel before pushing out the next one. My routine takes a long time, but do not rush it – a little slap on your bottom will let you know you when to push, but it should always be piecemeal." Having positioned himself as comfortably as possible relative to the object of his devotion, he seals his mouth to it, and I almost immediately deposit a lump of shit as large as a small egg: he sucks it, turns it over and over a thousand times in his mouth, chews it, savours it, and, after two or three

minutes, I clearly see him swallow it; I push again – the same ceremony, and as my need was great, his mouth fills and empties ten times in a row without him ever seeming satisfied.

[...] seeing him ready to carry out the operation himself, I asked him what necessity there was for me to kiss his arse. "The greatest, my dear," he replied, "for my arse, the most capricious of all arses, only shits when it is being kissed." I obey, but without taking any chances, and as he realizes this – "Closer, damn it! Closer, Milli!" he tells me imperiously. "Are you really afraid of a little shit?" Finally, to be obliging, I brought my lips close to the hole, but he had no sooner sensed this than he opened the floodgates, and the eruption was so violent that one of my cheeks was quite splattered – it only took one shot to fill the dish. In all my life I had never seen such a turd – it filled a very deep salad bowl all by itself; our man grabs it, lies down on the edge of the bed with it, shows me his shitty arse and orders me to fondle it vigorously while he immediately goes about filling his guts again with all he has just disgorged. As filthy as this backside was, I had to obey.] (*120J* 179, 183–4; 175, 180–1)

Did you see, smell, or even taste the shit as you read these passages? If so, my apologies. If not, imagine reading page after page of this: coprophagic scenes comprise a whole week of the *120 Journées* – from the 9th to the 16th Day – and amount to approximately sixty pages of our translation. Imagine slowly translating it, with all the endless rereading and rewriting that entails. It took me a month to produce a first draft of the thirty pages for which I was responsible, in part because I could not work on these passages for more than an hour without feeling nauseous and needing to get some fresh air. After three or four hours, the nausea would become overwhelming and I would have to stop for the day. Unlike the translation of obscenity, I never got used to the shit – indeed rather than becoming desensitized to it, I found the stench got worse with each day I spent translating it. Ploughing through those excremental Days from the first part of the novel, I felt rather like Andy Dufresne wading through the sewage in *The Shawshank Redemption* to freedom, or at least freedom from shit. While I had to spend longer in the sewage than a typical reader, my experience corroborated Annie Le Brun's claim regarding the *120 Journées*: 'c'est sûrement le texte le plus insupportable de Sade. Toute personne qui le lit sérieusement en est malade' [it is surely the most intolerable of Sade's texts. It makes anyone who reads it seriously feel ill].[66]

For obvious reasons, therefore, these are not passages that I wish to dwell on here. As with the extract from *Justine* in the previous chapter, my sense is that in the first passage the kinesic verbs are key once again, with the succession of 'suce', 'tourne', 'retourne', 'mâche', 'savoure', 'avaler' [suck, turns, turns again, savours, swallow] triggering the 'perceptual simulations'[67] of actions which Bolens describes, and grounding the disgust triggered by the visual images of defecating and eating. In the second paragraph, there is greater focus on seeing ('voyant', 'apercevant', 'je n'avais vu') and on the spectacle of the full 'saladier' [salad bowl] than there is on doing. How strong either passage smells or tastes will evidently depend on how vividly the reader imagines this scene: I suspect most readers are unlikely to linger over these descriptions, and may actively seek to outpace their imagination by increasing the pace of their reading. Fortunately, there will in any case be limits to what the reader can imagine: most of us do not know what shit tastes like. But somehow not knowing this is not enough to prevent a visceral reaction.[68] This reaction did have its uses, however: while the nausea was not helpful to the translating process, there was something reassuring about its return during the editing process – a somatic signal that we had succeeded in capturing the sights and smells of Silling.

On the rare occasions I have read material such as this aloud to an audience, I have noticed grimaces form and noses wrinkle – instinctive reactions to an unwanted smell. Modern sanitation means we are not used to lingering over excrement, as Sade makes us do for page after page of the *120 Journées*. Pierre Chauvet's 1797 *Essai sur la propriété de Paris* reminds us that Sade and his contemporaries were much more used to the smell: 'Il est étonnant que Paris, qui, depuis plus d'un siècle, est le centre des sciences, des arts, des modes et du goût, soit aussi le centre de la puanteur' [It is remarkable that Paris, which, for more than a century,

---

66 Annie Le Brun, 'Le secret de Juliette', interview with Jean-Luc Moreau, *Roman*, 15 (1986), 20.
67 See Chapter 2, 'Once More, with Einfühlung'.
68 This visceral reaction suggests an imaginative extrapolation based on our sensory knowledge of the smell, look and perhaps texture of excrement.

has been the centre of the sciences, the arts, fashion and taste, should also be the centre of stench].[69] As Mercier had complained a few years earlier in his *Tableau de Paris*, 'Les trois quarts des latrines sont sales, horribles, dégoûtantes : les Parisiens, à cet égard, ont l'œil et l'odorat accoutumés aux saletés' [Three quarters of the latrines are dirty, horrid, disgusting: Parisians, in this respect, are used to the sight and smell of ordure].[70] As used as they may have been to these sights and smells, I suspect they too would have responded somatically to Sade's excremental scenes. Although Sade's contemporaries were unaware of the existence of the *120 Journées*, their responses to *Justine* (which contains some less graphic scenes of coprophagia) suggest physical as well as moral revulsion. Charles Villers refers to *Justine* as 'cette production monstrueuse, dont personne n'a jamais pu lire dix pages sans que le cœur lui levât' [that monstrous production of which no one has ever been able to read ten pages without their stomach turning].[71] In marked contrast to Barthes, Joseph Joubert describes the novel in pungently olfactory terms:

> J'ai vu les loges de la Salpêtrière et les fureurs de la révolution, et il me semble toujours, par une liaison d'idées dont je ne distingue que le nœud, apercevoir, au fond de ces scènes monstrueuses, la chemise des folles et la houppelande de Marat. Je crois même y respirer quelque chose de l'odeur de ce livre infect, qui porte un beau nom dans son titre et un cloaque dans son sein. Ces livres honnêtes et ce livre infâme, que je ne veux pas nommer, de peur que l'air n'en soit souillé, sont nés visiblement sous la même atmosphère et dans le temps de la même peste ; ces papiers-là se sont touchés : ils sont marqués des mêmes taches, mélanges d'amour et de sang.

> [I have seen the cells of Salpêtrière and the furies of the revolution, and it feels to me I can still see, by an association of ideas of which I see only the knot, the madwomen's smock and Marat's cloak in the depths of those monstrous scenes. I even think I can breathe therein something of the smell of that revolting book which bears a pretty name in its title and a sewer in its heart. Those honourable books, and that foul one, which I do not wish to name, for fear of sullying the air, are quite visibly born in the same atmosphere and at the time of the same plague; those pages

---

69 Pierre Chauvet, *Essai sur la propriété de Paris* (Paris: Labrousse, 1797), 18.
70 Louis Sébastien Mercier, *Tableau de Paris*, ed. by Jean-Claude Bonnet, 2 vols. (Paris: Mercure de France, 1994–8), II, 1071.
71 Charles Villers, *Lettre sur le roman intitulé Justine ou les malheurs de la vertu* (Paris: Baur, 1877), 6–7 (reprinted from *Le Spectateur du Nord*, IV (1797)).

have brushed against each other: they are marked with the same stains, mixtures of love and blood.]⁷²

While such responses are evidently hyperbolic, they nonetheless reflect that Sade's early readers both understood and conveyed the power of fiction in sensory terms. Joubert's imagination ties the foul smell of *Justine*'s pages both to the plague of revolutionary violence and to the stench of the Parisian sewers – the latter, perhaps, hinting at that novel's excremental episodes.

Warning: the following section cites and analyses a passage of extreme violence, even by Sadean standards.

Back to Sodom

Prior to working on this chapter, I had not reread either the original text of the *120 Journées* or our translation since the publication of the latter in 2016, despite having taught the text every year since. I rationalized this to myself on the basis that the intimate knowledge of the text I had gained as a translator had made subsequent rereading unnecessary. If I did not feel the need – much less the desire – to return to the *120 Journées*, this was doubtless because I did not feel I had entirely left it behind. While the smell of the text had thankfully faded away, the translation of other passages, and in particular passages of extreme violence, had left a more enduring imprint, emotionally as well as sensorially. It is perhaps not by chance that I still remember precisely where I was when I translated a series of appalling tortures of mothers and babies (on a sofa in a foyer, laptop screen angled to avoid any unwitting gaze, while my young children were in the next room at a *bande dessinée* workshop). Nonetheless, as several years have now passed since I was immersed in the translation of this text, I no longer have a clear memory of the mental imagery I experienced while translating its scenes of violence. In order to capture some of that imagery and experience afresh, I therefore decided to go back to Silling and translate a short extract from it again. To find a suitably visceral passage, I reread our translation from cover to cover. I had resolved to read every line, but towards the end of the novel

---

72 Joseph Joubert, *Pensées, essais et maximes*, 2 vols. (Paris: Charles Gosselin, 1842), II, 224.

I came across an episode I could not bring myself to read in its entirety, so I skipped over it and ploughed on. I cannot definitively say that this is the most violent or visceral paragraph in the novel, but I can say that it was the one paragraph that stopped me in my tracks within a couple of lines. It is perhaps not coincidental that it is situated immediately after the sequence of tortures I just mentioned: if this paragraph felt like the final straw this time around, it was, I suspect, in part the cumulative effect of those preceding tortures.[73] Masochistically perhaps, I decided that the passage for me to retranslate had just chosen itself. It is up to you, obviously, whether to read on – if in doubt, feel free to skip ahead to the next section, 'From Translating to Rerererereading Sade'. For those who are staying, please note that for the purposes of this exercise I used the unmodernized and uncorrected Heine edition on which our published translation was based:

> Ce meme soir on presente Narcisse aux orgies, on acheve de lui couper tous les doigts des mains pendant que l'eveque l'encule et que Durcet opere, on lui enfonce une aiguille brulante dans le canal de l'urette, on fait venir Giton, on se le plotte et on joue a la balle avec, et on lui casse une jambe pendant que [le] duc l'encule sans decharger. Arrive Zelmire, on lui brule le clitoris, la langue, les gencives, on lui arrache quatre dents, on la brule en six endroits des cuisses par devant et par derrierre, on lui coupe les deux bouts des tetons, tous les doigts des mains et Curval l'encule en cet etat sans decharger. On ameine Fanchon a qui on creve un œil. Pendant la nuit le duc et Curval escortés de Desgranges et de Duclos descendent Augustine au caveau, elle avoit le cul tres conservé, on la fouette, puis chacun l'encule sans decharger, ensuite le duc lui fait cinquante huit blessures sur les fesses, dans chaqune desquelles il coule de l'huile bouillante, il lui enfonce un fer chaud dans le con et dans le cul et la fout sur les blessures avec un condom de peau de chien de mer qui redéchiroit les brulures, cela fait on lui decouvre les os et on les lui scie en differents endroits, puis l'on decouvre ses nerfs en quatre endroits formant la croix, on attache a un tourniquet chaque bout de ces nerfs, et on tourne, ce qui lui allonge ces parties delicates et la fait souffrir des douleurs inouies, on lui donne du relache pour la mieux faire souffrir, puis on reprend l'operation et a cette fois on lui egratigne les nerfs avec un canif a mesure qu'on les allonge, cela fait on lui fait un trou au gosier

---

[73] I am apparently not alone in finding this passage the most unbearable of the novel. A student on my 'Schools for Scandal' undergraduate module this year pinpointed the same passage as being the one she found the most extreme and difficult to read.

par lequel on rameine et fait passer sa langue, on lui brule a petit feu le teton qui lui reste, puis on lui enfonce dans le con une main armée d'un sca[l]pel, avec lequel on brise la cloison qui separe l'anus du vagin, on quitte le sca[l]pel, on renfonce la main, on va chercher dans ses entrailles et la force a chier par le con, ensuite par la meme ouverture on va lui fendre le sac de l'estomac, puis l'on revient au visage, on lui coupe les oreilles, on lui brule l'interieur du nés, on lui eteint les yeux en laissant distiller de la cire d'Espagne brulante dedans, on lui cerne le crane, on la pend par les cheveux en lui attachant des pierres aux pieds pour qu'elle tombe et que le crane s'arrache. Quand elle tomba de cette chute elle respirait encor et le duc la foutit en con dans cet etat, il dechargea et n'en sortit que plus furieux, on l'ouvrit, on lui brula les entrailles dans le ventre meme, et on passa une main armée d'un sca[l]pel qui fut lui piquer le cœur, en dedans, a differentes places. Ce fut la qu'elle rendit l'ame, ainsi perit a quinze ans et 8 mois, une des plus celeste creature qu'ait formée la nature &c. Son eloge.[74]

Below is the first (and only) draft of my retranslation:

That same evening, Narcisse is presented at the orgies. They manage to cut all his fingers off. While the bishop buggers him and while Durcet has his way, a red-hot needle is driven up his urethra. Giton is summoned, is groped, used as a ball to play with, and has his leg broken while the duke buggers him without coming. Zelmire arrives: they burn her clitoris, her tongue, her gums, they pull four teeth, they burn her thighs in six places in front and behind, they cut off both her nipples, all her fingers, and Curval buggers her in this state without coming. They bring out Fanchon, whose eye they put out. During the night, the duke and Curval, accompanied by Desgranges and Duclos, take Augustine down to the crypt. Her arse was still very fresh, she is flogged, then they each bugger her without coming; the Duc then wounds her buttocks 58 times, and in each wound he pours boiling oil. He drives a red hot poker into her cunt and into her arse, and fucks her rubbing against these wounds with a condom of dogfish skin which ripped open the burns. Once that was done they expose her bones and saw through them in different places. Then they exposed her nerves in four places forming a cross, they attach a tourniquet to the ends of each of these nerves, and start to turn, stretching these delicate fibres and making her suffer indescribable agonies. They give her some respite only to make her suffer even more, then they resume the operation, and, this time, they scrape her nerves with a penknife as they stretch them. Once that was done, they make

---

74 Sade, *Les 120 Journées de Sodome*, ed. by Maurice Heine, 3 vols. (Paris: Stendhal et cie, 1931–5), III, 480–1.

a hole in her throat through which they reach in and pull through her tongue; they slowly burn her remaining breast, then they thrust a hand armed with a scalpel into her cunt and break the partition that separates the anus from the vagina; they put down the scalpel, thrust the hand in again, rummage around her entrails and force her to shit through her cunt; next, through the same hole they split the stomach sac. Then they return to the face. They cut off her ears, they burn her nasal passages, they extinguish her eyes by allowing burning Spanish wax to trickle into them, they score her skull all around and hang her by the hair with stones attached to her feet so that she will fall and her skull will be ripped off. When she landed from this fall, she was still breathing, and the duke fucked her cunt in this state; he came, and left all the more furious for it. They open her up, they burn her entrails there in her belly, and they thrust a hand armed with a scalpel which pierces her heart into different places. There it was that she gave up the ghost. So perished at fifteen years of age one of the most heavenly creatures ever formed by nature. Her eulogy.

It may seem peculiar that I baulked at rereading an episode I had previously translated, and therefore evidently reread several times in the past. As I started to retranslate this passage, however, I was immediately reminded of the obvious differences between reading to translate and simply reading. Roger Shattuck, no admirer of Sade, grudgingly observes that 'The one stylistic effect that Sade has mastered is the crescendo. He knows how to turn the volume up slowly'.[75] But the power of a literary crescendo requires the reader to match the pace set by the author. As noted previously, the formation of mental imagery takes a certain amount of time. One of the advantages of reading over translating is indeed that one can speed up over the most challenging passages and thereby outpace the ability of the imagination to form unwanted images. Conversely, the crawling pace at which one reads as one translates can also disrupt the formation of mental imagery or the triggering of sensory responses. Stepping one's way through a sentence word by word, stopping to ponder the possibilities, perhaps consulting a thesaurus or an eighteenth-century dictionary, can mean one does not see the wood for the trees – which may be no bad thing when that wood is a scene of violence. When translating the *120 Journées* the first time, I generally did not practise what I would preach when

---

75 Shattuck, *Forbidden Knowledge*, 279.

teaching translation, namely that one should always read the whole of a passage before starting to translate it. The more violent the scene, the less I wanted to take in the view, so it became at times a case of 'eyes down' as I slowly shuffled my way forwards. Jeanne Holierhoek's account of her experience translating Jonathan Littell's holocaust novel *Les Bienveillantes* (2006) resonates in this regard in the strategies she used to help her 'cope with the horrors of the text world':[76] firstly, 'the act of collaborating' with a fellow translator, and secondly, 'the act of focussing on language and writing (e.g. word order)'.[77] As Hubscher-Davidson notes, Holierhoek describes 'deriving pleasure from specific linguistic and technical aspects of her translating work ("tinkering with words", "shifting sentence structures", etc.), even when the content of the text was harrowing'.[78] As this example shows, the task of translation thus offers some protection for the translator – some blinkers to keep unwelcome images at bay. In order to translate Sade, I thus found myself forced at times to read in precisely the way I have condemned Sade scholars for reading: focussing on words only as linguistic signs rather than as conjurors of images. This is why, as I suggested at the start of this chapter, translators should not necessarily be held up as model readers.

Even with blinkers on, one cannot help but catch glimpses of the horrors Sade depicts. There are clearly limits to how much self-reporting can capture of the translator's experience: a degree of immersion is required if one is to respond somatically to a text, while reporting those responses requires a degree of self-consciousness. While one cannot respond and narrate one's responses simultaneously, it is nonetheless possible to slip between the two. Retranslating the passage above, I found myself sufficiently engrossed in the task for images to come, whether I wanted them to or not, and would thus have to remind myself to jot these down whenever I came to a natural pause. If self-reporting cannot offer a complete picture of the experience of translating, it can at least offer glimpses – or, in this case, glimpses of those glimpses. Inserted

---

76 Hubscher-Davidson, *Translation and Emotion*, 93. See also Jeanne Holierhoek, 'De Memoires Van een Moordenaar: *Les Bienviellantes* Vertaald', *Filter*, 15.4 (2008), 3–11.
77 Hubscher-Davidson, *Translation and Emotion*, 167, 168.
78 Ibid., 168.

into the text below, in italics, are the mental images I noted down at the approximate points at which they occurred:[79]

> That same evening, Narcisse is presented at the orgies. They manage to cut all his fingers off. While the bishop buggers him and while Durcet has his way, a red-hot needle is driven up his urethra [*image of hand holding needle*] Giton is summoned, is groped, used as a ball to play with, and has his leg broken while the duke buggers him without coming. Zelmire arrives: they burn her clitoris, her tongue, her gums, they pull four teeth, they burn her thighs in six places in front and behind, they cut off both her nipples, all her fingers, and Curval buggers her in this state without coming [*images of nipples sliced off*]. They bring out Fanchon, whose eye they put out. During the night, the duke and Curval, accompanied by Desgranges and Duclos, take Augustine down to the crypt. Her arse was still very fresh, she is flogged, then they each bugger her without coming; the Duc then wounds her buttocks 58 times, and in each wound he pours boiling oil [*image of act of pouring from something like a gravy boat*]. He drives a red hot poker into her cunt and into her arse [*image of arm forcing something into a body*], and fucks her rubbing against these wounds [*image of grazed skin*] with a condom of dogfish skin which ripped open the burns. Once that was done they expose her bones and saw through them [*image of sawing motion*] in different places. Then they exposed her nerves in four places forming a cross, they attach a tourniquet [*image of twisting motion as if using a corkscrew*] to the ends of each of these nerves, and start to turn, stretching these delicate fibres and making her suffer indescribable agonies. They give her some respite only to make her suffer even more, then they resume the operation, and, this time, they scrape her nerves with a penknife as they stretch them [*image of scraping triggering discomfort including stab of pain to groin and discomfort – 'wincing' – in ear at sound like the scraping of chalkboard*]. Once that was done, they make a hole in her throat through which they reach in and pull through her tongue; they slowly burn her remaining breast, then they thrust a hand armed with a scalpel [*image of hand holding scalpel*] into her cunt and break the partition that separates the anus from the vagina; they put down the scalpel, thrust the hand in again, rummage around her entrails and force her to shit through her cunt; next, through the same hole they split the stomach sac [*vague sense of internal organs, of indistinct flesh, of a membrane being split*]. Then they return to the face. They cut off her ears, they burn her nasal passages, they extinguish her eyes by

---

79   The use of the term 'image' here, as elsewhere, should not be taken as an indication of visuality – it can apply to any of the senses, and indeed more than one sense.

allowing burning Spanish wax to trickle into them, they score her skull all around and hang her by the hair with stones attached to her feet so that she will fall and her skull will be ripped off. When she landed from this fall, she was still breathing [*image of woman on the floor breathing*], and the duke fucked her cunt in this state [*vague image of duke thrusting*]; he came, and left all the more furious for it. They open her up, they burn her entrails there in her belly, and they thrust a hand armed with a scalpel which pierces her heart into different places. There it was that she gave up the ghost. So perished at fifteen years of age one of the most heavenly creatures ever formed by nature. Her eulogy.

The images evoked as I translated ranged from the monosensory to the multisensory – from the fleeting visual image of grazed skin to the excruciating aural, visual, kinaesthetic image of the knife scraping against nerves. As noted in the previous chapter, research has shown that vicarious pain may be intensified by the belief that the suffering being observed will be in vain; that finding seems pertinent here.[80] At this late stage in the novel, the libertines have already started enacting murders inspired by Desgranges's narration, so it is clear the moment the paragraph begins that it will end in death. I suspect this is why I initially skipped over it in my rereading of the translation. The certainty that this scene of torture will be lethal unquestionably makes it a more painful and upsetting passage for the reader let alone the translator. I found myself once again at certain points attempting to block the formation of images, and, even if these were not kept entirely at bay, they remained for the most part vague rather than vivid. The torturing of nerves, however, evidently did break through my sensory defences, an example perhaps of what Hubscher-Davidson describes as the translator taking 'an (emotional) hit from "another" and attempt[ing] to regulate its impact before transferring it onto a third party'.[81] This idea of taking a hit, which echoes Maier's sense of being 'battered' by a source text, does indeed capture something of the somatic nature of translation, and in particular the way the body becomes a kind of sounding board. In order to inflict hits upon the readers of a translation, the translator needs to have felt those hits first, and in order to get those hits right, the translator's body becomes the site for the constant and continual testing of the affective force of words.

---

80   See Chapter 2, 'Bad Vibrations'.
81   Hubscher-Davidson, *Translation and Emotion*, 120.

From Translating to Rerererereading Sade

The first sign that we had succeeded in passing on at least some of those emotional hits was our commissioning editor's response to our first draft, which was to burst into tears the moment she reached the end. As bad as I felt about this, I was also relieved: it suggested we had succeeded in producing a translation as unreadable as the original – not something a translator would normally be proud to say. Unlike my co-translator and me, however, she only had to read our manuscript once. The act of translation is evidently only the first stage in the process of producing a published work, and in some respects the easiest. In our case, the first draft led to a second and eventually a third draft, and thus to a great deal of rereading and rewriting. In these stages our bodies served as soundings board again, as we read and shared drafts and tested words on each other and ourselves. And in this seemingly endless phase of revising our text, which spanned two years, and thus twice as long as the original draft took to complete, we no longer had the aforementioned protection afforded by the practical task of translation. For me at least, rereading our manuscript became increasingly difficult as our revisions progressed. While sharing the experience with a co-translator certainly helped, it also felt as if I was sharing it with Sade.

Prior to the translation I had always had quite an antagonistic attitude towards Sade, and I probably brought this into my work as a translator. During the course of the translation, my relationship to him at times felt passive, at others aggressive, and this probably settled into a slightly petulant passive-aggression. For the initial draft, I resigned myself to what felt like quite a submissive relationship to the text (and thus its author) in that I chose to err on the side of not erring, by adhering as closely as I could to the source text. There was perhaps an element of masochism too in willingly entering Sade's theatre of cruelty. Deleuze famously describes the masochist as 'a victim in search of a torturer and one who needs to educate, persuade and conclude an alliance with the torturer in order to realize the strangest of schemes'.[82] In some ways, Deleuze's recognition that the masochist is the one in charge might seem reassuring: imagined in these terms, translation might be an act of domination masquerading

---

82   Gilles Deleuze, 'Coldness and Cruelty', in Deleuze, *Masochism* (New York: Zone Books, 1991), 20.

as submission, rather as Steiner and others have indeed suggested. This would imply, however, a level of control that feels illusory at least to me: as translators we acted on Sade's text, but that text also certainly acted on us. It could moreover be said that we had to develop a sadistic as well as a masochistic streak in order to create a text that would make the reader suffer as we had during its translation.

If the original drafting of the translation felt submissive, the subsequent process of retranslation and revision did allow for some minor acts of rebellion, or micro-aggressions. As well as engaging in a little wordplay whenever the opportunity arose, I managed to sneak in a reference to Disney's *Frozen* (2013), which was ubiquitous at the time:

> « Un moment, dit Durcet ; ces excès-là me font toujours bander. Desgranges, continue-t-il, je te suppose un cul tout semblable à celui que Duclos vient de peindre : viens me l'appliquer sur la face. » La vieille maquerelle obéit. « Lâche, lâche ! lui dit Durcet, dont la voix paraissait étouffée sous ce duplicata de fesses épouvantables.
>
> ['One moment,' says Durcet. 'These excesses always make me hard. Desgranges,' he continues, 'I imagine your arse perfectly resembles the one Duclos has just described – come lay it on my face.' The old bawd obeys. 'Let it go! Let it go!' says Durcet, whose voice sounds stifled beneath this duplicate pair of dreadful buttocks.] (*120J* 192; 189)

While these occasional moments of playfulness served as a welcome reprieve from the grimness of the source text, it also provided discreet opportunities to make our presence felt as mediators, and to remind our readers that they were not entirely alone with Sade. Such moments became more fleeting, however, as the revision of the translation progressed, and the task of translation largely gave way to the task of seemingly endless rereading. Further evidence of the unreadable nature of our translation emerged in the later stages of this process. Overall, seven people were involved in the preparation of proofs, including a copy editor and two professional proofreaders. Rather than the usual two or three rounds of proofs, however, our manuscript went through seven as we kept discovering previously missed errors with each round. It became clear that even professional readers could not read the text as closely as the task required, and it was moreover striking that a disproportionate number of these errors were in the latter, most violent, stages of the novel. In the final week before the manuscript was sent to the printers, my co-translator and I received and read three rounds of proofs aimed at eliminating the last of these errors. Rather than becoming desensitized to the text, each round became more emotionally and sensorially unbearable than the last in what began to seem like my very own inescapable Silling. Finishing the text one day only to start it again the next, the novel's crescendo of violence became more pronounced and palpable each time. Those last few days of editing were the most difficult of the whole process, and the reason why I had not returned to Sade's novel prior to writing this chapter.

It would be remiss of me not to acknowledge, however, how fortunate we were as translators in one important regard, in that our commissioning editor granted us absolute authority over the manuscript of our translation. As Peter Fawcett notes, there are power dynamics at work in the process of publishing translations that are rarely discussed: 'Power in translation is not always exercised against the reader, of course; it can also be directed against the original text or author, and sometimes in the most mundane of ways, as in the unthinking use of target language norms or in-house conventions'.[83] This power can also, evidently, be directed against the translator, but Penguin thankfully embraced our aim to produce a version that captured the uncorrected and unpolished nature of our source text. There was only one very minor bump in the road when our copy editor moved hundreds of commas in our draft and deleted many others, citing Penguin's house style, which included the avoidance of Oxford commas. However, once we explained that these commas were not from Oxford but Paris, and that we had deployed them as far as possible in the same way that Sade had, we were allowed to put them back where they had previously been. And so I spent the next two days safely escorting each one back to its rightful home, wondering how I had come to care so much about the common comma.

Conclusion

In her discussion of the importance of 'emotion regulation' for translators, Hubscher-Davidson imagines two hypothetical translators' contrasting approaches to 'a particularly traumatic source text about genocide': Translator A, who 'uses *suppression* as a way to deal with the content, perhaps trying not to visualise or think too much about it while translating (effectively blocking emotions out)' and Translator B, who '*reappraises* the situation before starting the translation, perhaps

---

83 Peter Fawcett, 'Translation and Power Play', *The Translator*, 1.2 (1995), 187.

telling herself that spreading the word might encourage someone to take action to make a positive change to the situation' and possibly uses 'visualization to really "feel" the emotions'. She speculates that Translator A's use of suppression may 'lead him to express less negative emotion than he actually experiences', which could lead to 'a toning down of the target text' whereas Translator B's reappraisal strategy will lead her to 'share her negative/sad emotions in order to achieve a goal', which is likely to lead to 'an emotionally faithful rendition'.[84] While the latter's approach certainly sounds healthier, I would challenge the idea that one of these strategies is more likely than the other to produce a 'faithful' translation. When translating the *120 Journées*, I found a degree of suppression was necessary in order to be faithful to the depiction of violence, whereas the kind of visualization Hubscher-Davidson appears to encourage would have been detrimental to my progress. It could of course be said that translating fictional violence is a very different matter to translating actual violence. Hubscher-Davidson indeed states confidently, 'I would wager that translating a graphically detailed coroner's report on a violent murder is a vastly different experience to the description of a murder one might find in a novel or poem'.[85] While there is clearly a difference between the two, I would nonetheless argue that one should not underestimate the affective power of fictional – or fictionalized – violence for the translator, as Holierhoek's experience indeed reflects.

I would like to think translating and editing Sade has not done me any lasting damage. However, it is possible that the process – and perhaps all this time with Sade – may have changed me in more ways than I realize or wish to admit to myself. One change I am willing to admit to is that prior to our translation I had always been a rather lackadaisical editor of my own work. In the process of translating and editing our manuscript, however, I became increasingly meticulous (some might say anal) about every tiny detail of the text – including those pesky commas. If I owe becoming a more fastidious editor to Sade, then I

---

84 Ibid., 123. If I find the gendering of these two translators, one an emotionally repressed and inarticulate male and the other a woman in touch with her feelings, a little irksome, my approach to translating Sade arguably vindicates Hubscher-Davidson's stereotyping.
85 Ibid., 139.

am happy to give credit where it's due – and if this is the only 'sticky' affect left by my translating of the *120 Journées*, that seems a reasonably harmless outcome. As far as I am aware, the only other lingering trace left by my translation of Sade was a nightmare I experienced during the editing process that profoundly shocked me. A nightmare in which I found myself imprisoned with one of my children in Silling, desperately trying to find some way to protect him from the imminent threat of violence. As relieved as I was upon waking, I was also deeply disturbed by the sense that the text – and its author – had got to me, and into me, in a way that was far from healthy. I felt a little like Will Graham in the film *Manhunter* (1986), the FBI agent who had let Hannibal Lecter too far into his mind for his own wellbeing. Fortunately, this did not become a recurring nightmare, but there are very few dreams that stay with us more than a few minutes after we wake, and I still remember this one, and shudder as I do, almost a decade later.

4. Teaching with Sade

Not all pain is harm, and not all pleasure is good.
Ron Scapp, in bell hooks, *Teaching to Transgress*

Introduction

Looking back a quarter of a century, the circumstances in which I taught Sade for the first time now seem less than ideal. I was a doctoral student in my college room giving an individual tutorial to a female undergraduate having only read *Justine* – the text I was required to teach – the day before. Much as I cringe at the thought of this today, it did not even occur to me at the time that there might be something problematic about such an arrangement; it was doubtless that naivety and lack of self-consciousness that allowed me to muddle my way through that hour. As I was living in student accommodation, my college room served as both bedroom and study, and in those days at least lowly doctoral students were not generally provided with teaching rooms for their tutorials. That term, I had been entrusted with the students of a lecturer on research leave. He had left me a suggested reading list for a course of tutorials on libertine fiction that included the usual suspects, Crébillon fils's *Les Egarements du coeur et de l'esprit* and Laclos's *Les Liaisons dangereuses*, both of which I had read. It also, however, included Sade's *Justine*, a novel (and an author) I had not. I saw no reason to deviate from the reading list I had been given, and was happy to discover a new text along with my new student. That was until I started reading that text. My doctorate was on comic fiction, and I had never read anything like this before. A rather naive and sheltered reader, I was deeply shocked by the graphic depictions of sex and sexual violence, and throughout the novel had a genuine sense of reading something illicit. I kept wondering to myself, is this okay? Is it okay to read this? Twenty years later, I still find myself asking the same questions. This book, at its heart, is really an attempt to come to terms with that first encounter with *Justine*, and to explore those questions by focussing on what reading Sade does to us as readers. At the time, the arguably more pressing question was, how on earth was I going to teach this novel the next day?

Predictably, I chose the easy option: skipping over all the scenes of sexual violence and confining our discussion to the safer ground of the materialist philosophy espoused by the libertines in the novel. This has, in my defence, often been the approach of the few to have taught Sade in other institutions, as some have indeed admitted to me. In a survey I conducted a few years ago, it transpired that the most commonly taught Sadean text is not a complete text but an extract: the intercalated pamphlet, *Français, encore un effort si vous voulez être republications* [Frenchmen, one more effort if you wish to become Republicans], read aloud by Dolmancé in *La Philosophie dans le boudoir*. Excising the pamphlet from the surrounding text has evidently been a way to teach the philosophy while ignoring the pornography. It does not therefore seem like a great deal of progress has been made since the Aix conference, where Jean Fabre, one of the organisers, declared, 'Je crois que le moment n'est pas encore venu, je ne souhaite pas qu'il vienne, d'ailleurs, où l'œuvre de Sade sera matière d'examen pour étudiants!' [I believe the time has not yet come, nor indeed do I wish it to come, when Sade's œuvre will become an examination subject for students!].[1] Writing back in 1990, Camille Paglia berated the pusillanimity which was still keeping Sade out of the university classroom, describing him as 'a great writer and philosopher whose absence from university curricula illustrates the timidity and hypocrisy of the liberal humanities'.[2] Although Sade has been available for decades in paperback in France, and has made his way into mainstream classics collections in several other languages

---

1   Fabre, 'Allocution de M. J. Fabre', in *Le Marquis de Sade*, ed. by Centre aixois d'études et de recherches sur le dix-huitième siècle (Paris: Armand Colin, 1968), 10. See Introduction.
2   Camille Paglia, *Sexual Personae: Art and Decadence from Nefertiti to Emily Dickinson* (New Haven, CT: Yale University Press, 1990), 235.

including English, his works remain largely absent from university curricula. Implicit in Chantal Thomas's insistence that Sade should preferably be read in bed[3] is an attitude (shared by others such as Annie Le Brun) that he does not belong in the university classroom. If literature is simply what gets taught, as Barthes wryly suggested,[4] it seems that Sade is still not quite literary enough for some of his own apologists, let alone his many opponents.

Unsurprisingly, I have never shared the view that Sade's works were inappropriate for the university classroom. What bothered me after that first tutorial was my own inability to address the sexual violence that felt to me the most striking aspect of *Justine*. As I began to research Sade's works and their reception further, it soon became evident that my failure in this regard was the rule rather than the exception when it came to literary criticism on Sade.[5] As much as I disagreed with the censorious positions taken by Sadean opponents such as Andrea Dworkin or Roger Shattuck, I could at least recognize some of my own reading experience in the ways they had responded to Sade. At least they *got* it, I thought: at least they understood that the violence was the defining feature of Sadean fiction, their own visceral responses offering evidence of the power of that violence. The challenge was therefore to find a way to teach and write about Sade that addressed this violence rather than shied away from it, a challenge which led me to teach Sade on various courses at my university and, ultimately, to the writing of this book. This final chapter thus explores what the embodied approach delineated in previous chapters might mean for the ways in which Sade, as well as sexual and sexually violent material more broadly, is taught and studied in the university classroom.

---

3 Thomas, *Sade*, 8. See Introduction.
4 'La littérature, c'est ce qui s'enseigne' ('Réflexions sur un manuel', in *L'enseignement de la littérature*, ed. by Serge Doubrovsky and Tzvetan Todorov (Paris: Plon, 1971), 170).
5 The work of Peter Cryle offers a rare exception to this rule, despite Shattuck's misdirected accusation that he 'deals confidently with form and simply ignores the challenge of Sade's content' (*Forbidden Knowledge*, 255). See in particular Cryle's *Geometry in the Boudoir: Configurations of French Erotic Narrative* (Ithaca, NY and London: Cornell University Press, 1994).

Embodied Pedagogies

For well over a century, a significant strand of pedagogical theory and practice has been preoccupied by the role played by the body in the way we read, see and learn. Influential educationalists from John Dewey and Maria Montessori to Ken Robinson have argued for the importance of 'kinaesthetic learning'[6] for children, and since the 1980s it has been common practice to distinguish between three different 'learning styles': the visual, the auditory and the kinaesthetic.[7] While this separation of school-age learners according to different styles has not been without controversy, there has been broad agreement on the benefits of approaches that link learning to physical activity (and interactivity). In the last decade, however, there has been growing interest in developing an 'embodied pedagogy' that takes a 'more holistic mindbody approach to learning'[8] inspired by the same developments in neuroscience that have led to the cognitive and affective turns in literary and translation studies. A report by the OECD (Organisation for Economic Co-operation and Development) in 2018 identified embodied pedagogy as one of six 'clusters' of innovative pedagogies, and defined embodied learning as learning which 'connects the physical, artistic, emotional and social'.[9] While they focus primarily on embodied learning in the contexts of physical education, 'arts-integrated learning' and 'maker-culture', the authors stress its potential to foster 'curiosity, sensitivity, multiple perspective-taking, risk-taking, and metaphorical thinking' as well

---

6 Robinson's 'Do schools kill creativity?' is the most viewed TedTalk of all time, with almost seventy-eight million views (https://www.ted.com/talks/sir_ken_robinson_do_schools_kill_creativity?utm_campaign=tedspread&utm_medium=referral&utm_source=tedcomshare).

7 These styles form part of the 'VAK' model of learning designed by Walter Burke Barbe. See Thomas Fallace, 'The Long Origins of the Visual, Auditory, and Kinesthetic Learning Style Typology, 1921–2001', *History of Psychology*, 26.4 (2023), 334–354, https://doi.org/10.1037/hop0000240.

8 Lisa Clughen, '"Embodiment is the Future": What is Embodiment and is it the Future Paradigm for Learning and Teaching in Higher Education?', *Innovations in Education and Teaching International*, 61.4 (2024), 736, https://doi.org/10.1080/14703297.2023.2215226.

9 See Alejandro Paniagua and David Istance, *Teachers as Designers of Learning Environments: The Importance of Innovative Pedagogies* (Paris: OECD Publishing, 2018), 27, https://doi.org/10.1787/9789264085374-en. The other clusters include blended learning, gamification, computational thinking, experiential learning, and multiliteracies and discussion-based teaching.

as 'socio-emotional skills'.[10] Although the report betrays a degree of mind/body dualism in its separation of the cognitive and the affective, it strikingly suggests that imaginative play should be considered a form of embodied learning:

> in embodied learning the focus shifts from the cognitive to the emotional, physical and creative aspects. Activities revolving around the active role of students where the emotions play an important role (e.g. simulations and role-playing) are also forms of embodied learning.[11]

While the report only relates to the education of children, it does raise questions about what adults might be learning from the kind of simulation and role-playing that, as we have already seen, reading fiction demands of them – and in the case of Sade, whether that learning should necessarily be considered a good thing. It also raises questions about the role embodied pedagogy might play in the teaching of literature at university.

While the study and practice of some disciplines in higher education evidently come with the body 'built in', such as the creative arts or the sports sciences, the body in the literature classroom has typically been constrained in all sorts of ways. For the most part, students are required to be quiet, still and attentive during lectures, moving only to take notes, and speaking only to ask or answer questions. While seminars may offer scope for more active participation, from reading aloud or performing a scene from a play to discussions in small groups, the default remains an environment which addresses the mind while attempting to ignore the body. The body, indeed, is treated like a foreign body, an unwanted presence and distraction 'subversive of the serious work of the mind'[12] – and most noticeable when it interrupts that work (with a cough, or a stumble, or slamming of a door). Lisa Clughen, one of the few in recent years to explore what embodied pedagogy might look like in higher education, has challenged those who design and deliver university education with the simple question, 'How have I considered the body in this?'[13] Although she focusses on practical measures to improve the

---

10 Ibid., 27.
11 Ibid., 119.
12 Guy Claxton, *Intelligence in the Flesh: Why Your Mind Needs Your Body Much More Than It Thinks* (New Haven, CT: Yale University Press, 2015), 11.
13 Clughen, '"Embodiment is the Future"', 737.

learning experience, from breathing exercises to classrooms that allow more freedom of movement, she stresses the importance of engaging and reflecting upon the emotions and the senses:

> Embodied learning research may, for instance, consider how we can use the senses in knowledge construction (as in kinaesthetic learning), or it may look at issues of empowerment through the body and ask how bodies can play a part in resisting dominant cultural structures and their material effects.[14]

As Clughen's allusion to empowerment and cultural hierarchies reflects, the current and growing interest in embodied pedagogy marks a return to, rather than a break from, the recent (feminist) past: 'It seems that hooks' clarion call for embodied pedagogies might usefully be reissued and modernized for today's educational contexts'.[15] Claxton's complaints about the 'somatically impoverished' classroom indeed echo bell hooks's expression of frustration two decades earlier that 'individuals enter the classroom to teach as though only the mind is present, and not the body'.[16] hooks's own approach was rooted in a feminist critical pedagogy, one of the central tenets of which was 'the insistence on not engaging the mind/body split'.[17] As hooks admits, however, this holistic approach was facilitated by the context which inspired it, and which it in turn inspired: the rise of Women's Studies in the United States. She notes, 'since so many of our early classes were taken almost exclusively by female students, it was easier for us to not be disembodied spirits in the classroom'.[18] An anecdote recounted by Jane Gallop, whose own work on pedagogy influenced hooks, chimes with the latter's suggestion that female embodiment required – at least at that time – the absence of male bodies. Gallop recalls a feminist event held in 1971 which included a women-only dance that male students unsuccessfully attempted to gatecrash: 'we stripped off our shirts in triumphant defiance of the men we had kept out. With no men around to ogle our breasts, we were as free as men to take off our shirts in public; so we were asserting equal

---

14 Ibid., 738.
15 Ibid., 737.
16 bell hooks, *Teaching to Transgress: Education as the Practice of Freedom* (New York and London: Routledge, 1994), 191.
17 Ibid., 193.
18 Ibid., 194.

rights. But our breasts were not just political'.[19] With characteristic honesty, Gallop notes her own ogling of 'the most beautiful breasts I had ever seen',[20] and her desire to touch them, in order to show the ways in which her own form of feminist pedagogy was rooted in a feminism suffused with eroticism from the start.

If men in those early days had to disappear in order for women to appear to each other and themselves, hooks's 'engaged pedagogy' – as anticolonial as it is feminist – is driven by a desire to make the university classroom a more inclusive as well as embodied space. The challenge, as she puts it, is how to let 'eros' – and with eros, the body – into that classroom. While she does not exclude the sexual from her definition of eros, she stresses the need to 'move beyond thinking of those forces solely in terms of the sexual'.[21] For her, it is much more about 'passionate teaching', and she cites as one such passion, 'The quest for knowledge that enables us to unite theory and practice'.[22] At the heart of hooks's pedagogy is a desire to break down 'the false dichotomy between the world outside and the inside world of the academy',[23] and the belief that the classroom can be a nurturing – and thus loving – space for social as well as imaginative transformation. Gallop, who has been described as 'the ur-theorist of teaching-as-seduction',[24] embraces a more sexualized version of eros than hooks, however, claiming that 'at its most intense – and I would argue, its most productive – the pedagogical relation between teacher and student is, in fact, a "consensual amorous relation"'.[25]

As Elspeth Probyn wryly observes, 'In terms of writing that forefronts and problematizes "the personal" in teaching, it's hard to ignore Jane Gallop'.[26] Gallop's conceptualization of teaching as seduction proved both influential and controversial during the 1990s, when feminist interest in embodied pedagogy was at its peak. In her contribution to a

---

19 Jane Gallop, *Feminist Accused of Sexual Harassment* (Durham, NC: Duke University Press, 1997), 13.
20 Ibid. 13.
21 hooks, *Teaching to Transgress*, 194.
22 Ibid., 199, 195.
23 Ibid., 195.
24 Kate Levin, '"The Only Beguiled Person": Accessing *Fantomina* in the Feminist Classroom', *ABO: Interactive Journal for Women in the Arts, 1640–1830*, 2.1 (2012), 3.
25 Gallop, *Feminist Accused of Sexual Harassment*, 57.
26 Elspeth Probyn, 'Teaching Bodies: Affects in the Classroom', *Body and Society*, 10.4 (2004), 39.

volume on *The Erotics of Instruction*, Rebecca Pope spoke for many when she insisted that 'Some of the most effective teaching and motivating is, in effect, a process of seduction, whereby the teacher hopes to bring the student to a love of the subject by displaying her own passion for it'.[27] Others, however, offered a note of caution about the potential risks inherent in such attempts to seduce students into a love of literature. Elaine Marks, for example, warned that 'desire is the central force in teaching, a force that can be dangerous if it is not recognized and controlled but without which the language and literature classroom is a dry and boring place'.[28] Although she acknowledged that 'all teaching (or at least all *effective* teaching) involves some kind of seduction by the teacher', Kate Levin could also see 'nightmarish' as well as 'utopian' possibilities in this model of teaching.[29] The same dichotomy is expressed – rather oddly – in John Glavin's assertion that 'All teaching, all successful teaching, falls into one of two kinds: abusive or seductive'.[30] Quite how abuse might constitute a successful model is unclear to say the least, but Glavin may be on stronger ground when he suggests that the classroom stages 'a clash of narcissisms': on the one hand, 'the resistant, adolescent or post-adolescent narcissism of the student, demanding to be wooed', and on the other, 'the exhibitionist-performative narcissism of the teacher, setting out to conquer'. The 'good teacher', Glavin provocatively suggests, will be the 'superior narcissist'.[31]

If a sense of unease is discernible in many of these explorations of teaching as seduction, it is because the risks of such an approach were being played out not just on the page but on a college campus, with Gallop accused of sexual harassment by two of her students (and found guilty of a 'consensual amorous relation' with one of those students). Rather than shrink into the shadows, Gallop characteristically tackled the case against her head-on in *Feminist Accused of Sexual Harassment* (1997), and in so doing arguably offered further evidence of the very

---

27   Pope, 'Hayley, Roz, and Me', in *The Erotics of Instruction*, ed. by Regina Barreca and Deborah Denenholz Morse (Hanover, NH: University Press of New England, 1997), 34.
28   Elaine Marks, 'In Defense of Modern Languages and Literatures, Masterpieces, Nihilism, and Dead European Writers', *MLA Newsletter*, 25 (1993), 2–3.
29   Levin, '"The Only Beguiled Person"', 3.
30   John Glavin, 'The Intimacies of Instruction', in *The Erotics of Instruction*, ed. by Barreca and Morse, 13.
31   Ibid., 12.

quality Glavin identifies as being the hallmark of the good teacher. Probyn accurately notes that Gallop's writing on pedagogy 'is a mixture of the savvy and bold and the self-indulgent – and as such reveals both the strengths and limitations of deploying the personal', but she finds herself in agreement with Gallop's insistence on the need for a pedagogy that allows for sensation as well as sense-making: 'It is no more possible to really teach without at the same time eliciting powerful and troubling sensations than it is to powerfully write without producing the same sort of sensations'.[32] Clearly, however, Gallop's own experience suggests that an embodied pedagogical approach has ethical consequences ignored at the peril of both teachers and students.

While Gallop's openness inevitably left her open to criticism, it at least reflected an honest attempt to explore the nature of the teacher-student relationship. By contrast, a degree of evasiveness marks many if not most of her contemporaries' contributions to the theme of teaching-as-seduction at the time. Most of the contributors to *The Erotics of Instruction*, for example, steer clear of any discussion of their own experiences as teachers to focus on literary representations of teaching instead.[33] Any sense that these 'erotics' pose a risk is further tempered by an underlying confidence among the contributors in the nobility of the cause – that to seduce students into a love of literature is to seduce them into a relationship worthy of their love. The canonicity of the literary texts chosen – not to mention the teachers' devotion to them – precludes any consideration that there might be dangers lurking within their pages. In the few contributions to offer anecdotal glimpses into the campus classroom, eros remains at most a discreet presence – something to be sensed, and perhaps even enjoyed, but never mentioned let alone acted upon. The literary classroom is thus cast in the same respectable mould as the literature it exists to serve.

---

32 Gallop, *Feminist Accused of Sexual Harassment*, 100.
33 This is indeed the complaint of one reviewer at the time: 'The biggest mistake made by many of the book's contributors (most of whom are professors) is their shared decision to focus primarily on how "the erotics of instruction" has been portrayed through the ages in literature and film, rather than turning to their own experiences, and those of their colleagues, in the classroom' (Henry Gonshak, *The Erotics of Instruction* (Review), *The Montana Professor*, 8.2 (1998), http://mtprof.msun.edu/spr1998/gonshak.html.

But what happens when eros is a less nebulous presence in the classroom? When it is there in black and white on the pages of the books being studied and discussed? What happens to the idea of teaching as seduction when those books are themselves attempting to seduce – or coerce – the reader into sex? Very little if any attention has been paid to the teaching of textual pornography in the classroom, no doubt because works of this kind no longer provoke the kind of concern they did a few decades ago. That concern waned in the wake of a threat perceived to be more urgent: the rise of visual forms of pornography in the 1960s and 1970s. When *Hard Core*, Linda Williams's landmark work on film pornography appeared in 1989, it paved the way for visual pornography to become a field of research in the humanities as well as the social sciences; this in turn led to pornography's entry into American university classrooms in various disciplinary contexts including law, sociology, gender studies, media studies and film. It was perhaps inevitable that the arrival of pornography in the classroom would itself become the subject of academic essays, with those teaching pornography – labelled 'Porn Profs'[34] in the media – keen to share their experiences with their peers. While these essays typically offer sober warnings of the pedagogic problems and professional risks involved,[35] one account that stands out for its self-assurance is that of Dennis Waskul, a Professor of Sociology at Minnesota State University.

Waskul adopts what he describes as a 'performative' approach to his course on sexualities by 'embracing sensuality in the academic setting rather than repressing it'.[36] He aims to stimulate his students' senses as well as their intellects, a process he describes as 'sensual learning', and to this end his classroom presentations include

> a plethora of images, sound files, music, digital video and internet resources in powerpoint productions which are often choreographed and synchronized so that visuals are timed to text, oration, lyrics, or the

---

34 Anna Reading, 'Professing Porn or Obscene Browsing? On Proper Distance in the University Classroom', *Media Culture & Society*, 27.1 (2005), 131.

35 See, for example, Henry Jenkins, 'Foreword: So You Want to Teach Pornography?', in *More Dirty Looks: Gender, Pornography and Power*, ed. by Pamela Church Anderson (London: BFI, 2004), 1–8.

36 Dennis Waskul, 'My Boyfriend Loves it when I Come Home from this Class: Pedagogy, Titillation, and New Media Technologies', *Sexualities*, 12 (2009), 655.

beat of music. The combined result is a *new media performance* that, I think, represents a powerful and innovative aesthetic of knowledge transfer.[37]

Although he insists his course is 'extremely rigorous', Waskul admits that when his students provide anonymous feedback on his course, his use of erotic media is 'the subject of choice'.[38] The more of that feedback he cites, the more it appears that this use of media has displaced sexuality itself as the primary focus of the course for the students if not their instructor. Although he insists he is 'more interested in what students learn in scholarly and academic terms' than he is in his students' affective responses to sexual content, he does so only after spending half a page quoting students talking about those responses:

> 'my boyfriend always knew when I had class . . . certain images are meant to be provocative and turn you on. I think it worked well' [...]
>
> 'This class has successfully turned me on almost everyday of class.'
>
> 'I won't lie. Some of the presentations with seductive photos and sounds are slightly arousing to me.'
>
> 'I sometimes find myself leaving class aroused.'
>
> 'I find myself masturbating after class more frequently than other times of the day.'[39]

Like the title he chooses for his article, 'My Boyfriend Loves it when I Come Home from this Class', the impression given here is of a teacher rather too interested in, and proud of, the sexual responses of his students to his classes – responses he seems to offer as a measure of the success of his teaching methods. His form of 'porn pedagogy' thus duplicates the strategies and dynamic of the very pornography it purports to teach, apparently with the same erotic designs.

Waskul represents both his course and the pornography that it includes as part of a liberatory narrative in which pleasure is offered as the answer that negates all other questions – a narrative with distinctly Sadean undertones. In contrast to Sade, however, Waskul's method requires a certain kind of pornography – the non-violent kind – to sell its

---

37   Ibid., 655.
38   Ibid., 657.
39   Ibid., 658.

sex-positive vision. He makes no mention of the prevalence of violence in online pornography in his article, and it is difficult to imagine he would include scenes of sexual violence in his *'new media performances'*. If his particular brand of embodied pedagogy has been useful to me, it has been as a reverse barometer for my own approach to teaching Sade and other works of early modern pornography, almost all of which depict acts of sexual aggression and violence. While, as a repressed English academic, I have a certain admiration for Waskul's apparent lack of self-consciousness, I have found my own self-consciousness to be more of an asset than a liability when it comes to teaching pornographic texts. As Karen Boyle observes,

> The contentious—and potentially litigious—decision to teach pornography involves academics in a process of self-reflection that is rarely required of those of us teaching outside of this field. As a result, the following issues are consistently foregrounded for staff and students alike:
>
> - Class dynamics: boundaries, power, safety, respect, difference, tolerance.
> - Self-reflective learning: why, how and what we study.
> - Moral and ethical decisions about learning.
> - Canonicity, cultural and intellectual value.
> - The place of affective response in academic criticism.
> - The context of viewing and the construction of meaning.
> - Students' relative agency in constructing their curriculum.
> - Intellectual freedom versus academic accountability.
> - Censorship (including self-censorship) and regulation of media images in public and educational contexts.[40]

Boyle's list, which could serve as a template for the teaching of literature let alone pornography, raises questions that extend beyond teaching to the practice of criticism, and indeed raises questions that the teaching of pornography asks of the practice of criticism. In my own case, it was indeed teaching Sade that led me to explore – and address in this book – the exclusion of affect from both the literature classroom and literary

---

40 Karen Boyle, 'The Boundaries of Porn Studies: On Linda Williams' *Porn Studies*', *New Review of Film and Television Studies*, 4.1 (2006), 13.

criticism. Perhaps surprisingly, gender is not explicitly raised as an issue by Boyle, although it evidently looms large in the class dynamics to which she alludes. It has also, inevitably, loomed large in my own self-consciousness as a straight male teacher of predominantly female cohorts of students. As Williams wisely cautions,

> It is also worth noting that male teachers need to exercise special discretion in teaching this material because of long-standing presumptions, feminist and otherwise, that pornography is for men and only about women. I do not think this should deter male teachers, but it does mean that they need to take different sorts of precautions that are probably best acknowledged up front. A tone of frank sexual interest accepting the fact that sexuality and sexual representation have become compelling to all, but tempered by an awareness that we are still learning a proper pedagogy of pornography, seems the best course.[41]

There is, of course, one very obvious historical precedent for any would-be pedagogue of pornography, male or female...

Teaching in the Boudoir

The self-consciousness that teaching Sade's works both elicits and demands is compounded by the fact that so many of those works are about teaching, and moreover about men teaching women. It is no coincidence that Jane Gallop began her career as a scholar of Sade given their shared preoccupation with the theory and practice of pedagogy. Teaching is indeed the theme in Sade's works to which Gallop is evidently most drawn, and which she claims as the most important: 'there may be some sense in treating the entirety of Sade's writing as a meditation on teaching'.[42] For Gallop, who admits to having been seduced by works such as *La Philosophie dans le boudoir* as a young woman, Sade is arguably the 'ur-theorist' of teaching as seduction that she has been held up to be. The prominence of teaching as a theme is evident, as Gallop herself notes, simply in the titles of his works, from the subtitle of the *120 Journées* – *l'école du libertinage* [the school of libertinage] – to that

---

41 Linda Williams, 'Porn Studies: Proliferating Pornographies On/Scene: An Introduction', in *Porn Studies*, ed. by Williams (Durham, NC: Duke University Press, 2004), 21.
42 Gallop, 'The Immoral Teachers', *Yale French Studies*, 63 (1982), 117.

of *La Philosophie dans le boudoir* – *les instituteurs immoraux* [the immoral teachers]. However, it is worth making the obvious point that an interest in pedagogy was far from unique to Sade as an eighteenth-century thinker: how we learn, and how we should be taught, were fundamental questions for the Enlightenment philosophers who preceded Sade; the same questions were also explored by the pornographers who preceded him. Aretino's *Ragionamenti* (1534, 1536), in which an experienced older woman provides life – and sex – lessons to a younger woman, provided the template for so-called whore dialogues including *L'Ecole des filles* (1655), the *Satyra sotadica* (1660)[43] and *Vénus dans le cloître* (1683). Although, or rather because, these were written by men for men, these dialogues are exclusively between women:[44] men are to be talked about rather than talked to, as these conversations unfold in a safe female space that serves as a metaphorical antechamber – or boudoir – to the bedroom, where men, and sex, lie in wait.

La Philosophie dans le boudoir is perhaps best described as a Sadean version of a whore dialogue – one, indeed, in dialogue with *L'Ecole des filles*. The latter, subtitled *La Philosophie des dames*, opens with an 'Epître' [epistle] addressed to 'Belles et curieuses demoiselles' whom it invites 'à lire soigneusement ces préceptes et à bien étudier les enseignements que Suzanne donne à Fanchon' [to read these precepts carefully and to study the lessons Suzanne teaches Fanchon].[45] Sade's dialogue opens with an appeal 'Aux libertins', and an entreaty of its own: 'Voluptueux de tous les âges et de tous les sexes, c'est à vous seuls que j'offre cet ouvrage ; nourrissez-vous de ses principes' [Voluptuaries of all ages and all sexes, it is to you alone I offer this work; feast yourselves on its principles] (*PB* 3). Whereas *L'Ecole* ostensibly addresses itself to young women, *La Philosophie* addresses both sexes, from 'Jeunes filles' [young girls] and 'Femmes lubriques' [lubricious women] to the 'aimables débauchés' [amiable debauchees] (*PB* 3) who no doubt more closely resemble the actual readership Sade anticipated. This introduction of men into

---

43 Adapted into French as *L'Académie des dames* (1680) and, partially, into English as *The Duell* (1676), *The School of Women* (1688) and *Dialogue between a Married Lady and a Maid* (1740).

44 The only exception to this exclusion of men being one of the seven dialogues that comprise the *Satyra sotadica*.

45 Anon., *L'Ecole des filles*, in *L'Enfer de la Bibliothèque Nationale Tome 7: Œuvres érotiques du XVIIe siècle* (Paris: Fayard, 1988), 169, 170.

the previously female paratextual space anticipates what is to come in the subsequent dialogues. The boudoir offers the ideal setting for a whore dialogue because it too is a predominantly female space – a 'cabinet orné avec élégance, à l'usage particulier des dames, et dans lequel elles se retirent, lorsqu'elles veulent être seules ou s'entretenir avec des personnes intimes' [a closet decorated with elegance, for the particular use of ladies, and to which they may retire, when they wish to be alone or to talk to those close to them].[46] However, while Sade's pairing of Mme de Saint-Ange and Eugénie follows the familiar template of an older, sexually experienced woman teaching a young and innocent girl, it soon becomes clear that this dialogue is not going to be bound by precedent. As Jane Gallop observes, when Saint-Ange leads Eugénie into her boudoir she is shocked to find a man there, in the form of Dolmancé: 'The entrance of philosophy into the boudoir is thus represented as a male penetration into female space, one which the women did not consent to but which they very quickly accept and warm to'.[47] Dolmancé's presence in the boudoir demotes Saint-Ange to a lesser role than her whore-dialogue predecessors: less a teacher than a teacher's assistant, and at times little more than a prop – or blank page – to be used to demonstrate the theory. Offering herself to Dolmancé, she tells him, 'me voilà toute nue, dissertez sur moi tant que vous voudrez' [here I am quite naked, hold forth about me for as long as you wish] (*PB* 16).

While this male intrusion marks a departure from the conventions of the whore dialogue, it nonetheless adheres to the androcentric logic that is characteristic of the genre. The two dialogues of *L'Ecole des filles* are preceded by a brief 'argument' which situates the text historically ('Sous le règne de Louis treizième'[48]) before explaining that Suzanne's conversation with Fanchon is prompted by a young man named Robinet, who has enlisted her to 'mettre l'amour dans la tête de sa cousine' [place

---

46 *Dictionnaire de l'Académie française*, 6th edn. (1835). Accessed online at: http://www.dictionnaire-academie.fr/article/A6B1067.
47 Gallop, 'The Liberated Woman', *Narrative*, 13.2 (2005), 94.
48 There is possible an echo of *L'Ecole des filles* at the start of the *120 Journées*, which opens with 'Les guerres considérables que Louis XIV eut à soutenir pendant le cours de son règne' [The extensive wars that Louis 14 had to wage throughout the course of his reign] (*120J* 15; 3).

love in her cousin's head].⁴⁹ Education is not – as it is in Aretino – for the benefit of the young woman receiving the lesson, but for the man standing by to turn theory into practice. There is an echo of this line and logic in *La Philosophie* when Saint-Ange tells her brother, 'nous placerons dans cette jolie petite tête, tous les principes du libertinage le plus effréné, nous l'embraserons de nos feux, nous l'alimenterons de notre philosophie, nous lui inspirerons nos désirs' [we will place in that pretty little head all the principles of the most unbridled libertinage, we shall set her ablaze with our flames, we shall feed her with our philosophy, we shall inspire in her our desires] (*PB* 9). As Gallop remarks on the teacher-student relationship in Sade,

> The student is an innocent, empty receptacle, lacking his own desires, having desires 'introduced' into him by the teacher. If the phallus is a sign of desire, then the student has no phallus of his own, no desires, is originally innocent. The loss of innocence, the loss of ignorance, the process of teaching, is the introduction of desire from without into the student, is the 'introduction' of the teacher's desire.⁵⁰

Like Saint-Ange's body, Eugénie's mind is a tabula rasa upon which the libertine teacher is free to inscribe desire. Eugénie herself thus becomes for the reader what Saint-Ange becomes for her: the page upon which the lesson is inscribed rather than the student for whom the lesson is intended.

While this form of pedagogy might appear to be centred on the teacher rather than the student, this is not quite the case. Once again, there is a parallel with *L'Ecole des filles*, where the task of the teacher is to imbue her pupil with desires not for herself but for men, including of course the man who has entrusted her with the lesson. In *La Philosophie*, although Dolmancé does engage in sex with Eugénie on several occasions, his lessons are not driven by any great desire for her. As Gallop points out, Dolmancé is 'a man's man, a man who insistently prefers men to women'.⁵¹ His education of Eugénie might perversely be described as altruistic in being for the benefit of those other men who

---

49   Anon., *L'Ecole des filles*, 171.
50   Gallop, 'The Immoral Teachers', 118.
51   Ibid., 94.

desire women. This is indeed borne out by the anatomy lesson with which that education begins:

> DOLMANCÉ (*il touche à mesure, sur Mme de Saint-Ange, toutes les parties qu'il démontre*) : Je commence.
> Je ne parlerai point de ces globes de chair, vous savez aussi bien que moi, Eugénie, que l'on les nomme indifféremment *gorge, seins, tétons* ;[52] leur usage est d'une grande vertu dans le plaisir, un amant les a sous les yeux en jouissant, il les caresse, il les manie, quelques-uns en forment même le siège de la jouissance, et leur membre se nichant entre les deux monts de Vénus, que la femme serre et comprime sur ce membre, au bout de quelques mouvements, certains hommes parviennent à répandre là le baume délicieux de la vie dont l'écoulement fait tout le bonheur des libertins... Mais ce membre sur lequel il faudra disserter sans cesse, ne serait-il pas à propos, madame, d'en donner dissertation à notre écolière ?

> [DOLMANCÉ (*as he proceeds, he touches Mme de Saint-Ange upon all the parts he is demonstrating*): I shall begin.
> I will not speak of those fleshy globes: you know as well as I do, Eugénie, that they are called either *bosom, breasts,* or *tits*; they may be used to great effect in matters of pleasure; a lover casts his eyes upon them with ardour, he caresses them, fondles them, some even make it the seat of their pleasure and, their member nestling between these two mounts of Venus that the woman squeezes together and presses around it, after a few repeated movements some men are able to spray right there that delicious balm of life that brings libertines the greatest joy when it pours out... But regarding this member on which we shall have to hold forth at great length, would it not be an opportune moment, Madame, to provide our pupil with a disquisition?] (*PB* 17)

Breasts are described purely in terms of the various uses to which they can be put by men, from objects to be seen and touched to a potential site of male *jouissance*. Dolmancé's subsequent *dissertation* regarding the male anatomy is predictably far more thorough than his cursory glance at the female body, and this shift of attention to his own sex creates a temporary gap in Eugénie's anatomical knowledge that Saint-Ange subsequently fills by instructing her pupil, 'examine mon *con*' [examine my cunt] (*PB* 21). The brevity of these lessons is ultimately reflective of Dolmancé's philosophical attitude towards women: 'c'est en un mot,

---

52 The naming of sexual parts also suggests the text's debt to *L'Ecole des filles* (see *L'Ecole des filles*, 192–4).

pour être foutue que vous êtes née' [it is, in a word, to be fucked that you are born] (*PB* 83–4).

As we have already seen, no author is quite as adept as Sade at showing the dark potentialities that lurk in our capacity to be moved by what we read. The pleasures taken by readers in the suffering of those heroines of sentimental fiction no longer seem quite so innocent after a novel like *Justine*. Reading Sade makes one wonder about things one had previously assumed could only be good for us – things like literature, and, indeed, education. The pedagogical theories touched on earlier in this chapter are evidently based on the assumption that learning is a Good Thing. But what is striking is how much they share with the pedagogic model that we find in *La Philosophie* and other works by Sade. Dolmancé too practises an embodied pedagogy that takes what Clughen describes as a 'more holistic mind/body approach to learning'.[53] Eugénie learns her lessons kinaesthetically as well as visually and aurally by putting theory into practice. One could imagine Dolmancé, and perhaps Sade, nodding approvingly at Clughen's suggestion that embodied learning offers the potential to explore 'issues of empowerment through the body and ask how bodies can play a part in resisting dominant cultural structures and their material effects'.[54] Dolmancé would perhaps claim that this is precisely what his education of Eugénie achieves: by teaching materialist philosophy through the body, he shows Eugénie how to resist the hegemony of religious, moral and social strictures. His liberation of her, however, is also an act of subjugation and appropriation: she is freed only to be put into service.[55] *La Philosophie* thus suggests that an embodied pedagogy has the power to corrupt as well as educate, and indeed that corruption is itself a form of education.

Gallop's two articles on *La Philosophie*, 'The Immoral Teachers' and 'The Liberated Woman', were published in 1982 and 2005 respectively, and in the latter she offers not just a rereading of Sade but a rereading of her own original reading of Sade. Having not looked at *La Philosophie*

---

53   Clughen, '"Embodiment is the Future"', 736.
54   Ibid., 738.
55   Gallop draws a parallel between the emancipation of Eugénie and the sexual revolution of the 1960s which 'freed women to be totally available and perfectly responsive to men's desire for them' ('The Liberated Woman', 92). Eugénie de Franval's education similarly offers a form of liberation which enslaves the pupil to her teacher's desires.

for twenty years, Gallop finds herself 'stunned' by what she finds there: 'What shocked me were things about the text that were glaringly obvious and yet which I had not seen before, not in the multiple careful readings I had devoted to this text, over the course of a decade of studying Sade'.[56] What Gallop failed to see in those readings was the mother-hating that is at the heart of *La Philosophie* and which culminates in the brutal, and imminently fatal, violence committed against Eugénie's mother.[57] Looking back on her first encounter with *La Philosophie* as a fifteen-year-old, Gallop casts her younger self in the image of Sade's willing student:

> a girl the very same age as Eugénie bought the Grove translation of Sade. She read it with an attitude remarkably similar to Sade's fictional ingenue – that is, with a readiness to question all her prejudices, to break with conventional morality, to explore sexual radicalism. She was, like Eugénie, an apt, enthusiastic pupil. That girl, who was of course adolescent me back in the late sixties, did not in fact identify with Eugénie, and she was unaware of how strikingly she resembled Sade's ingenue in her earnest desire to be a good student of those instructing her to be a bad girl.[58]

A text that had so influenced Gallop's own embodied – and indeed sexualized – conception of pedagogy now leaves her feeling 'creepy' for the violence with which it pitches daughters against mothers:

> This is what, upon my most recent reading, gave me the creeps. I felt creepy in part because this book of Sade's has always turned me on, inspired me to masturbate, and it still does. My arousal makes me complicit in this mother-hating. Reading it now that I am the mother-of-a-daughter makes me particularly uncomfortable.[59]

With her usual candour, Gallop does not pretend that the misogyny of the text negates its somatic power over her. As a scholar steeped in psychoanalytical theory, she knows not to expect desires and fantasies

---

56   Gallop, 'The Liberated Woman', 89. Although she does not mention it in this article, what makes Gallop's earlier blind spot even more surprising is that she had, in the course of completing her doctorate on Sade, published an article on 'Sade, Mothers, and Other Women' two years prior to 'The Immoral Teachers' – albeit an article that focusses on the hatred of mothers in some of Sade's other writings. See Gallop, 'Sade, Mothers, and Other Women', *enclitic*, 4.2 (1980), 60–8.
57   See Chapter 1, 'Eugénie and Myrrha'.
58   Gallop, 'The Liberated Woman', 91.
59   Ibid., 97.

to be politically correct. But that power is now a source of discomfort as well as pleasure, as the ethical and the erotic mingle and disrupt each other. It leaves Gallop returning to a question asked of her in 1977 that she had previously dismissed: 'How can a feminist read Sade?'[60] She does not reflect, however, on what the ramifications of her changed view of Sade's 'immoral teachers' might be for her own conception of pedagogy as seduction, even though her rereading of Sade, and indeed her own experience as a teacher, suggest its potential dangers. Another question therefore remains: how can a feminist teach Sade?

Sade in the Classroom

Like Gallop, the Sadean pedagogic model delineated in *La Philosophie* has shaped my own approach to teaching, albeit in a rather different way. The aforementioned self-consciousness that the teaching of pornographic texts inspires, and requires, is particularly acute when it comes to dealing with works which stage the pedagogic scene as an encounter between an older male instructor and young female students – a scene duplicated in most of my classes, given that women typically outnumber men on my courses by ten to one. My own approach has therefore been to use the Sadean scene of teaching as a template of everything I need to avoid as an instructor, particularly when considering the inextricably connected classroom dynamics of gender and power. The need to consider these is evidently all the greater given that the sexual violence at the heart of the Sadean texts I have taught most often – *Justine* and the *120 Journées* – is typically perpetrated by men on women.

While the world Sade creates is one in which the male body poses a perpetual threat to the female body, my role as a teacher is evidently to create a classroom that feels as safe as possible for my students. Safe not just from the Sadean world in which sexual violence is part of the fiction, however, but also from the world outside the classroom where it is a fact of life. The latter, evidently, is a world which the students and I cannot help but bring with us into the classroom, and indeed bring up in the classroom. Each time I teach my *Schools for Scandal* course, which features Sade's fiction alongside works such as *L'Ecole des Filles*, *Fanny Hill* and

---

60   Ibid., 90.

Venus in Furs, some news story of sexual abuse by a man in a position of power inevitably offers a contemporary frame for our discussions about masculinity and misogyny. And, of course, the stories my students bring into the classroom will include ones that are closer to home. One student suggested in class a few weeks ago in response to a question about the relevance of these old works of fiction today, 'there is not a woman in this room who has not experienced some form of sexual harassment'. In recent years, two survivors of rape have to my knowledge attended the module (against my advice), and perhaps others without my knowing. This known unknown looms large not only when dealing with Sade's most explicitly violent works but also the relatively polite Sade of the *Crimes de l'amour*. Although 'Eugénie de Franval' is a far from graphic text, its incestuous storyline risks causing distress: over a period of a few years I taught it to increasingly large cohorts of first year undergraduates, and consequently became increasingly and uncomfortably aware I was in all likelihood teaching a story of child sexual abuse in the presence of survivors of abuse.[61] Although there were never any complaints, and Sade was often the author students chose to wrote essays on over others, it seemed to me at a certain point a risk not worth taking, particularly for students newly arrived at university.

Teaching, like translation, is instinctive to some extent, so to describe my 'approach' to teaching Sade and other pornographic texts risks overstating the degree of deliberation – and deliberateness – behind what I am about to describe. Thinking about this approach, it is clear to me that much of it has been driven by a desire – part conscious, part unconscious – to model a form of masculinity that contrasts with the aggressive one Sade symbolically represents for my students. It may not be entirely by chance that the wallpaper on my laptop, which is projected onto a large screen at the start of lectures, features a photograph of my three boys: an attempt, albeit a clumsy one perhaps, to signal a reassuringly paternal rather than sexual presence. As part of class discussions about the visceral nature of Sadean violence, I have on occasion mentioned the way in which having children changed my experience of reading Sade – how it made me feel the violence against

---

61   Recent NSPCC research suggests around one in twenty children in the UK have been sexually abused. See https://learning.nspcc.org.uk/research-resources/statistics-briefings/child-sexual-abuse.

children more keenly, particularly in those passages of the *120 Journées* described in the previous chapter. In the opening lecture of the course, I address the gender dynamics of the classroom explicitly, and ask the class what the risks might be for students and instructors alike when dealing with pornographic materials. Here too, I define myself in opposition to another male presence when I use Waskul as an example of the kind of 'ickiness' – to use the technical term – that I am determined to avoid. When I do so, the subtext is clearly to signal to the students that I have no prurient interest in them, or in any blurring of the boundaries of the teacher-student relationship.

The fine line I am walking, however, as I set out my stall in the first week is to allay these potential student concerns without wholly retreating into the disembodied approach to literary criticism and pedagogy that the course is aiming to challenge. As Probyn eloquently and succinctly puts it, 'The hyper-awareness of the proscription of actual sexual behaviour in pedagogy is a major factor in the avoidance of the body's affective nature in teaching. It produces a situation where "theory" is safer than grounded analysis and discussion'.[62] The risk here is an avoidance of risk that undermines the embodied approach for which I am advocating, and that avoids addressing the ways in which the texts studied speak to, as well as about, the body – an evasiveness which, as Probyn notes, 'is bound to veer towards abstraction, and at times a lifeless rendition of hot subjects'.[63] Signalling my own determination to avoid ickiness from the start, however, clears the way for me to make my case for a critical and pedagogic approach that acknowledges rather than avoids the body. That I regard such an approach as a necessity is evident in the warning with which my opening lecture begins: a warning that the texts on the syllabus are sexually explicit, that they may provoke a range of affective responses from arousal to revulsion, and that they include scenes of violence that students may – and perhaps should – find troubling if not upsetting. Drawing on bell hooks, I stress the need for an approach that acknowledges these embodied responses and reflects on them. I tell students they will not just be reading texts, but reading themselves reading texts.

---

62 Probyn, 'Teaching Bodies', 34.
63 Ibid., 35.

This shift to the body also entails a shift in the power dynamics of the classroom. Although it would be impossible, and indeed undesirable, to abdicate all authority as an instructor, the focus on affect and reception in my courses circumscribes some of that authority. As Barry Kanpol reminds us, the teacher is not the only bringer of knowledge to the classroom: 'First, the teacher is an authority over his or her subject area. Second, the teacher is not the only authority in the classroom. Teachers and students share each other's knowledge'.[64] While I may retain some authority as a specialist of the material I teach, and as an assessor of assignments, the course privileges students' embodied encounters with the primary sources. Class discussions focus on their affective responses to the texts and the ethical questions raised by those responses. The authority of the students is further reinforced by the emphasis placed on the lived experience of a first reading of a text (which outside the academy is often the only reading of a text). While, with one or two exceptions, I struggle to remember my first encounters with the books I teach, students come to class with their impressions still vivid and fresh. I am of course reliant on their willingness to share these impressions, and, given the sexual nature of the materials studied, this is asking them to accept a degree of vulnerability. No one, ever, is obliged to speak, but as students gain confidence, and trust, in me and each other, they generally become more comfortable describing their responses. As the *Schools for Scandal* course progresses, it moreover moves away from my period of specialization and towards the present day. This year, the final week was devoted to *50 Shades of Grey*, a class which had me (happily) relegated to the position of bystander, as students conversed amongst themselves, and to the position of student, as they enlightened me on recent trends in erotic fiction. In that hour it certainly felt we had shaken off the kind of authoritarian pedagogic model we had uncovered in our set texts, and that I could put my anxiety about duplicating that model to rest for another year.

It may not be coincidental that being a bystander in a literal sense is the position to which I revert whenever possible in the classroom. Although I inevitably spend a fair amount of time standing at the front of the class as I lecture on various subjects, much of the work done in

---

64 Barry Kanpol, *Critical Pedagogy: An Introduction*, 2nd edn. (Westport, CT and London: Bergin and Garvey, 1999), 51.

class revolves around extracts and images projected onto a large screen, and for this work I generally stand off to the side. I may be rationalizing, but I think this is because I want the students' focus to be on the text, and their responses to it, and do not want my presence to be a distraction. But it may also be another small way of signalling a relinquishing of at least some teacherly authority, a spatial cue to suggest I am one of many readers exploring a text rather than an instructor explaining one. There is perhaps a parallel here with my approach to translating the *120 Journées*, which was driven by a desire to stay out of the way of the text and its readers – to be, *pace* Laurence Venuti, as invisible as possible. Similarly, in the classroom, I find myself consciously or unconsciously making myself as quiet and as invisible as I possibly can. One could evidently say this sounds like a very disembodied form of pedagogy. I would argue, however, that it is fundamentally embodied in its self-reflective emphasis on students' affective responses, and that these are more likely to emerge when the teacher's body is relegated to the background.

Eric Detweiler has recently made the case for 'responsibility as an alternate relational trope to authority and agency' in the higher education classroom.[65] If I have been happy to abdicate some of the authority traditionally ascribed to the teacher, it is doubtless because I have indeed seen my relationship with my students as one defined by responsibility. On courses which encourage students to explore and reflect on their own affective experiences, the instructor evidently has a particular responsibility to ensure the wellbeing of those students. Probyn, who calls for 'an ethics of the affective in the classroom', emphasizes the importance of 'providing safety structures for students for whom a triggered affective response may be deeply disturbing'.[66] If this is true of the relatively respectable material Probyn studies with her students, it is evidently no less essential for students engaging with sexual, and sexually violent, material. My responsibility begins with ensuring students have a clear sense of what lies ahead before the course even starts: each enrolled student thus receives a cautionary email with the suggestion they skim through some of *Justine* (a set text) so they can

---

65 Eric Detweiler, *Responsible Pedagogy: Moving Beyond Authority and Mastery in Higher Education* (University Park, PA: Penn State University Press, 2022), 17.
66 Probyn, 'Teaching Bodies', 30, 29.

make an informed decision on whether this is the kind of material they really want to spend a term exploring. The opening lecture then begins with a slide featuring a list of reasons not to study the course (identical to the list of reasons to study the course that follows on the next slide) and, as already mentioned, a further warning of the content that lies in store. As the nature of the course, and this book, reflect, I am acutely conscious not only that what is read cannot be unread, but that what is read is also seen, heard and felt and so cannot be unseen, unheard and unfelt: images can outstay their welcome in our imagination and be hard to dislodge. Students are therefore encouraged to proceed with caution, and to come to me if they need more information before the course begins, or if they need support as the course unfolds. They are also warned that in the case of the *120 Journées* – an optional text to which I devote an optional seminar – they should stop reading the moment they find the material too difficult, particularly as the escalatory logic of that text means the material will not get any easier.

So far these precautions and warnings appear to have done their job, but teaching this kind of material remains unpredictable. Over the last fifteen years, there has only been one occasion when a student has shown any sign of distress in class, and this occurred when I was teaching *La Philosophie* on an optional course for French finalists. The student burst into tears in a seminar before we had even opened the book. When I asked what was wrong, she said she had been upset by the following line uttered by Saint-Ange: 'Ô Lucifer ! seul et unique Dieu de mon âme, inspire-moi quelque chose de plus, offre à mon cœur de nouveaux écarts, et tu verras comme je m'y plongerai !' [Oh Lucifer! Only and unique God of my soul, inspire in me something more, offer my heart new aberrations, and you will see how I take the plunge!] (*PB* 88). Apparently untroubled by the previous hundred pages of sex, obscenity and misogyny, it was at this point that the student, a devout Christian, asked herself – and then me – 'how could anyone say such a thing?' At which point a devout student of a different faith began to berate her for not having heeded my warnings at the start of the course until I swiftly interceded. To be fair to the distressed student, it had never occurred to me to warn of blasphemy, and I was thus given a salutary reminder of the intensely individual and thus unpredictable nature of our responses to Sade.

Offering warnings, and condemnations of misogyny, and positioning myself in opposition to self-evidently problematic models of masculinity is, in a way, the easy part. But doing so can create as well as solve some of the problems that arise when teaching Sade and other early modern pornographic texts. First of all, the opposition may be reassuring, but it is also facile in its binary juxtaposition of diabolical author (dangerous, misogynistic, sexual, immoral) and angelic teacher (safe, feminist, sexless, moral). While it may have its value in providing initial reassurance, as my courses unfold I pick away at the presumptions underpinning the contrast I have knowingly or unknowingly encouraged students to draw. When we come to Sade, for example, I trace the history of his critical reception to show the ways in which a *happy few* have hidden their fascination behind a veneer of respectable motives, from the bibliographic interests of bibliophiles to the scientific interests of sexologists and surrealists and the linguistic and historicist interests of academic literary critics. As part of that history, I implicate myself – particularly when I suggest to my students that I distrust all those who have claimed they find Sade 'boring', from the lawyers and judges of the Pauvert trial to my fellow academics. While Eve Sedgwick and Rita Felski have justifiably exposed some of the limitations of 'paranoid' and 'suspicious reading',[67] in my experience undergraduate students tend to be rather too trusting of, and deferential to, authors and critics; Sade and his scholars thus provide instructive examples of reasons to be circumspect of both. Prior to their encounter with Sade, the idea that authors might have anything other than the best of intentions – that they might, for example, be on the side of the 'baddies' – is a novel one for most students. As if sowing the seed of doubt about critics and teachers, as well as authors, were not unsettling enough, it also serves as an invitation for students to reflect on their own motivations for choosing a course on Sade and other writers of sexual fiction.

It goes without saying, even if it is hard for students to say, that among their motivations there lurks the promise of pleasure. Another of the risks of positioning myself in opposition to Sade at the outset of the

---

[67] See Eve Kosofsky Sedgwick, 'Paranoid Reading and Reparative Reading, or, You're So Paranoid, You Probably Think This Essay Is About You', in Sedgwick, *Touching Feeling: Affect, Pedagogy, Performativity* (Durham, NC: Duke University Press, 2003), 123–52, and Rita Felski, 'Suspicious Minds', *Poetics Today*, 32.2 (2011), 215–34.

course is that it makes it harder for students to talk about the pleasures of reading his fiction. This is most acutely the case for straight male students, for whom speaking – let alone speaking about pleasure – is already something of a challenge on a course about pornography. Linda Williams notes that straight men – 'the group that has been the most vilified for its interest in pornography' – have been 'understandably slower to acknowledge their "vulnerability" to pornography',[68] and slower too than women and gay men to engage in the academic study of pornography. The same reticence is evident in the classroom, and my emphasis on the misogyny of early modern pornography – and my (self-?)righteous condemnation of it – do not really help the straight male student in this regard. When I raised this issue in an essay tutorial with a female student, she told me she had asked a male student (and close friend) why he had not said a word in any of our class discussions that semester. His reply was that he did not feel he had the right to speak. That one of the few intended readers of the texts studied on the course felt this way suggests that my framing had turned the classroom into a female space from which he felt excluded, or at least relegated to the role of bystander – as if the course were part of a Women's Studies programme, with me serving as a kind of emissary, offering early modern male artefacts for the sole benefit of modern female students. As much as I understand and respect that male student's desire to be sensitive to the feelings of the female students around him, his silence speaks volumes about my failure to provide the classroom he needed.

As this example makes clear, I am still learning how to teach Sade, and still making mistakes along the way. That the male student in question was comfortable enough talking one-to-one to his friend suggests the need for more discussions to take place in small groups or pairs as a less intimidating alternative to our collective discussions. This is likely to be of broader benefit, as straight men are not the only ones to find talking about the pleasures of pornography difficult. However, as I have grown in experience, and confidence, I have found ways to make it a little easier for students to express themselves without, as it were, exposing themselves. Once again, in marked contrast to Sade, the ambition is less *tout dire* than *dire assez*: I do not wish to know the details of my students'

---

68   Linda Williams, *Hard Core: Power, Pleasure, and the 'Frenzy of the Visible'*, 2nd edn. (Berkeley and Los Angeles, CA: University of California Press, 1999), xii.

own embodied responses to the sexual scenes we discuss nor to reveal my own – and nor, I am sure, do my students wish to know the latter. At the same time, a course that advocates an embodied approach needs to explore the ways in which texts manage to elicit physical responses. So rather than ask the intrusive question – 'do you find this scene erotic?' – I tend to ask more neutrally phrased questions such as 'Can you understand why some readers might find this scene erotic?', 'How might this scene trigger an erotic response?' or 'What kind of fantasy is this scene appealing to?' Questions such as these offer both teacher and students a way to talk about responses in less personal terms, and, just as importantly, a way to listen to, and imagine, responses other than their own. The language may sound a little evasive, but, as in matters of taxation, evasion is better than avoidance, and avoidance has largely been the norm in terms of teaching and writing about Sade.

The choice of scenes from Sade is evidently important when it comes to these kinds of class discussions. In recent years the scene that has proved most conducive to discussion – among male as well as female students – has been the following one from *Justine* between the Comte de Bressac and his manservant, Jasmin:

> Ils s'approchent, ils se placent tellement en face de moi, qu'aucun de leurs propos, aucun de leurs mouvements ne peut m'échapper, et je vois... [...] L'un de ces hommes, celui qui se prêtait, était âgé de vingt-quatre ans, assez bien mis pour faire croire à l'élévation de son rang, l'autre à peu près du même âge paraissait un de ses domestiques. L'acte fut scandaleux et long. Appuyé sur ses mains à la crête d'un petit monticule en face du taillis où j'étais, le jeune maître exposait à nu au compagnon de sa débauche l'autel impie du sacrifice, et celui-ci plein d'ardeur à ce spectacle en caressait l'idole, tout prêt à l'immoler d'un poignard bien plus affreux et bien plus gigantesque que celui dont j'avais été menacée par le chef des brigands de Bondy ; mais le jeune maître nullement craintif, semble braver impunément le trait qu'on lui présente ; il l'agace, il l'excite, le couvre de baisers ; s'en saisit, s'en pénètre lui-même, se délecte en l'engloutissant ; enthousiasmé de ses criminelles caresses, l'infâme se débat sous le fer et semble regretter qu'il ne soit pas plus effrayant encore ; il en brave les coups, il les prévient, il les repousse... Deux tendres et légitimes époux se caresseraient avec moins d'ardeur... Leurs bouches se pressent, leurs soupirs se confondent, leurs langues s'entrelacent, et je les vois tous deux enivrés de luxure, trouver au centre des délices le complément de leurs perfides horreurs. L'hommage se renouvelle, et pour en rallumer l'encens, rien n'est épargné par celui

qui l'exige ; baisers, attouchements, pollutions, raffinements de la plus insigne débauche, tout s'emploie à rendre des forces qui s'éteignent, et tout réussit à les ranimer cinq fois de suite ; mais sans qu'aucun des deux changeât de rôle. Le jeune maître fut toujours femme, et quoiqu'on pût découvrir en lui la possibilité d'être homme à son tour, il n'eut pas même l'apparence d'en concevoir un instant le désir.

[They approach, they place themselves right in front of me so that not one of their words, not one of their actions can escape me, and I see... [...] One of these men, the one who submitted himself, was twenty-four years of age, well enough attired to make me believe in the nobility of his rank, the other, about the same age, seemed to be one of his servants. The act was scandalous and long. Resting on his hands, on the ridge of a small mound facing the thicket I was in, the young master laid bare the impious altar of sacrifice to his companion in debauchery, and the latter, filled with ardour at the sight, caressed its idol, quite ready to immolate it with a dagger far more dreadful and far more gigantic than the one with which I had been threatened by the chief of the brigands of Bondy; but the young master, not fearful at all, seems to brave with impunity the proffered shaft; he teases it, he excites it, covers it in kisses; grabs it, penetrates himself with it, delights in engulfing it; spurred on by his criminal caresses, the scoundrel writhes beneath the blade and seems to lament that it is not even more daunting; he braves its blows, he anticipates them, he pushes back against them... Two tender and legitimate spouses would caress each other with less ardour... Their mouths press against each other, their sighs mingle, their tongues intertwine, and I see the two of them drunk with lust, finding in the midst of ecstasy the complement to their perfidious atrocities. Tribute was paid again, and to revive the incense, nothing is spared by the one who demands it; kisses, caresses, defilements, refinements of the most unparalleled debauchery, every effort is made to restore those flagging powers, and every effort succeeds in reviving them five times in a row; but without either of the two changing role. The young master was always the woman, and although one could see he was capable of taking his turn to be the man, he did not seem for a moment to have the slightest desire to do so.] (J 174–5)

Perhaps because it is a rare scene of consensual sex, and one in which no women come to harm, male students tend to be more vocal in class discussions about this scene than one might have expected. By this time in the course, the class has been introduced to the embodied cognition research that has also shaped this book, and so we can trace together the ways in which Sade invites the reader sensorially into this scene: the phrase 'aucun de leurs mouvements ne peut m'échapper' [not one of their actions can escape me] applies as much to the reader as it does to Justine. Guided by the action verbs, the reader instinctively enacts as well as observes these 'mouvements', feels as well as sees the kisses that cover Jasmin's 'poignard' [dagger], perhaps even grabs hold and feels it penetrate ('s'en saisit, s'en pénètre'), before seeing, hearing and feeling the embrace, the sighs and the interlacing of tongues ('Leurs bouches se pressent, leurs soupirs se confondent, leurs langues s'entrelacent') exchanged between these two, tender lovers.

Linda Williams has described a moment that arose as she was teaching a course on visual pornography to a largely female cohort of students: it followed the first screening of gay and bisexual porn films on the course. She notes that 'a few men made dramatic, door-slamming exits' and that 'some of the women students took this opportunity to take revenge on the males who had finally been made to squirm by the use of male bodies as sexual objects of desire'.[69] One such student

> precipitated the most traumatic of our class discussions by pointedly asking the men in the class how they felt in response to the gay porn. Up until this moment, no one had asked this question. Though there had been ample discussion of the political implications of various sexual acts and positions, no one had been willing to say publicly either 'this turns me on' or 'this disgusts me' without giving either a safe political or aesthetic reason for such a reaction (nor did I ever ask anyone to say what turned them on, though the issue was lurking in the background throughout the class). Though the question was obvious and important, it thus represented something of a breach of class etiquette, made no less serious by the fact that it was uttered, and was understood to be uttered, in a spirit of revenge. [...] All but one of the men denied feeling anything but a healthy, virile disgust either at the aesthetic crudeness of the film or at what today are judged unsafe sex practices. The exception was a young biology major, new to the kind of media study conducted in this class, who admitted, with disarming honesty, that the film made him uncomfortable because he was afraid that if he liked it, it would mean he was gay.[70]

Williams is quick to condemn the male student's confession as homophobic in her essay (although she did not do so in class) and points to it as evidence that homophobia is rooted not in 'irrational fear

---

69   Linda Williams, 'Porn Studies', 16.
70   Ibid., 16–17.

of homosexuality, but fear of becoming homosexual'.[71] As much as I agree, I do have some sympathy – as I think she did – for the young man surprised, and discomfited, by his sexual response to a scene that did not match his sexual orientation. I remember a similar sense of surprise at my own response to the scene between Bressac and Jasmin when I first read *Justine* all those years ago – a valuable lesson for the naïf I then was that sexuality is far less predictable than we may lazily assume, and that sexual orientation does not necessarily determine sexual response. When I teach this scene now, I suspect this is a lesson some of my straight male students may be learning too, although, if that is the case, they have thus far done so without expressing any homophobic anxiety.

The scene between Bressac and Jasmin also offers students an opportunity to reflect on the relevance – or otherwise – of gender as well as orientation when it comes to erotic responses to pornography. As we saw in Chapter 2, with Sévérino's rape of Justine, action verbs appear to act kinaesthetically upon the reader regardless of gender, placing female readers as well as male readers in the uncomfortable – and potentially upsetting – position of rapist as well as victim. In the scene between Bressac and Jasmin, the female reader, like her male counterpart, is invited or rather instructed to embody the male characters, to feel and give those kisses herself – to be, like Bressac, *toujours femme* – and thus to be a woman playing a man playing a woman in a dizzying *mise-en-abîme*. It is a scene that raises intriguing questions not just for the classroom but also for future research into our embodied responses to what we read and watch. Do female readers in this scene imagine themselves into male bodies, or do they supplant those bodies with their own? Do male readers of Justine's rape imagine their own male bodies being penetrated, or imagine themselves into female bodies? I suspect there is no single answer to such questions, but clearly there is more work to be done. Bear with me while I ask my students...

Conclusion

It should be obvious by now that I could not have written this book without my students. Their contribution extends far beyond the

---

71   Ibid., 17.

questionnaires many of them have completed. In literary studies, much of our research tends to be conducted in relative isolation, and perhaps that is not conducive to thinking about the lived experiences of other readers. Perhaps our tendency to focus on the text is to some extent a product of the context in which we conduct much of our research – alone in a room with books. One of the reasons it took me so long to be in a position to write this book is that it took years of ongoing dialogue with successive cohorts of students before I knew what I needed to write. And years of thinking about how to make that dialogue possible. Teaching Sade's works forces you to think about how actual readers – namely, your students – will respond to them, even if, as we have already seen, some of those responses may be unpredictable. It forces you to confront what is most obvious about the experience of reading Sade – the extremity of the violence, and its visceral force – and forces you to think about how you will address that violence in class. And at that point the inadequacy, and indeed perversity, of the disembodied approach practised by scholars in academic papers and books becomes very clear. The fact that such an approach is not fit for purpose when it comes to teaching Sade should have us wondering how it has endured in literary criticism for so long, and how little that criticism has had to say even to committed and enthusiastic students of literature.

As suggested earlier in this chapter, the students on my courses read Sade in the context of the world around them. They see literary study not as a means of escaping the world but as a way of understanding it better. It is in this spirit that they read Sade's novels and the other works of sexual fiction I teach alongside his. In marked contrast to the Barthesian tradition of Sade scholarship, the violence of Sade's fiction is not simply a matter of reading words from the past but sensing and feeling them in the present. It is for this reason – simultaneously heartening and depressing – that Sade in particular matters to students. It is difficult to imagine anyone disagreeing with Henri Giroux's claim that 'it is crucial to connect classroom knowledge to the experiences, histories, and resources that students bring to the classroom but also to link such knowledge to the goal of furthering their capacities to be critical agents'.[72] With Sade, students need little encouragement to

---

72 Henri Giroux, *On Critical Pedagogy* (London: Continuum, 2011), 7.

make those connections, and to link what they learn to what they see happening both around and to them. I am writing these words a week after the end of a term which saw the trial of Gisèle Pelicot's rapists unfold, and the election of an American President found liable in a civil court for the sexual assault of a journalist, E. Jean Carroll. This context has unsurprisingly made itself felt in the essays I am currently marking, a good few of which are by students visiting from America. More students than ever this year chose to write an essay on whether pornography belongs in the literature classroom. It seems appropriate to leave one of them, Riley, with the last word here, taken from the last lines of her conclusion: 'Pornography in the literature classroom facilitates students' ability to critically engage with sexual content, preparing them to talk about sex and its societal impacts. Ignorance and silence on these matters only maintains the status quo, so for all those who are dreaming of a better world, it's time to get to class and speak up'.

Conclusion

The violence in Sade is not senseless, but sensory. His libertines are driven, and driven to violence, by an unquenchable desire for ever more intense sensations – as indeed is his fiction. In the *Histoire de Juliette*, Madame de Donis recognizes that her friend Juliette suffers from a problem she knows all too well herself: 'N'est-il pas vrai, ma belle amie, que vous avez déjà trouvé vos désirs bien supérieurs à vos moyens' [Is it not true, my fine friend, that you have already found your desires far superior to your means?] (*HJ* 752). All of Sade's libertines indeed desire beyond their means, but perhaps none expresses this more spectacularly than the Président de Curval in the *120 Journées*: 'Combien de fois, sacredieu, n'ai-je pas désiré qu'on pût attaquer le soleil, en priver l'univers, ou s'en servir pour embraser le monde ?' [How many times, good God, have I not wished it were possible to attack the sun, to deprive the universe of it, or to use it to set the world ablaze?] (*120J* 158–9; 154). When Durcet confides in the same conversation to his fellow libertines, 'j'ai toujours mille fois plus conçu que je n'ai fait' [I have always conceived a thousand times more than I have carried out] (*120J* 158; 153), it is to acknowledge both his failure, and the inevitability of that failure. His confession ironically echoes his author's famous declaration of innocence in his *grande lettre* from prison, written four years earlier:

> Oui, je suis libertin, je l'avoue ; j'ai conçu tout ce qu'on peut concevoir dans ce genre-là, mais je n'ai sûrement pas fait tout ce que j'ai conçu et ne le ferai sûrement jamais. Je suis un libertin, mais je ne suis pas *un criminel* ni *un meurtrier*.
>
> [Yes, I am a libertine, I admit; I have imagined all that one can imagine in that vein, but I have certainly not done all that I have imagined, and certainly never will. I am a libertine, but I am not *a criminal* or *a murderer*.][1]

---

1   Sade, *Lettres à sa femme*, 20 February 1781, 229.

Libertinage, Durcet and Sade suggest for different reasons, has more to do with fantasy than reality, more to do with what can be imagined than what can be done. The remedy that Donis offers Juliette for her frustrated desires seems to confirm this:

> Soyez quinze jours entiers sans vous occuper de luxures, distrayez-vous, amusez-vous d'autre chose ; mais jusqu'au quinzième ne laissez pas même d'accès aux idées libertines. Cette époque venue, couchez-vous seule, dans le calme, dans le silence et dans l'obscurité la plus profonde ; rappelez-vous là tout ce que vous avez banni depuis cet intervalle, et livrez-vous mollement et avec nonchalance à cette pollution légère par laquelle personne ne sait s'irriter ou irriter les autres comme vous. Donnez ensuite à votre imagination la liberté de vous présenter par gradation différentes sortes d'égarements ; parcourez-les tous en détail ; passez-les successivement en revue ; persuadez-vous bien que toute la terre est à vous... que vous avez le droit de changer, mutiler, détruire, bouleverser tous les êtres que bon vous semblera ; vous n'avez rien à craindre là ; choisissez ce qui vous fait plaisir, mais plus d'exception, ne supprimez rien ; nul égard pour qui que ce soit ; qu'aucun lien ne vous captive ; qu'aucun frein ne vous retienne ; laissez à votre imagination tous les frais de l'épreuve, et surtout ne précipitez pas vos mouvements ; que votre main soit aux ordres de votre tête et non de votre tempérament. Sans vous en apercevoir, des tableaux variés que vous aurez fait passer devant vous, un viendra vous fixer plus énergiquement que les autres, et avec une telle force que vous ne pourrez plus l'écarter ni le remplacer ; l'idée acquise par le moyen que je vous indique, vous dominera, vous captivera, le délire s'emparera de vos sens ; et vous croyant déjà à l'œuvre, vous déchargerez comme une Messaline. Dès que cela sera fait, rallumez vos bougies, et transcrivez sur vos tablettes l'espèce d'égarement qui vient de vous enflammer, sans oublier aucune des circonstances qui peuvent en avoir aggravé les détails ; endormez-vous sur cela, relisez vos notes le lendemain, et en recommençant votre opération, ajoutez tout ce que votre imagination un peu blasée sur une idée qui vous a déjà coûté du foutre, pourra vous suggérer de capable d'en augmenter l'irritation. Formez maintenant un corps de cette idée, et, en la mettant au net, ajoutez-y de nouveau tous les épisodes que vous conseillera votre tête ; commettez ensuite, et vous éprouverez que tel est l'écart qui vous convient le mieux, et que vous exécuterez avec le plus de délices. Mon secret, je le sens, est un peu scélérat, mais il est sûr ; et je ne vous le conseillerais pas si je n'en avais éprouvé le succès.[2]

---

[2] This passage has been cited by several Sade critics: see, for example, Barthes, *Sade Fourier, Loyola*, 167–9; Marcel Hénaff, *Sade, l'Invention du corps libertin*, 102–11, Josua

[Spend an entire fortnight without indulging in lechery, entertain yourself, amuse yourself in other ways; but until the fifteenth day do not allow any libertine thoughts to enter your mind. When that time has come, go to bed alone, in tranquillity, in silence, and in the most profound darkness; then remember all that you had banished in the meantime, and surrender slowly, nonchalantly, to that gentle fondling by which no one knows better than you how to excite yourself and others. Next, give your imagination free rein to present you, gradually, with different kinds of excess; study them all in detail; go over them one by one, convince yourself that the whole earth is yours... that you have the right to change, mutilate, destroy, upset as many individuals as you see fit; you have nothing to fear on that score; choose what gives you pleasure, but without exception, suppress nothing; have no regard for anyone at all; let no ties constrain you; let no brake restrain you; let your imagination cover the cost, and above all do not rush your movements; let your hand be at the command of your head and not of your temperament. Without you noticing, of the various scenes you will have let pass before you, one will take hold of you with greater energy than the others, and with such force that you will no longer be able to keep it at bay or replace it with another; this idea acquired in the manner I have indicated, will dominate you, captivate you, delirium will take hold of your senses; and believing you are already hard at it, you will come like a Messalina. As soon as this is done, relight your candles, and copy down in your notebook the kind of excess which just inflamed you, without forgetting any circumstances that might exacerbate the details; sleep on it, reread your notes the next day, and as you begin the process all over again, add all that your imagination, a little jaded by an idea that has already cost you your come, may suggest to you to heighten your excitation. Now form a body from this idea, and, as you copy it out, add once again all the episodes your head advises; next, carry it out and you will find that this is the excess which suits you best, and which you will execute with the greatest delight. My secret, I know, is a little wicked, but it may be relied upon; and I would not advise it had I not successfully put it to the test.] (*HJ* 752–3)

Donis thus provides Juliette with a manual for both the creation and reception of erotic material, one which enlists the senses in order to stimulate them further. External stimuli are shut down in silence and

---

Harari, 'Sade's Discourse on Method: Rudiments for a Theory of Fantasy', *Modern Language Notes*, 99.5 (1984), 1057–71; Annie Le Brun, *On n'enchaine pas les volcans* (Paris: Gallimard, 2006), 153–4; and Lucienne Frappier-Mazur, *Sade et l'écriture de l'orgie*, 89–91. Chantal Thomas's depiction of her own youthful reading of Sade echoes this scene quite closely (see Introduction).

darkness to give the imagination dominion over the body. Hume's image of the mind as a theatre where perceptions 'pass, repass, glide away and mingle in an infinite variety of postures and situation'[3] here gives way to a gallery of 'tableaux variés' to be viewed and reviewed until one takes hold. Though these images are in the mind, Donis tells Juliette, you see them 'devant vous' [before you], assisted by a hand that tricks you into believing you are already 'à l'œuvre' [hard at it]. At this point, seeing in the dark gives way to writing by candlelight, as the fantasy is inscribed in words only to be read and thereby reinscribed in the imagination. The cycle then begins once more: reading recreates the previously visualized images, inner eye and hand combine again to form 'un corps de cette idée' [a body from this idea], and new material is added and committed to the page, then to be enacted. Although on the surface of it, this would appear to be a model of sexual fantasy in service of actual violence, 'commettez ensuite' [next, carry it out] reads more like an afterthought than a climax. The true end, and ending, here is accomplished when the 'notes' have become the finished article.

This secret formula for satisfying one's desires is accompanied by an authorial footnote:

> Toutes les personnes qui ont quelque penchant au crime, voient leur portrait dans ce paragraphe ; qu'elles profitent donc soigneusement de tout ce qui précède, et de tout ce qui suit sur la manière de vivre délicieusement, dans le genre de vie pour lequel les a créées la nature ; et qu'elles se persuadent que la main qui donne ces avis a l'expérience pour elle.

> [All those who have some penchant for crime will see their own likeness in this paragraph; may they therefore studiously profit from all that has come before, and from all that follows on how to live the delectable life for which Nature created them; and may they be assured that the hand that pens this advice knows of what it writes.] (*HJ* 752)

Lucienne Frappier-Mazur is not the first of Sade's critics to read Donis's advice, and this footnote, autobiographically: 'Le caractère autobiographique de cette «recette» ne ferait aucun doute, même si une note en bas de page, attribuée au scripteur, ou à Sade, ne l'accompagnait' [There would be no doubt about the autobiographical nature of this

---

3   Hume, *A Treatise of Human Nature*, I.iv.6: 165.

'recipe', even without the accompanying note at the foot of the page attributed to the scriptor, or to Sade].[4] If it is indeed an insight into Sade's creative process, this advice seems to acknowledge that the enactment of the fantasy is itself just a fantasy, and that there is no ambition to see the violence conjured by the imagination escape into the real world. Fantasy here is a private, solipsistic affair, with the libertine author his own and only reader – another Pygmalion, creating a 'corps' from an idea for his own satisfaction.

Donis makes clear to Juliette that her imagination will have to work hard to create the sensations she craves. It is probably only a matter of time, however, before technology finds a way to obviate the need for such hard imaginative labour. Recent advances in neurotechnology already suggest that our mental imagery may not remain our private domain forever: scientists are proving increasingly successful at decoding and reconstructing individual subjects' mental imagery from brain scans so that, as one article rather chillingly puts it, 'I can see what you see'.[5] Brain implants have also been developed that can decode inner speech, so in time it will also be possible to say, 'I can hear what you hear'.[6] For now, the possibility of decoding one person's sensory experience to encode it sensorially for someone else may seem like the realm of science fiction. The time will doubtless come, however, when the pornographic dream of a consumer experiencing a sex scene directly rather than vicariously through the senses becomes a reality. Kathryn Bigelow's first film, *Strange Days* (1995), explores the nightmarish potential of such a dream in ways even more disturbing than the kinds of sensory experience offered by Sadean fiction.

---

4   Frappier-Mazur, *Sade et l'écriture de l'orgie*, 91.
5   Kendrick N. Kay and Jack L. Gallant, 'I Can See What You See', *Natural Neuroscience*, 12 (2009), 245–6. Much progress has been made on refining these mental image reconstructions since. See Naoko Koide-Majima, Shinji Nishimoto and Kei Majima, 'Mental Image Reconstruction from Human Brain Activity: Neural Decoding of Mental Imagery via Deep Neural Network-based Bayesian Estimation', *Neural Networks*, 170 (2024), 349–63; Tomoyasu Horikawa and Yukiyasu Kamitani, 'Generic Decoding of Seen and Imagined Objects Using Hierarchical Visual Features', *Nature Communications*, 8 (2017), 1–15.
6   See Sarah Kim Wandelt and David Bjånes, 'Brain–Machine-Interface Device Translates Internal Speech into Text', *Natural Human Behaviour*, 8 (2024), 1014–15. Eventually, such advances could offer an alternative to the kind of self-reporting questionnaires upon which this book has drawn.

Written by James Cameron and Jay Cocks, *Strange Days* imagines a form of technology that can record, transmit and play life experiences in a manner which captures the entire sensorium. As Lenny, a dealer in the 'clips' made from these devices, puts it to a prospective client: 'This isn't like TV only better. This is life. It's a piece of somebody's life. Pure and uncut, straight from the cerebral cortex. You're there. You're doing it, seeing it, hearing it... feeling it'. The film opens with a clip recorded by the perpetrator of a robbery, which ends as he falls to his death; other clips we see include one of an able-bodied man running, bought by a double-amputee, and a pornographic one of 'a woman writhing above us in ecstasy' before the surprise reveal: 'We look down, see OUR BODY, a woman's body...'[7] The surprise, presumably, being that two women could be having sex – and that the very male 'We' envisaged by the writers could be one of them. In another scene, we watch a prospective client wearing the playback 'wire' of electrodes as he gingerly touches various parts of his body, but are not privy to the clip he sees; once it has finished playing, Lenny seems to address the audience as well as his client when he says, 'You were just an eighteen-year-old girl taking a shower. Are you beginning to see the possibilities here?' Some of these possibilities are later revealed in a scene which prompted one critic to declare, 'Conceptually, this is the sickest sequence in modern movies, and I came away from it feeling unclean'.[8]

The scene in question sees Lenny playing a clip recorded by the perpetrator of a rape that ends with the murder of the victim, a friend of Lenny's called Iris. The film plays the clip so that the audience, like Lenny, experiences the rape from the rapist's perspective, as the script captures with disconcerting relish in its use of the first-person plural:

> We lower [the knife] toward her and cut up the middle of her T-shirt, laying it open. Exposing her torso. We then look down and slide the knife under the side band of her panties, slicing them off. We put the knife up to her throat, and she whimpers, afraid to cry out, and then we draw the flat side of the blade across her body as if to tease her with the prospect of her death.[9]

---

[7] James Cameron and Jay Cocks, *Strange Days* script (unpublished), 13. Script downloaded from Scriptslug.com (https://www.scriptslug.com/script/strange-days-1995).

[8] David Denby, 'People Are Strange', *New York Magazine*, 16 October 1995, 61.

[9] Cameron and Cocks, *Strange Days* script, 63.

In contrast to the ever-shifting perspectives offered to the reader of Sade, Lenny is inescapably locked into the single perspective of the rapist, and we along with him; our only moments of reprieve are a few intermittent shots of his squirming reactions to the scene as it unfolds.

Fig. 6 *Strange Days* © 1995 Lightstorm Entertainment Inc. © 2017 Universal Studios © Mediumrare Entertainment

It gets even worse, however. As the clip plays, we realize that during the rape Iris too has been forced to adopt the perspective of the rapist, who has blindfolded her and placed a playback 'wire' on her head connected to his recording 'wire'. Throughout her ordeal, therefore, 'Iris is feeling and seeing what he sees and feels' until the moment she dies, at which point the script somehow manages to sink even lower, describing in overblown prose what the film can only suggest: 'Her death comes at the moment of his orgasm which is fed to her... blasting off the planet on total overload... terror, pain, death merging with ecstasy and exultation at the same instant'.[10] Having watched the scene to its conclusion, Lenny removes his wire and vomits on the pavement.

As someone who has been reading Sade for two decades, I tend to agree with the sentiment Lenny expresses when he tells his friend Max

---

10   Ibid., 63.

(who, unbeknown to him, is the rapist), 'I've seen a lot [...] But this is a bad one'. There are indeed echoes of Sade in the simultaneity of the rapist's climax and the victim's death in *Strange Days* – a scenario that features in several of the 'crimes meurtrières' in the *120 Journées*. The film, however, arguably surpasses the sadistic cruelty of the episodes we find in Sade. As we saw in Chapter 2, the Sadean libertine inflicts pain on the victim and experiences that pain as pleasure; in order to extract maximal pleasure, he or she strives to be as close as sensorially possible to that pain. In *Strange Days*, the rapist not only inflicts pain on the victim, but also his pleasure at causing that pain: as the script puts it, 'She feels her own pain and humiliation swirling with the killer's exhilaration'.[11] Even before her death, there is an erasure of the blindfolded victim as her experience is no longer entirely her own but enmeshed with that of her rapist. Although the film positions the spectator as rapist in a manner which recalls the reader's experience of sexual violence in Sade, this is a very un-Sadean rape fantasy. It is nonetheless a common one, as its inclusion in the Rice study reflects: a fantasy in which the victim enjoys her own rape – a rape myth 'perpetuated in many pornographic films'.[12] In contrast to the Sadean scenario of the rapist experiencing pain as pleasure, in *Strange Days* it is the victim who does so.

Lenny's revulsion at the scene he has not just witnessed but sensorially enacted – and thus enjoyed – is meant to stand in for that of the audience, and presumably that of the filmmakers. But these are the same filmmakers who, like the rapist, have recorded a rape scene in order to show it to an audience, and have made that audience watch it from beginning to end from the rapist's point of view. As Denby remarks, 'We're meant to be turned on by violence or sex and then turned off by our righteous disapproval'.[13] The justification for doing so is apparently to show the audience the danger of their own appetites: the film ostensibly shows us violent pornography only to warn us of its dangers. If the message appears to chime with the work of the anti-pornography campaigners of the time, the scenario it envisages suggests worse is still to come: a world where the campaigners' slogan that 'Pornography is the theory, rape is the practice' no longer applies, because pornography has

---

11   Ibid., 63.
12   Rice et al., 'Empathy for the Victim', 436.
13   Denby, 'People Are Strange', 61.

become both the theory and practice of rape. Ultimately, however, the film resists the logic of campaigners such as Catharine MacKinnon, who had claimed a few years earlier that pornography 'makes' its consumers 'want to rape'.[14] Although Lenny is 'made' to feel sensorially what the rapist in the clip feels, it does not turn him into a rapist. The film's ostensible warning thus seems like a hollow excuse for the filmmakers to indulge in the very violence they purport to deplore.

There is little to redeem the depiction of rape in *Strange Days*. It does, however, serve as a stark reminder of the ways in which words on a page, or images on a screen, may coerce us into adopting deeply uncomfortable positions, physically and ethically. It reminds us of what the reading of scenes from Sade in this book have aimed to show – that we are not the bystanders we may imagine or wish ourselves to be as readers of fiction. There is still much we do not know about what happens to us when we read, and thus much to discover about the effects and affects of fictional violence. What should already be clear, however, is that the better we understand how texts acts upon us, the better equipped we are to react to, and 're-act' upon, those texts – and the better equipped we are to translate, teach and study those texts. Reading Sade, and reading ourselves reading Sade, continually reminds us that, as Judith Butler observes, our critical agency is 'inflicted with impurity from the start'. Our attempts to make sense of what we read, and what we translate and teach, will thus never be 'an exercise of agency at a distance, but precisely a struggle from within the constraints of compulsion'.[15] But while we may not be able to control the instinctive responses of our embodied mind to the sensory cues we encounter as we read, an awareness of those cues brings us closer to understanding those responses, and, in the case of Sade, closer to making sense, as well as sensations, of violence.

---

14 MacKinnon, *Only Words*, 12.
15 Judith Butler, *Excitable Speech: A Politics of the Performative* (London and New York: Routledge, 1997), 96, 37.

Digital Appendix

Additional Resource 1 Spreadsheet of 'Eugénie' questionnaire and responses. Created by the author. http://hdl.handle.net/20.500.12434/1cfb4442

Additional Resource 2 Spreadsheet of *Justine* questionnaire and responses. Created by the author. http://hdl.handle.net/20.500.12434/b16981a3

Bibliography

Primary Sources

Anon., 'La neuvaine de Versailles', in anon., *L'art de plumer la poule sans crier* ('Cologne: Chez Robert le Turc, au Cocq hardi', 1710), 37–45.

Anon., *L'Ecole des filles*, in *L'Enfer de la Bibliothèque Nationale Tome 7 : Œuvres érotiques du XVIIe siècle* (Paris: Fayard, 1988), 167–288.

Anon., *Thérèse philosophe, ou Mémoires pour server à l'histoire du Père Dirrag et de Mademoiselle Éradice*, ed. by Florence Lotterie (Paris: Flammarion, 2007).

Baculard d'Arnaud, François-Thomas-Marie, 'Liebman, histoire allemande', in *Pygmalions des Lumières*, ed. by Henri Coulet (Paris: Desjonquères, 1998), 111–71.

Boureau-Deslandes, André-François, 'Pygmalion ou la statue animée', in *Pygmalions des Lumières*, ed. by Henri Coulet (Paris: Desjonquères, 1998), 47–70.

Cameron, James, and Cocks, Jay, *Strange Days* script (unpublished), www.Scriptslug.com, https://www.scriptslug.com/script/strange-days-1995).

Canler, Louis, *Mémoires de Canler*, vol. 1 (Paris: F. Roy, 1882).

Chantelou, Paul Fréart de, *Journal du voyage du Cavalier Bernin en France*, ed. by Ludovic Lalanne (Paris: Gazette des beaux-arts, 1885).

Chauvet, Pierre, *Essai sur la propriété de Paris* (Paris: Labrousse, 1797).

Condillac, Etienne Bonnot de, *Essai sur l'origine des connoissances humaines*, in *Œuvres philosophiques*, ed. by Georges Le Roy, 3 vols. (Paris: Presses universitaires de France, 1947).

Coulet, Henri (ed.), *Pygmalions des Lumières* (Paris: Desjonquères, 1998).

Denon, Dominique Vivant, *Point de Lendemain, suivi de* Jean-Francois de Bastide, *La Petite maison*, ed. by Michel Delon (Paris: Gallimard, 1995).

Diderot, Denis, *Salon de 1767*, in *Salons III: Ruines et paysages*, ed. by Else Marie Bukdahl, Michel Delon and Annette Lorenceau (Paris: Herman, 1995).

Dubos, Jean-Baptiste, *Réflexions critiques sur la poésie et la peinture*, 2 vols. (Paris: Jean Mariette, 1719).

Dupuy La Chapelle, *Instruction d'un père à sa fille, tirée de l'Écriture sainte, sur les plus importans sujets concernant la religion, les mœurs, & la manière de se conduire dans le monde* (Paris: Frères Estienne, 1743).

Evelyn, John, *The Diary of John Evelyn*, ed. by William Bray, 2 vols. (New York and London: Walter Dunne, 1901).

Goethe, Johann Wolfgang von, *Roman Elegies and Venetian Epigrams*, trans. by L. R. Lind (Wichita, KA: University Press of Kansas, 1974).

Grimod de La Reynière, Alexandre-Balthazar-Laurent, Imbert de Boudeaux, Guillaume, Métra, François, *Correspondence secrète, politique et littéraire* (London: John Adamson, 1787), vol. 5.

Hélvetius, Claude-Adrien, *De l'homme, de ses facultés intellectuelles et de son éducation*, 2 vols. (Paris: Fayard, 1989).

Herder, Johann Gottfried, *Auch eine Philosophie der Geschichte zur Bilding der Menschheit* (Riga: Hartknoch, 1774).

—— *Sculpture: Some Observations on Shape and Form from Pygmalion's Creative Dream*, ed. and trans. by Jason Gaiger (Chicago, IL: University of Chicago Press, 2002), https://doi.org/10.7208/chicago/9780226328003.001.0001

Hume, David, *A Treatise of Human Nature*, ed. by David Fate Norton and Mary Jane Norton (Oxford: Oxford University Press, 2000), https://doi.org/10.1093/actrade/9780199596348.book.1

Laclos, Choderlos de, *Les Liaisons dangereuses* (Paris: Gallimard, 1972).

Joubert, Joseph, *Pensées, essais et maximes*, 2 vols. (Paris : Charles Gosselin, 1842).

La Mettrie, Julien Offray de, *L'Homme machine* (Leiden: Élie Luzac, 1748).

—— *Machine Man and Other Writings*, ed. by Ann Thomson (Cambridge, UK: Cambridge University Press, 1996), https://doi.org/10.1017/cbo9781139166713

Lucian, *Soloecista. Lucius or The Ass. Amores. Halcyon. Demosthenes. Podagra. Ocypus. Cyniscus. Philopatris. Charidemus. Nero. Amores*, trans. by M. D. Macleod, Loeb Classical Library, 432 (Cambridge, MA: Harvard University Press, 1967).

Marivaux, Pierre Carlet de, *La Vie de Marianne*, ed. by Frédéric Deloffre (Paris: Garnier, 1957).

Mercier, Louis Sébastien, *Tableau de Paris*, ed. by Jean-Claude Bonnet, 2 vols. (Paris: Mercure de France, 1994–8).

Molière, Jean-Baptiste Poquelin de, *L'Ecole Des Femmes, L'Ecole Des Maris, La Critique de L'Ecole Des Femmes, L'Impromptu de Versailles*, ed. by Jean Serroy (Paris: Gallimard, 2019).

Nabokov, Vladimir, *Lolita* (London: Penguin, 1995).

Ovid, *Metamorphoses*, ed. by R. J. Tarrant (New York: Oxford University Press, 2004), https://doi.org/10.1093/actrade/9780198146667.book.1

—— *Metamorphoses*, trans. by A. D. Melville (Oxford: Oxford University Press, 1986), https://doi.org/10.1093/actrade/9780199537372.book.1

Rabelais, François de, *The Third Book*, trans. by Thomas Urquhart and Peter Anthony Motteux (London: Richard Baldwin, 1693–4).

Rousseau, Jean-Jacques, *Œuvres complètes*, ed. by Bernard Gagnebin and Marcel Raymond, vol. 4 (Paris: Gallimard, 1969).

Rétif de la Bretonne, Nicolas, 'Le nouveau Pygmalion', in Henri Coulet (ed.), *Pygmalions des Lumières* (Paris: Desjonquères, 1998), 173–207.

Roscommon, Wentworth Dillon, Earl of, *An Essay on Translated Verse* (London: Jacob Tonson, 1684).

Sade, Donatien-Alphonse-François, Marquis de, 'Liste des différents objets de moral traités dans les lettres du comte', *Les 120 Journées de Sodome* manuscript, Ms-15877 Réserve, Bibliothèque de l'Arsenal.

—— *Justine, or the Misfortunes of Virtue*, trans. by Harold Berman (New York: Risus Press, 1931).

—— *Les 120 Journées de Sodome*, ed. by Maurice Heine, 3 vols. (Paris: Stendhal et cie, 1931–5).

—— *The 120 Days of Sodom and other Writings*, ed. and trans. by Austryn Wainhouse and Richard Seaver (New York: Grove Press, 1966).

—— *The Complete Marquis de Sade*, trans. by Paul J. Gillette (San Francisco: Holloway House, 1966).

—— *Œuvres complètes*, ed. by Gilbert Lely, 16 vols. (Paris: Cercle du livre précieux, 1966–7).

—— *Œuvres*, ed. by Michel Delon, 3 vols. (Paris: Gallimard, 1990–8).

—— *La Marquise de Gange*, ed. Jean Goldzinck (Paris: Autrement, 1993).

—— *Les Crimes de l'amour*, ed. by Eric Le Grandic (Paris: Zulma, 1995).

—— *Lettres à sa femme*, ed. by Marc Buffat (Arles: Actes Sud, 1997).

—— *The Crimes of Love*, ed. and trans. by David Coward (Oxford: Oxford University Press, 2005).

—— *Jûstîn*, trans. by Mohamed Eid Ibrahim (Libya [city unspecified]: Ishraqat Publishing, 2006).

—— *Justine, or the Misfortunes of Virtue*, ed. and trans. by John Phillips (Oxford: Oxford University Press, 2012), https://doi.org/10.1093/owc/9780199572847.001.0001

—— *The 120 Days of Sodom*, ed. and trans. by Will McMorran and Thomas Wynn (London: Penguin, 2016).

Schiller, Friedrich, *On the Aesthetic Education of Man*, ed. and trans. by E. M. Wilkinson and L. A. Willoughby (Oxford: Oxford University Press, 1982).

Smith, Adam, *The Theory of Moral Sentiments*, 2nd edn. (London: A Millar, 1761).

Smollett, Tobias, *Travels Through France and Italy*, ed. by Frank Felsenstein (Oxford: Oxford University Press, 1981), https://doi.org/10.1093/actrade/9780198126119.book.1

Secondary Sources

Sade and the Eighteenth Century

Abramovici, Jean-Christophe, '« Avec une telle violence que... » : Sade's Use of the Term Violence', in *Representing Violence in France, 1760–1820*, ed. by Thomas Wynn, *Studies on Voltaire and the Eighteenth Century*, 2013: 10 (Oxford: Voltaire Foundation, 2013), 221–8.

—— *Encre de sang: Sade écrivain* (Paris: Garnier, 2013).

Astbury, Katherine, 'The Marquis de Sade and the Sentimental Tale: *Les Crimes de l'amour* as a Subversion of Sensibility', *Australian Journal of French Studies*, 39.1 (2002), 47–59, https://doi.org/10.3828/ajfs.39.1.47

Barthes, Roland, 'L'arbre du crime', in *La Pensée de Sade, Tel Quel*, 28 (1967), 22–37.

—— *Sade, Fourier, Loyola* (Paris: Seuil, 1971).

Beauvoir, Simone de, 'Faut-il brûler Sade?', in Beauvoir, *Privilèges* (Paris: Gallimard, 1972), 9–29.

Bennington, Geoffrey, 'Sade: Laying Down the Law', *Oxford Literary Review*, 6.2 (1984), 38–56, https://doi.org/10.3366/olr.1984.002

Bloch, Iwan, *Neue Forschungen über den Marquis de Sade und seine Zeit* (Berlin: Harrwitz, 1904).

Bongie, Laurence, *Sade: A Biographical Essay* (Chicago, IL: University of Chicago Press, 1998), https://doi.org/10.4000/books.pum.10862

Bour, Isabelle (ed.), *Noise and Sound in Eighteenth-Century Britain* (special issue), *Études Épistémè : Revue de littérature et de civilisation (XVIe-XVIIIe siècles)*, 29 (2016), https://doi.org/10.4000/episteme.962

Brochier, Jean-Jacques, *Sade* (Paris: Editions universitaires, 1966).

—— 'Sade et le langage', in *Œuvres complètes*, ed. by Gilbert Lely, 16 vols. (Paris: Cercle du livre précieux, 1966–7), vols. 15–16, 511–9.

Carter, Angela, *The Sadeian Woman: An Exercise in Cultural History* (London: Virago, 2000).

Centre aixois d'études et de recherches sur le dix-huitième siècle (ed.), *Le Marquis de Sade* (Paris: Armand Colin, 1968).

Coward, David, 'Down with Sade?', *Paragraph*, 23.1 (2000), 4–15, https://doi.org/10.3366/para.2000.23.1.4

Cussac, Hélène, 'Anthropologie du bruit au siècle des lumières', in *Bruits* (special issue), *L'Autre musique*, 4 (2016), https://www.lautremusique.net/images/Page/90/56f945375f047.pdf

—— (ed.), *Le paysage sonore dans la littérature d'Ancien Régime, ou du son comme topos de scènes narratives* (special issue), *Topiques, études satoriennes*, 6 (2022), https://www.erudit.org/fr/revues/topiques/2022-v6-topiques07705/

Cryle, Peter, *Geometry in the Boudoir: Configurations of French Erotic Narrative* (Ithaca, NY and London: Cornell University Press, 1994), https://doi.org/10.7591/9781501733925

—— *The Telling of the Act: Sexuality as Narrative in Eighteenth- and Nineteenth-Century France* (Newark, DE: University of Delaware Press, 2001).

Delon, Michel, *L'Idée d'énergie au tournant des lumières, 1770–1800* (Paris: P.U.F., 1988).

—— 'L'obsession anale de Sade', *Annales historiques de la Révolution française*, 361 (2010), 131–44, https://doi.org/10.4000/ahrf.11710

Démoris, René, 'Peinture et belles antiques dans la première moitié du siècle. Les statues vivent aussi', *Dix-huitième siècle*, 27 (1995), 129–42, https://doi.org/10.58282/colloques.632

Edmiston, William, 'Irony, Unreliability and the Failure of the Sadean Project: *Les Infortunes de la vertu*', *French Forum*, 12 (1987), 147–56.

—— *Sade: Queer Theorist, Studies on Voltaire and the Eighteenth Century,* 2013: 03 (Oxford: Voltaire Foundation, 2013).

Faye, Jean-Pierre, 'Changer la mort (Sade et la politique)', *Obliques*, 12–13 (1977), 47–58.

Frappier-Mazur, Lucienne, *Sade et l'écriture de l'orgie* (Paris: Nathan, 1991).

Gaillard, Aurélia, *Le Corps des statues: Le vivant et son simulacre à l'âge classique (de Descartes à Diderot)* (Paris: Champion, 2003).

Gallop, Jane, 'Sade, Mothers, and Other Women', *enclitic*, 4.2 (1980), 60–8.

—— 'The Immoral Teachers', *Yale French Studies*, 63 (1982), 117–28, https://doi.org/10.2307/2929835

—— *Thinking through the Body* (New York: Columbia University Press, 1990), https://doi.org/10.7312/gall94366

—— 'The Liberated Woman', *Narrative*, 13.2 (2005), 89–104, https://doi.org/10.1353/nar.2005.0009

Gambacorti, Chiara, 'Un Pygmalion des Lumières ? Inceste et émancipation féminine dans « Eugénie de Franval »', in *Sade et les femmes*, ed. by Stéphanie Genand (Paris: Itinéraires, 2014), 113–24, https://doi.org/10.4000/itineraires.716

Goulemot, Jean Marie, '"Divin Marquis" ou objet d'études?', *Revue des sciences humaines*, 124 (1966), 413–21.

—— 'Beau marquis parlez-nous d'amour', in *Sade, écrire la crise*, ed. by Michel Camus and Philippe Roger (Paris: Belfond, 1983), 119–32.

Harari, Josué, 'Sade's Discourse on Method: Rudiments for a Theory of Fantasy', *Modern Language Notes*, 99.5 (1984), 1057–71, https://doi.org/10.2307/2905400

Hénaff, Marcel, *Sade, l'Invention du corps libertin* (Paris: Presses universitaires de France, 1978).

Hulbert, James, 'The Problems of Canon Formation and the "Example" of Sade: Orthodox Exclusion and Orthodox Inclusion', *Modern Language Studies*, 18.1 (1988), 120–33, https://doi.org/10.2307/3194706

Laugaa-Traut, Françoise, *Lectures de Sade* (Paris: Armand Colin, 1973).

Le Brun, Annie, 'Le secret de Juliette', interview with Jean-Luc Moreau, *Roman*, 15 (1986), 7–25.

—— *Soudain un bloc d'abîme, Sade* (Paris: Gallimard, 1993).

—— *On n'enchaine pas les volcans* (Paris: Gallimard, 2006).

Lynch, Lawrence, *The Marquis de Sade* (Boston, MA: Twayne, 1984).

Margolin, Jean-Claude, 'Lectures de Sade', *Études Françaises*, 3.4 (1967), 410–3, https://doi.org/10.7202/036284ar

Martin, Christophe, 'Agnès et ses sœurs : belles captives en enfance, de Molière à Baculard d'Arnaud', *Revue d'Histoire littéraire de la France*, 2 (2004), 343–62, https://doi.org/10.3917/rhlf.042.0343

McMorran, Will, 'Intertextuality and Urtextuality: Sade's Justine Palimpsest', *Eighteenth-Century Fiction*, 19.4 (2007), 367–90, https://doi.org/10.1353/ecf.2007.0025

—— 'The Sound of Violence: Listening to Rape in Sade', in *Representing Violence in France, 1760–1820*, ed by Thomas Wynn, *Studies on Voltaire and the Eighteenth Century*, 2013: 10 (Oxford: Voltaire Foundation, 2013), 229–49.

—— 'Behind the Mask? Sade and the *Cent Vingt Journées de Sodome*', *Modern Language Review*, 108 (2013), 1121–34, https://doi.org/10.1353/mlr.2013.0060

—— 'Introducing the Marquis de Sade', *Forum for Modern Language Studies*, 51.2 (2015), 133–51, https://doi.org/10.1093/fmls/cqv025

Miller, Nancy K., *The Heroine's Text: Readings in the French and English Novel 1722–1782* (New York: Columbia University Press, 1980), https://doi.org/10.7312/mill91404

—— 'Libertinage and Feminism', in *Libertinage and Modernity* (special issue), *Yale French Studies*, 94 (1988), 17–28, https://doi.org/10.2307/3040695

—— *French Dressing: Women, Men and Ancien Régime Fiction* (London and New York: Routledge, 1995), https://doi.org/10.4324/9781315865980

Paulhan, Jean, 'Sade, ou le pire est l'ennemi du mal', *Labyrinthe*, 11 (1945), 1–2.

—— *Le Marquis de Sade et sa complice ou Les Revanches de la pudeur* (Brussels: Editions Complexe, 1987).

Pauvert, Jean-Jacques (ed.), *L'Affaire Sade* (Paris: Pauvert, 1957).

Phillips, John, *Sade: The Libertine Novels* (London and Stirling, VA: Pluto Press, 2001), https://doi.org/10.2307/j.ctt18fsb6x

Roger, Philippe, *Sade: La philosophie dans le pressoir* (Paris: Bernard Grasset, 1976).

Sheriff, Mary, *Moved by Love: Inspired Artists and Deviant Women in Eighteenth-century France* (Chicago, IL and London: University of Chicago Press, 2004), https://doi.org/10.7208/chicago/9780226752846.001.0001

St-Martin, Armelle, *Sade, la Révolution et la finance* (Paris: Garnier, 2021).

Thomas, Chantal, *Sade* (Paris: Seuil, 1994).

—— *Sade, La Dissertation et l'orgie*, 2nd edn. (Paris: Payot & Rivages, 2002).

Tort, Michel, 'L'effet Sade,' *Tel quel*, 28 (1967), 66–83.

Vallenthini, Michèle, *Sade dans l'histoire : Du temps de la fiction à la fiction du temps* (Paris: Garnier, 2019).

Warman, Caroline, *Sade: From Materialism to Pornography*, *Studies on Voltaire and the Eighteenth Century*, 2002: 01 (Oxford: Voltaire Foundation, 2002).

Wrigley, Richard, 'Sculpture and the Language of Criticism', in *Augustin Pajou et ses contemporains*, ed. by Guilhem Scherf (Paris: Musée du Louvre, 1999), 77–89.

Wynn, Thomas, *Sade's Theatre: Pleasure, Vision, Masochism, Studies on Voltaire and the Eighteenth Century*, 2007: 02 (Oxford: Voltaire Foundation, 2007).

—— (ed.), *Representing Violence in France, 1760–1820, Studies on Voltaire and the Eighteenth Century*, 2013: 10 (Oxford: Voltaire Foundation, 2013).

General Criticism and Theory

Abbott, H. Porter, *The Cambridge Introduction to Narrative* (Cambridge, UK: Cambridge University Press, 2002).

Aczel, Richard, 'Hearing Voices in Narrative Texts', *New Literary History*, 29.3 (1998), 467–500, https://doi.org/10.1353/nlh.1998.0023

Ahmed, Sara, 'Happy Objects', in *The Affect Theory Reader*, ed. by Melissa Gregg and Gregory J. Seigworth (Durham, NC: Duke University Press, 2010), 29–51, https://doi.org/10.1215/9780822393047-001

Baal, Mieke, *Narratology: Introduction to the Theory of Narrative*, 2nd edn. (Toronto: University of Toronto Press, 1997).

Barthes, Roland, *Critique et vérité* (Paris: Seuil, 1966).

—— *L'obvie et l'obtus. Essais critiques III* (Paris: Seuil, 1982).

Bolens, Guillemette, *The Style of Gestures: Embodiment and Cognition in Literary Narrative* (Baltimore, MD: Johns Hopkins University Press, 2012), https://doi.org/10.56021/9781421405186

—— 'Relevance Theory and Kinesic Analysis in *Don Quixote* and *Madame Bovary*', in *Reading Beyond the Code: Literature and Relevance Theory*, ed. by Terence Cave and Deirdre Wilson (Oxford: Oxford University Press, 2018), 55–70, https://doi.org/10.1093/oso/9780198794776.003.0004

Booth, Wayne C., *The Company We Keep: An Ethics of Fiction* (Berkeley and Los Angeles, CA: University of California Press, 1988), https://doi.org/10.1525/9780520351981

Bortolussi, Marisa and Dixon, Peter, *Psychonarratology: Foundations for the Empirical Study of Literary Response* (Cambridge, UK: Cambridge University Press, 2003), https://doi.org/10.1017/cbo9780511500107

Brundage, James A., *Law, Sex, and Christian Society in Medieval Europe* (Chicago and London: University of Chicago Press, 1987), https://doi.org/10.7208/chicago/9780226077895.001.0001

Butler, Judith, *Excitable Speech: A Politics of the Performative* (London and New York: Routledge, 1997), https://doi.org/10.4324/9781003146759

Calvino, Italo, *Six Memos for the Next Millenium*, trans. by Geoffrey Brock (London: Penguin, 2016).

Carroll, Noel, *Beyond Aesthetics: Philosophical Essays* (Cambridge, UK: Cambridge University Press, 2001), https://doi.org/10.1017/cbo9780511605970

Cave, Terence, *Thinking with Literature: Towards a Cognitive Criticism* (Oxford: Oxford University Press, 2016), https://doi.org/10.1093/acprof:oso/9780198749417.001.0001

Classen, Constance, 'Museum Manners: The Sensory Life of the Early Museum', *Journal of Social History*, 40.4 (2007), 895–914, https://doi.org/10.1353/jsh.2007.0089

Coleman, Robert, 'Structure and intention in the *Metamorphoses*', *The Classical Quarterly*, 21.2 (1971), 461–77, https://doi.org/10.1017/s0009838800033644

Crawford, Lucas, '"Woolf's 'Einfühlung": An Alternative Theory of Transgender Affect', *Mosaic: An Interdisciplinary Critical Journal*, 48.1 (2015), 165–81, https://doi.org/10.1353/mos.2015.0004

Culler, Jonathan, *Structuralist Poetics: Structuralism, Linguistics and the Study of Literature* (London: Routledege, 1975), https://doi.org/10.4324/9781003260080

—— 'Prolegomena to a Theory of Reading', in *The Reader in the Text: Essays on Audience and Interpretation*, ed. by Susan R. Suleiman and Inge Crossman (Princeton, NJ: Princeton University Press, 1980), 46–66, https://doi.org/10.1515/9781400857111.46

Deleuze, Gilles, 'Coldness and Cruelty', in Deleuze, *Masochism* (New York: Zone Books, 1991), 7–138.

Denby, David, 'People Are Strange', *New York Magazine*, 16 October 1995, 60–1.

Dworkin, Andrea, *Pornography: Men Possessing Women* (New York: Plume, 1989).

Dworkin, Andrea and MacKinnon, Catharine A., *Pornography and Civil Rights: A New Day for Women's Equality* (Minneapolis, MN: Organizing Against Pornography, 1988)

Eagleton, Terry, *Literary Theory: An Introduction* (Oxford: Blackwell, 1983).

Elliot, R. K., 'Imagination in the Experience of Art', *Royal Institute of Philosophy Supplement*, 6 (1972), 88–105, https://doi.org/10.4324/9781315263250-3

Esrock, Ellen J., *The Reader's Eye: Visual Imaging as Reader Response* (Baltimore, MD: Johns Hopkins University Press, 1994).

Felski, Rita, 'Suspicious Minds', *Poetics Today*, 32.2 (2011), 215–34, https://doi.org/10.1215/03335372-1261208

—— *The Limits of Critique* (Chicago, IL: University of Chicago Press, 2015), https://doi.org/10.7208/chicago/9780226294179.001.0001

Fetterley, Judith, *The Resisting Reader: A Feminist Approach to American Fiction* (Bloomington, IN and London: Indiana University Press, 1978), https://doi.org/10.2979/2812.0

Fish, Stanley, *Is there a Text in this Class? The Authority of Interpretive Communities* (Cambridge, MA: Harvard University Press, 1980).

Gaiger, Jason, 'Projective and Ampliative Imagining', in *Philosophy of Sculpture*, ed. by Kristin Gjesdal, Fred Rush, Ingvild Torsen (New York: Routledge, 2020), 17–32, https://doi.org/10.4324/9780429462573-2

Gallop, Jane, *Feminist Accused of Sexual Harassment* (Durham, NC: Duke University Press, 1997), https://doi.org/10.2307/j.ctv1134g39

—— *Anecdotal Theory* (Durham, NC: Duke University Press, 2002), https://doi.org/10.2307/j.ctv120qrts

Genette, Gérard, *Figures III* (Paris: Seuil, 1972).

Glass, Loren, *Counterculture Colophon: Grove Press, the Evergreen Review and the Incorporation of the Avant-Garde* (Stanford, CA: Stanford University Press, 2013).

Glass, William H., *Fiction and the Figures of Life* (Boston, MA: Nonpareil Books, 1979).

Groth, Helen, 'Literary Soundscapes', in *Sound and Literature*, ed. by Anna Snaith (Cambridge, UK: Cambridge University Press, 2020), 135–153, https://doi.org/10.1017/9781108855532.007

Harrison, Nicholas, *Circles of Censorship: Censorship and its Metaphors in French History, Literature, and Theory* (Oxford: Oxford University Press, 1995), https://doi.org/10.1093/acprof:oso/9780198159094.001.0001

Holland, Norman N., *The Dynamics of Literary Response*, 2nd edn. (New York: Norton, 1975), https://doi.org/10.7312/holl93354

—— *5 Readers Reading* (New Haven, CT: Yale University Press, 1975).

—— *Literature and the Brain* (Gainsville, FL: The PsyArt Foundation, 2009).

Gregg, Melissa and Seigworth, Gregory J., 'An Inventory of Shimmers', in *The Affect Theory Reader*, ed. by Gregg and Seigworth (Durham, NC and London: Duke University Press, 2010), 1–25, https://doi.org/10.1515/9780822393047-002

Horeck, Tanya, *Public Rape: Representing Violation in Fiction and Film* (London: Routledge, 2004), https://doi.org/10.4324/9780203604182

Iser, Wolfgang, *Prospecting: From Reader Response to Literary Anthropology* (Baltimore, MD: Johns Hopkins University Press, 1993), https://doi.org/10.56021/9780801837920

Jameson, Fredric, *The Prison-House of Language* (Princeton, NJ: Princeton University Press, 1972), https://doi.org/10.2307/j.ctv10crf9x

Johnson, Geraldine A., 'Touch, Tactility, and the Reception of Sculpture in Early Modern Italy', in *A Companion to Art Theory*, ed. by Paul Smith and Carolyn Wilde (Oxford: Blackwell, 2002), 61–74, https://doi.org/10.1002/9780470998434.ch6

Kipnis, Laura, *Bound and Gagged: Pornography and the Politics of Fantasy in America* (Durham, NC: Duke University Press, 2003), https://doi.org/10.2307/j.ctv1198z19

Kivy, Peter, *The Performance of Reading: An Essay in the Philosophy of Literature* (Oxford: Blackwell, 2009), https://doi.org/10.1002/9780470776650

Kukkonen, Karin and Caracciolo, Marco, 'Introduction: What is the "Second Generation"?', *Style*, 48.3 (2014), 261–74, https://www.jstor.org/stable/10.5325/style.48.3.261

—— *With Bodies: Narrative Theory and Embodied Cognition* (Columbus, OH: Ohio University Press, 2021), https://doi.org/10.26818/9780814214800

Kuzmičová, Anežka, 'The Words and Worlds of Literary Narrative: The Trade-off Between Verbal Presence and Direct Presence in the Activity of Reading', in *Stories and Minds: Cognitive Approaches to the Theory of Narrative*, ed. by Lars Bernaerts, Dirk de Geest, Luc Herman and Bart Vervaeck (Lincoln, NE: University of Nebraska Press, 2013), 191–231, https://doi.org/10.2307/j.ctt1ddr7zh.9

—— 'Literary Narrative and Mental Imagery: A View from Embodied Cognition', *Style*, 48.3 (2014), 275–93, https://www.jstor.org/stable/10.5325/style.48.3.275

Langfeld, Herbert S., *The Aesthetic Attitude* (Port Washington, NY: Kennikat Press, 1920).

Lipps, Theodor, 'Einfühlung, innere Nachahmung und Organempfindungen', in *Archiv für die gesamte Psychologie*, 1 (1903), 185–204.

—— '"Empathy", Inward Imitation, and Sense Feelings', in *Philosophies of Beauty: From Socrates to Robert Bridges, being the Sources of Aesthetic Theory*, ed. by E. F. Carritt (Oxford: Oxford University Press, 1931), 252–6.

Littau, Karin, *Theories of Reading: Books, Bodies, and Bibliomania* (Cambridge, UK: Polity Press, 2006).

MacKinnon, Catharine A., *Only Words* (Cambridge, MA: Harvard University Press, 1993), https://doi.org/10.2307/j.ctvjk2xs7

McHale, Brian, *Postmodernist Fiction* (New York: Methuen, 1987), https://doi.org/10.4324/9780203393321

Mellmann, Katja, 'Voice and Perception: An Evolutionary Approach to the Basic Functions of Narrative', in *Towards a Cognitive Theory of Narrative Acts*, ed. by Frederick Luis Aldama (Austin, TX: University of Texas Press, 2010), 119–41, https://doi.org/10.7560/721579-006

Miall, David S., 'On the Necessity of Empirical Studies of Literary Reading', *Frame. Utrecht Journal of Literary Theory*, 14.2–3 (2000), 43–59, https://sites.ualberta.ca/~dmiall/MiallPub/Miall_Necessity_1990.htm

—— 'Empirical Approaches to Studying Literary Readers: The State of the Discipline', *Book History*, 9 (2006), 291–311, https://doi.org/10.1353/bh.2006.0010

Miller, J. Hillis, *Versions of Pygmalion* (Cambridge, MA: Harvard University Press, 1990).

Morgan, Benjamin, 'Critical Empathy: Vernon Lee's Aesthetics and the Origins of Close Reading', *Victorian Studies*, 55.1 (2012), 31–56, https://doi.org/10.2979/victorianstudies.55.1.31

Morgan, Robyn, *Going Too Far: The Personal Chronicle of a Feminist* (New York: Vintage, 1978).

O'Neill, Patrick, *Fictions of Discourse: Reading Narrative Theory* (Toronto: University of Toronto Press, 1996), https://doi.org/10.3138/9781442674868

Paglia, Camille, *Sexual Personae: Art and Decadence from Nefertiti to Emily Dickinson* (New Haven, CT: Yale University Press, 1991), https://doi.org/10.12987/9780300182132

Paraskos, Michael, 'Bringing into Being: Vivifying Sculpture through Touch', in *Sculpture and Touch*, ed. by Peter Dent (Farnham: Ashgate, 2014), 61–9.

Poulet, Georges, 'Phenomenology of Reading', *New Literary History*, 1.1 (1969), 53–68, https://doi.org/10.2307/468372

Richardson, Alan, 'Studies in Literature and Cognition: A Field Map', in *The Work of Fiction: Cognition, Culture, and Complexity*, ed. by Ellen Spolsky and Alan Richardson (London: Routledge, 2004), 1–29.

Rimmon-Kenan, Shlomith, *Narrative Fiction: Contemporary Poetics* (London: Methuen, 1983), https://doi.org/10.4324/9780203130650

Rose, Margaret A., *Parody: Ancient, Modern, and Post-Modern* (Cambridge, UK: Cambridge University Press, 1993).

Ryan, Marie-Laure, *Narrative as Virtual Reality: Immersion and Interactivity in Literature and Electronic Media* (Baltimore, MD: Johns Hopkins University Press, 2001).

Sedgwick, Eve Kosofsky, 'Paranoid Reading and Reparative Reading, or, You're So Paranoid, You Probably Think This Essay Is About You', in Sedgwick, *Touching Feeling: Affect, Pedagogy, Performativity* (Durham, NC: Duke University Press, 2003), 123–52, https://doi.org/10.2307/j.ctv11smq37.9

Segal, Charles, 'Ovid's Metamorphic Bodies: Art, Gender, and Violence in the Metamorphoses', *Arion: A Journal of Humanities and the Classics*, 5.3 (1998), 9–41.

Segal, Naomi, *The Unintended Reader: Feminism and Manon Lescaut* (Cambridge, UK: Cambridge University Press, 1986).

Shattuck, Roger, *Forbidden Knowledge: From Prometheus to Pornography* (San Diego, CA: Harcourt Brace, 1997).

Soble, Alan, *Pornography, Sex and Feminism* (Amherst, NY: Prometheus Books, 2002).

Sontag, Susan, 'The Pornographic Imagination', in Sontag, *Styles of Radical Will* (London: Secker and Warburg, 1969), 35–73.

Steiner, George, 'Night Words', in Steiner, *Language and Silence: Essays 1958–1966* (London: Faber, 1967), 89–99.

—— 'To Civilize our Gentleman', in *Language and Silence: Essays 1958–1966* (London: Faber, 1967), 75–88.

Stewart, Garrett, *Reading Voices: Literature and the Phonotext* (Berkeley, CA: University of California Press, 1990), https://doi.org/10.1525/9780520342682

Stoichita, Victor, *The Pygmalion Effect: From Ovid to Hitchcock* (Chicago, IL: Chicago University Press, 2008).

Sunder Rajan, Rajeswari, *Real and Imagined Women: Gender, Culture and Postcolonialism* (London: Routledge, 1993), https://doi.org/10.4324/9780203359662

Todorov, Tzvetan, *Poétique de la prose* (Paris: Seuil, 1971).

Tompkins, Jane, 'The Reader in History', in *Reader-Response Criticism*, ed. by Tompkins (Baltimore, MD: Johns Hopkins University Press, 1980), 201–32.

Urmson, J. O., 'Literature', in *Aesthetics: A Critical Anthology*, ed. by George Dickie and Richard Sclafani (New York: St Martin's Press, 1977), 334–41, https://doi.org/10.4324/9781315303673-71

Walsh, Richard, 'Person, Level, Voice: A Rhetorical Reconsideration', in *Postclassical Narratology*, ed. by Jan Alber and Monika Fludernik (Columbus, OH: Ohio State University Press, 2010), 31–57.

Walton, Kendall, 'Spelunking, Simulation, and Slime: On Being Moved by Fiction', in *Emotion and the Arts*, ed. by Mette Hjort, and Sue Laver (New York: Oxford University Press, 1997), 37–49, https://doi.org/10.1093/oso/9780195111040.003.0003

Wicke, Jennifer, 'Through a Glass Darkly: Pornography's Academic Market', *Transition*, 54 (1991), 68–89.

Williams, Linda, *Hard Core: Power, Pleasure, and the 'Frenzy of the Visible'*, 2nd edn. (Berkeley and Los Angeles, CA: University of California Press, 1999).

Wimsatt, W. K. and Beardsley, Monroe C., 'The Affective Fallacy', in Wimsatt, *The Verbal Icon: Studies in the Meaning of Poetry* (Lexington, KY: University of Kentucky Press, 1954), 21–39.

Wittgenstein, Ludwig, *Zettel*, 2nd edn. (Oxford: Blackwell, 1981).

Zuckert, Rachel, 'Sculpture and Touch: Herder's Aesthetics of Sculpture', *Journal of Aesthetics and Art Criticism*, 67.3 (2009), 285–99, https://doi.org/10.1111/j.1540-6245.2009.01359.x

Translation Studies

Anderson, Jean, 'The Double Agent: Aspects of Literary Translator Affect as Revealed in Fictional Work by Translators', *Linguistica Antverpiensia, New Series – Themes in Translation Studies*, 4 (2021), 171–82, https://doi.org/10.52034/lanstts.v4i.134

Arrojo, Rosemary, 'Fidelity and the Gendered Translation', *TTR : Traduction, terminologie, rédaction*, 7.2 (1994), 147–63, https://doi.org/10.7202/037184ar

Baer, Brian James, 'Translation, Gender and Sexuality', in *The Cambridge Handbook of Translation*, ed. by Kirsten Malmkjær (Cambridge, UK: Cambridge University Press, 2022), 277–97, https://doi.org/10.1017/9781108616119.015

Batista, Carlos, *Bréviaire d'un traducteur* (Paris: Arléa, 2003).

Bell, Sharon and Massardier-Kenney, Françoise, 'Black on White: Translation, Race, Class and Power', in *Translating Slavery: Gender and Race in French Women's Writing, 1783–1823*, ed. by Doris Y. Kadish and Françoise Massardier-Kenney (Kent, OH: Kent State University Press, 1994), 168–84.

Chamberlain, Lori, 'The Metaphorics of Translation', *Signs*, 13.3 (1988), 454–72, https://doi.org/10.1086/494428

Cole, Peter, 'Making Sense in Translation: Towards an Ethics of the Art', in *In Translation: Translators on their Work and What it Means*, ed. by Esther Allen and Susan Bernofsky (New York: Columbia University Press, 2013), 3–16.

Davis, Lydia, 'Eleven Pleasures of Translating', *The New York Review*, 8 December 2016, https://www.nybooks.com/articles/2016/12/08/eleven-pleasures-of-translating/?lp_txn_id=1531994

de León, Celia Martín, 'Mental Imagery in Translation Processes', *HERMES - Journal of Language and Communication in Business* (2017), 201–20, https://doi.org/10.7146/hjlcb.v0i56.97232

Fawcett, Peter, 'Translation and Power Play', *The Translator*, 1.2 (1995), 177–92, https://doi.org/10.1080/13556509.1995.10798956

Gavronsky, Serge, 'The Translator: From Piety to Cannibalism', *SubStance*, 6/7.16 (1977), 53–62, https://doi.org/10.2307/3684124

Holierhoek, Jeanne, 'De Memoires Van een Moordenaar: *Les Bienviellantes* Vertaald', *Filter*, 15.4 (2008), 3–11.

Honig, Edwin, *The Poet's Other Voice: Conversations on Literary Translation* (Amherst, MA: University of Massachusetts Press, 1985).

Hubscher-Davidson, Séverine, *Translation and Emotion: A Psychological Perspective* (New York and Abingdon: Routledge, 2018), https://doi.org/10.4324/9781315720388

Hubscher-Davidson, Séverine and Lehr, Caroline (eds.), *The Psychology of Translation: Interdisciplinary Approaches* (Abingdon: Routledge, 2022), https://doi.org/10.4324/9781003140221

Kaminski, Johannes D., *Erotic Literature in Adaptation and Translation* (Cambridge, UK: Legenda, 2018), https://doi.org/10.2307/j.ctv16km1h6

Koskinen, Kaisa, *Translation and Affect: Essays on Sticky Affects and Translational Affective Labour* (Amsterdam: John Benjamins, 2020), https://doi.org/10.1075/btl.152

Levi, Primo, 'Translating and Being Translated', trans. by Harry Thomas and Marco Sonzogni, *Berfrois*, 26 July 2017, https://www.berfrois.com/2017/07/primo-levi-translating-and-being-translated/

Levine, Suzanne Jill, 'Translation As (Sub) Version: On Translating Infante's *Inferno*', 13.1 (1984), 85–94.

Maier, Carol, 'A Woman in Translation, Reflecting', *Translation Review*, 17 (1985), 4–8, https://doi.org/10.1080/07374836.1985.10523344

—— 'Translation, *Dépaysement*, and their Figuration', in *Translation and Power*, ed. by Maria Tymoczko and Edwin Gentzler (Amherst, MA: University of Massachussetts Press, 2002), 184–94, https://www.jstor.org/stable/j.ctt5vk30h.14

—— 'Translating as a Body: Meditations on Mediation (Excerpts 1994–2004)', in *The Translator as Writer*, ed. by Susan Bassnett and Peter Bush (London and New York: Continuum, 2006), 137–48.

McMorran, Will, 'We Translated the Marquis de Sade's Most Obscene Work – Here's How', *The Independent*, 2 November 2016, https://www.independent.co.uk/arts-entertainment/books/we-translated-the-marquis-de-sade-s-most-obscene-work-here-s-how-a7393066.html

Newmark, Peter, *About Translation* (Clevedon: Multilinguial Matters, 1991).

Robinson, Douglas, *The Translator's Turn* (Baltimore, MD: Johns Hopkins University Press, 1991).

Roscommon, Wentworth Dillon, Earl of, *An Essay on Translated Verse* (London: Jacob Tonson, 1684).

Santaemilia, José, 'The Translation of Sex, The Sex of Translation: *Fanny Hill* in Spanish', in *Gender, Sex and Translation: The Manipulation of Identities*, ed. by Santaemilia (Manchester: St Jerome, 2015), 117–36, https://doi.org/10.4324/9781315760261

Spivak, Gayatri Chakravorty, 'Translation as Culture', *Parallax* 6.1 (2000), 13–24, https://doi.org/10.1080/135346400249252

Steiner, George, *After Babel: Aspects of Language and Translation* (Oxford: Oxford University Press, 1975).

Venuti, Lawrence, *The Translator's Invisibility: A History of Translation* (London: Routledge, 1995), https://doi.org/10.4324/9780203360064

Von Flotow, Luise, *Translation and Gender: Translating in the 'Era of Feminism'* (Ottowa: University of Ottowa Press, 1997), https://doi.org/10.4324/9781315538563

—— 'Feminist Translation: Contexts, Practices and Theories', *TTR : Traduction, terminologie, rédaction*, 4.2 (1991), 69–84, https://doi.org/10.7202/037094ar

Wilson, Emily, 'Epilogue: Translating Homer as a Woman', in *Homer's Daughters: Women's Responses to Homer in the Twentieth Century and Beyond*, ed. by Fiona Cox and Elena Theodorakopoulos (Oxford: Oxford University Press, 2019), 279–97, https://doi.org/10.1093/oso/9780198802587.003.0016

Wynn, Thomas, 'Translation, Ethics and Obscenity', in *Erotic Literature in Adaptation and Translation*, ed. by Johannes D. Kaminski (Cambridge, UK: Legenda, 2018), 13–32, https://doi.org/10.2307/j.ctv16km1h6.5

Pedagogy

Barreca, Regina and Morse, Deborah Denenholz (eds.), *The Erotics of Instruction* (Hanover, NH: University Press of New England, 1997).

Barthes, Roland, 'Réflexions sur un manuel', in *L'enseignement de la littérature*, ed. by Serge Doubrovsky and Tzvetan Todorov (Paris: Plon, 1971), 170–7.

Boyle, Karen, 'The Boundaries of Porn Studies: On Linda Williams' Porn Studies', *New Review of Film and Television Studies*, 4.1 (2006), 1–16, https://doi.org/10.1080/17400300600577286

Clughen, Lisa, '"Embodiment is the future": What is Embodiment and is it the Future Paradigm for Learning and Teaching in Higher Education?', *Innovations in Education and Teaching International*, 61.4 (2024), 735–47, https://doi.org/10.1080/14703297.2023.2215226

Detweiler, Eric, *Responsible Pedagogy: Moving Beyond Authority and Mastery in Higher Education* (University Park, PA: Penn State University Press, 2022), https://doi.org/10.1515/9780271093796

Fallace, Thomas, 'The Long Origins of the Visual, Auditory, and Kinesthetic Learning Style Typology, 1921–2001', *History of Psychology*, 26.4 (2023), 334–54, https://doi.org/10.1037/hop0000240

Giroux, Henry, *On Critical Pedagogy* (London: Continuum, 2011).

Glavin, John, 'The Intimacies of Instruction', in *The Erotics of Instruction*, ed. by Regina Barreca and Deborah Denenholz Morse (Hanover, NH: University Press of New England, 1997), 12–27.

hooks, bell, *Teaching to Transgress: Education as the Practice of Freedom* (New York and London: Routledge, 1994), https://doi.org/10.4324/9780203700280

Jenkins, Henry, 'Foreword: So You Want to Teach Pornography?', in *More Dirty Looks: Gender, Pornography and Power*, ed. by Pamela Church Anderson (London: BFI, 2004), 1–8.

Kanpol, Barry, *Critical Pedagogy: An Introduction*, 2nd edn. (Westport, CT and London: Bergin and Garvey, 1999), https://doi.org/10.5040/9798400634093

Levin, Kate, '"The Only Beguiled Person": Accessing *Fantomina* in the Feminist Classroom', *ABO: Interactive Journal for Women in the Arts, 1640–1830*, 2.1 (2012), 3, 1–12, https://doi.org/10.5038/2157-7129.2.1.5

Marks, Elaine, 'In Defense of Modern Languages and Literatures, Masterpieces, Nihilism, and Dead European Writers', *MLA Newsletter*, 25 (1993), 2–3.

Paniagua, Alejandro and Istance, David, *Teachers as Designers of Learning Environments: The Importance of Innovative Pedagogies* (Paris: OECD Publishing, 2018), https://doi.org/10.1787/9789264085374-en

Pope, Rebecca, 'Hayley, Roz, and Me', in *The Erotics of Instruction*, ed. by Regina Barreca and Deborah Denenholz Morse (Hanover, NH: University Press of New England, 1997), 28–51.

Probyn, Elspeth, 'Teaching Bodies: Affects in the Classroom', *Body and Society*, 10.4 (2004), 21–43, https://doi.org/10.1177/1357034x04047854

Reading, Anna, 'Professing Porn or Obscene Browsing? On Proper Distance in the University Classroom', *Media Culture & Society*, 27.1 (2005), 123–30, https://doi.org/10.1177/0163443705049061

Waskul, Dennis, 'My Boyfriend Loves it when I Come Home from this Class: Pedagogy, Titillation, and New Media Technologies', *Sexualities*, 12 (2009), 654–61, https://doi.org/10.1177/1363460709340374

Williams, Linda, 'Porn Studies: Proliferating Pornographies On/Scene: An Introduction', in *Porn Studies*, ed. by Williams (Durham, NC: Duke University Press, 2004), 1–23, https://doi.org/10.1215/9780822385844-001

Sexology, Psychology and Neuroscience

Abramson, Marianne and Goldinger, Stephen D., 'What the Reader's Eye Tells the Mind's Ear: Silent Reading Activates Inner Speech', *Perception & Psychophysics*, 59.7 (1997), 1059–68, https://doi.org/10.3758/bf03205520

Ardizzi, Martina, Erroni, Francesca, Umiltà, Maria Alessandra, Pinardi, Chiara, Errante, Antonino, Ferri, Francesca, Fadda, Elisabetta and Gallese, Vittorio, 'Visceromotor Roots of Aesthetic Evaluation of Pain in Art: An fMRI Study', *Social Cognitive and Affective Neuroscience*, 16.11 (2021), 1113–22, https://doi.org/10.1093/scan/nsab066

Avenanti, Alessia, Minio-Pauello, Ilaria, Bufalari, Ilaria and Aglioti, Salvatore M., 'Stimulus-Driven Modulation of Motor-Evoked Potentials During Observation of Others' Pain', *Neuroimage*, 32.1 (2006), 316–24, https://doi.org/10.1016/j.neuroimage.2006.03.010

Avenanti, Alessia, Bueti, Domenica, Galati, Gaspare and Aglioti, Salvatore M., 'Transcranial Magnetic Stimulation Highlights the Sensorimotor Side of Empathy for Pain', *Nature Neuroscience*, 8.7 (2005), 955–60, https://doi.org/10.1038/nn1481

Baars, Bernard, *In the Theatre of Consciousness: The Workspace of the Mind* (New York: Oxford University Press, 1997), https://doi.org/10.1093/acprof:oso/9780195102659.001.1

Batson, C. Daniel, 'These Things Called Empathy: Eight Related but Distinct Phenomena', in *The Social Neuroscience of Empathy*, ed. by Jean Decety and William Ickes (Cambridge, MA: MIT Press), 3–15, https://doi.org/10.7551/mitpress/9780262012973.003.0002

Beilock, Sian L. and Lyons, Ian M., 'Expertise and the Mental Simulation of Action', in *Handbook of Imagination and Mental Simulation*, ed. by Keith D. Markman, William M. P. Klein and Julie A. Suhr (New York: Taylor and Francis, 2009), 21–34, https://doi.org/10.4324/9780203809846.ch2

Blackmore, Susan, *Consciousness: An Introduction*, 2nd edn. (London: Routledge, 2010).

Bloch, Iwan, *Beiträge zur Aetiologie der Psychopathia sexualis*, 2 vols. (Dresden: Dohrn, 1902–3).

—— *Das Sexualleben unserer Zeit in seinen Beziehungen zur modernen Kultur* (Berlin: Louis Marcus, 1907).

Bond, Susan B. and Mosher, Donald L., 'Guided Imagery of Rape: Fantasy, Reality and the Willing Victim Myth', *Journal of Sex Research*, 22.2 (1986), 162–83, https://doi.org/10.1080/00224498609551298

Boring, Edwin G., Langfeld, Herbert S. and Weld, Harry Porter, *Introduction to Psychology* (New York: John Wiley and Sons, 1939), https://doi.org/10.1037/11332-000

Claxton, Guy, *Intelligence in the Flesh: Why Your Mind Needs Your Body Much More Than It Thinks* (New Haven, CT: Yale University Press, 2015), https://doi.org/10.12987/9780300215977

Craver-Lemley, Catherine and Reeves, Adam, 'How Visual Imagery Interferes with Vision', *Psychological Review*, 99 (1992), 633–49, https://doi.org/10.1037//0033-295x.99.4.633

Dennett, Daniel, *Consciousness Explained* (Boston, MA and London: Little Brown, 1991).

Donnerstein, Edward and Linz, Daniel, 'Mass Media, Sexual Violence, and Male Viewers: Current Theory and Research', *American Behavioural Scientist*, 29.5 (1986), 601–18; republished in *Men Confront Pornography*, ed. by Michael S. Kimmel (New York: Crown, 1990), 219–32, https://doi.org/10.1177/000276486029005007

Downey, June, *Creative Imagination: Studies in the Psychology of Literature* (London: Harcourt Brace, 1929), https://doi.org/10.1037/11391-000

Ellis, Havelock, *Studies in the Psychology of Sex*, vols. 4 and 5 (Philadelphia, PN: F. A. Davis., 1905–6).

Eulenberg, Albert, *Sexuale Neuropathie* (Leipzig: F. C. W. Vogel, 1895).

Frith, Chris, *Making Up the Mind: How the Brain Creates Our Mental World* (Oxford: Blackwell, 2007).

Gerrig, Richard, *Experiencing Narrative Worlds: On the Psychological Activities of Reading* (New Haven, CT: Yale University Press, 1998), https://doi.org/10.4324/9780429500633

Grice-Jackson, Thomas, Critchley, Hugo D., Banissy, Michael J. and Ward, Jamie, 'Common and Distinct Neural Mechanisms Associated with the Conscious Experience of Vicarious Pain', *Cortex*, 94 (2017), 152–63, https://doi.org/10.1016/j.cortex.2017.06.015

González, Julio, Barros-Loscertales, Alfonso, Pulvermüller, Friedemann, Meseguer, Vanessa, Sanjuán, Ana, Belloch, Vicente and Ávila, César, 'Reading Cinnamon Activates Olfactory Brain Regions', *NeuroImage*, 32.2 (2006), 906–12, https://doi.org/10.1016/j.neuroimage.2006.03.037

Hirschfeld, Magnus, *Sexualpathologie: Ein Lehrbuch für Ärzte und Studierende* (Bonn: A. Marcus & E. Webers, 1920).

Horikawa, Tomoyasu and Kamitani, Yukiyasu, 'Generic Decoding of Seen and Imagined Objects Using Hierarchical Visual Features', *Nature Communications*, 8 (2017), 1–15, https://doi.org/10.1038/ncomms15037

Kaan, Heinrich, *Psychopathia sexualis*, in *Heinrich Kaan's 'Psychopathia sexualis' (1844): A Classic Text in the History of Sexuality*, ed. by Benjamin Kahan and trans. by Melissa Haynes (Ithaca, NY and London: Cornell University Press, 2016), 27–161, https://doi.org/10.7591/cornell/9781501704604.001.0001

Kalisch, Raffael, Wiech, Katja, Critchley, Hugo D., Seymour, Ben, O'Doherty, John P., Oakley, David A., Allen, Philip and Dolan, Raymond J., 'Anxiety Reduction Through Detachment: Subjective, Physiological, and Neural Effects', *Journal of Cognitive Neuroscience*, 17 (2005), 874–83, https://doi.org/10.1162/0898929054021184

Kay, Kendrick N. and Gallant, Jack L., 'I Can See What You See', *Natural Neuroscience*, 12 (2009), 245–6, https://doi.org/10.1038/nn0309-245

Koide-Majima, Naoko, Nishimoto, Shinji and Majima, Kei, 'Mental Image Reconstruction from Human Brain Activity: Neural Decoding of Mental Imagery via Deep Neural Network-based Bayesian Estimation', *Neural Networks*, 170 (2024), 349–63, https://doi.org/10.1016/j.neunet.2023.11.024

Kosslyn, Stephen M., Thompson, William L. and Ganis, Giorgio, *The Case for Mental Imagery* (New York: Oxford University Press, 2006), https://doi.org/10.1093/acprof:oso/9780195179088.001.0001

Lacey, Simon, Stilla, Randall and Sathian, K., 'Metaphorically Feeling: Comprehending Textural Metaphors Activates Somatosensory Cortex', *Brain and Language*, 120.3 (2012), 416–21, https://doi.org/10.1016/j.bandl.2011.12.016

Lamm, Claus, Batson, C. Daniel and Decety, Jean, 'The Neural Substrate of Human Empathy: Effects of Perspective-Taking and Cognitive Appraisal', *Journal of Cognitive Neuroscience*, 19.1 (2007), 42–58, https://doi.org/10.1162/jocn.2007.19.1.42

Langfeld, Herbert S., *The Aesthetic Attitude* (Port Washington, NY: Kennikat Press, 1920), https://doi.org/10.1037/10922-000

Lanzoni, Susan, *Empathy: A History* (New Haven, CT: Yale University Press, 2018), https://doi.org/10.2307/j.ctv5cgb7s

Laplanche, Jean and Pontalis, Jean Bertrand, 'Fantasy and the Origins of Sexuality', in *Formations of Fantasy*, ed. by Victor Burgin, James Donald and Cora Kaplan (London: Routledge, 1987), 5–34.

Malamuth, N. M. and Check, J. V. P., 'Sexual Arousal to Rape and Consenting Depictions: The Importance of the Woman's Arousal', *Journal of Abnormal Psychology*, 89.6 (1980), 763–66, https://doi.org/10.1037//0021-843x.89.6.763

Moore, Alan Tonnies and Schwitzgebel, Eric, 'The Experience of Reading', *Consciousness and Cognition*, 62 (2018), 57–68, https://doi.org/10.1016/j.concog.2018.03.011

Nell, Victor, *Lost in a Book: The Psychology of Reading for Pleasure* (New Haven, CT: Yale University Press, 1988), https://doi.org/10.2307/j.ctt1ww3vk3

Osborn, Jody and Derbyshire, Stewart W. G., 'Pain Sensation Evoked by Observing Injury in Others', *Pain*, 148 (2010), 268–74, https://doi.org/10.1016/j.pain.2009.11.007

Pinker, Steven, How the Mind Works (London: Penguin, 1998).

Rice, Marnie E., Chaplin, Terry C., Harris, Grant T. and Coutts, Joanne, 'Empathy for the Victim and Sexual Arousal Among Rapists and Nonrapists', *Journal of Interpersonal Violence*, 9.4 (1994), 435–49, https://doi.org/10.1177/088626094009004001

Sartre, Jean-Paul, *L'Imaginaire: Psychologie phénoménologique de l'imagination* (Paris: Gallimard, 1966).

Scobie, A. and Taylor, A. J. W, 'Perversions Ancient and Modern: I. Agalmatophilia, the Statue Syndrome', *The History of the Behavioral Sciences*, 11.1 (1975), 49–54, https://doi.org/10.1002/1520-6696(197501)11:1<49::aid-jhbs2300110112>3.0.co;2-6

Shephard, Roger and Metzler, J., 'Mental Rotation of Three-Dimensional Objects', *Science* (1971), 701–703, https://doi.org/10.1126/science.171.3972.701

Singer, Tania, Seymour, Ben, O'Doherty, John, Kaube, Holger, Dolan, Raymond J. and Frith, Chris D., 'Empathy for Pain Involves the Affective but Not Sensory Components of Pain', *Science*, 303 (2004), 1157–62, https://doi.org/10.1126/science.1093535

Socarides, C. W., 'A Psychoanalytic Study of the Desire for Sexual Transformation ("Transsexualism"): The Plaster-of-Paris Man', *International Journal of Psychoanalysis*, 51 (1970), 341–9.

Tarnowksky, Veniamin, *The Sexual Instinct and its Morbid Manifestation*, trans. by W. C. Costello and Alfred Allinson (Paris: Charles Carrington, 1898).

Titchener, Edward, *Lectures on the Experimental Psychology of the Thought-Processes* (New York: Macmillan, 1909), https://doi.org/10.1037/10877-000

Wandelt, Sarah Kim and Bjånes, David, 'Brain–Machine-Interface Device Translates Internal Speech into Text', *Natural Human Behaviour*, 8 (2024), 1014–15, https://doi.org/10.1038/s41562-024-01869-w

White, Murray, 'The Statue Syndrome: Perversion? Fantasy? Anecdote?', *The Journal of Sex Research*, 14.4 (1978), 246–9, https://doi.org/10.1080/00224497809551011

Wulffen, Erich, *Der Sexualverbrecher* (Berlin: P. Langenscheidt, 1910).

Yao, Bo and Scheepers, Christoph, 'Inner Voice Experiences During Processing of Direct and Indirect Speech', in *Explicit and Implicit Prosody in Sentence Processing: Studies in Honor of Janet Dean Fodor*, ed. by Lyn Frazier and Edward Gibson, Studies in Theoretical Psycholinguistics, 46 (Cham: Springer, 2015), 287–307, https://doi.org/10.1007/978-3-319-12961-7_15

Index

Abbott, H. Porter 99
Abramovici, Jean-Christophe 84
actors and acting 20, 89, 130, 141–142
affect 5, 7, 10–12, 14, 16–17, 23–24,
   60, 87, 100, 130, 139, 145, 157,
   168, 172–173, 178–179, 185–186,
   196–198
Ahmed, Sara 145
Anderson, Jean 142
Aretino, Pietro 188, 190
Arrojo, Rosemary 151
author 3, 5–6, 9, 13, 19, 36, 43, 47–48,
   54–55, 62, 75, 92, 94, 97–98, 100,
   102, 104–105, 107–108, 135,
   140–144, 147, 150–151, 153, 165,
   169, 171, 173, 175, 178, 192, 195,
   200, 209, 212–213

Baars, Bernard 17
Baculard d'Arnaud, François-Thomas-
   Marie 33
Baer, Brian James 153
Barthes, Roland 3–5, 11, 13, 57, 87,
   111, 141, 157, 161, 177, 206
Bataille, Georges 7
Batista, Carlos 142
Batson, C. Daniel 124–125, 130–131
Beardsley, Monroe C. 12, 15–16
Beaumarchais, Pierre Augustin Caron
   de 30
Beauvoir, Simone de 2, 5–6, 8, 11
Bell, Sharon 152, 154–155
Bennington, Geoffrey 5
Berman, Harold 146–147
Blackmore, Susan 17
Blanchot, Maurice 2
Bloch, Iwan 74–76
body 5, 8, 16, 20, 22–23, 25, 30, 47,
   53, 56–57, 60–61, 72–73, 78, 84,
   87–88, 91–92, 94, 109, 112, 114–115,
   117, 119–120, 122, 124–126, 128,
   134–135, 138–140, 143, 150, 153,
   167–169, 178–181, 190–192, 194,
   196–198, 204–205, 211–212, 214
Bolens, Guillemette 23, 115, 119, 160
Bongie, Laurence 9
Booth, Wayne C. 7–8, 117
Bortolussi, Marisa 22, 100
Boureau-Deslandes, André François
   31, 48
Boyle, Karen 186–187
Brochier, Jean-Jacques 3–5
Butler, Judith 217

Calvino, Italo 19
Cameron, James 214
Canler, Louis 74
Carroll, Noel 116–117
Carter, Angela 134
Cave, Terence 23, 115, 117, 129
censorship 2, 5, 49, 55–56, 154–156,
   177, 186
   self-censorship 55, 155–156, 186
Cervantes, Miguel de
   30, 84
Chamberlain, Lori 143
Chantelou, Paul Fréart de 63
Chauvet, Pierre 160
Classen, Constance 63–64
Claxton, Guy 180
Cleland, John
   Fanny Hill 100, 194
Clughen, Lisa 179–180, 192
Cocks, Jay 214
cognition 7, 14, 16–18, 21–23, 99, 115,
   117, 130, 138–139, 178–179, 203
   embodied 17–18, 23, 115, 203
Cole, Peter 144
Condillac, Etienne Bonnot de 88, 128
Coward, David 9
Crébillon fils, Claude Prosper Jolyot
   de 175

Cryle, Peter 46
Culler, Jonathan 13–15

Davis, Lydia 140–143
de León, Celia Martín 145
Deleuze, Gilles 169
Delon, Michel 68
Denby, David 216
Dennett, Daniel 17
Detweiler, Eric 198
Dewey, John 178
Diderot, Denis 69, 85
Dixon, Peter 22, 100
Downey, June 116–117
Dubos, Jean-Baptiste 124–126
Dworkin, Andrea 78–79, 98, 177

Eagleton, Terry 12
L'Ecole des filles 149, 188–191
editors and editing 47–48, 147–150, 156–157, 160, 169–173
Elliot, R.K. 132–133, 135
ellipsis 46–47, 49, 91
Ellis, Havelock 76
embodied cognition. *See* cognition: embodied
emotion 12, 16, 25, 66, 92, 110, 129, 135, 138–139, 144–145, 157, 168–169, 171–172, 178–180
empathy 25, 96–97, 107, 110, 113–114, 128, 131, 140
Esrock, Ellen J. 18, 58
ethics 5, 7, 11, 23, 109, 132, 137–138, 150, 183, 186, 194, 197–198, 217
Evelyn, John 63

Fawcett, Peter 171
Faye, Jean-Pierre 4
Felski, Rita 108, 200
feminism 7, 25, 138, 143–144, 151–153, 180–181, 187, 194, 200
Fish, Stanley 13
Frappier-Mazur, Lucienne 106, 118, 212
Frith, Chris 128–129
Frozen (2013) 170

Gaiger, Jason 65, 133–135
Gaillard, Aurélia 31
Gallop, Jane 25, 180–183, 187, 189–190, 192–194
Gambacorti, Chiara 40
Gavronsky, Serge 143
Genand, Stéphanie 40
gender 53, 100, 104–105, 107, 113, 142–143, 153–154, 172, 184, 187, 194, 196, 205
Genette, Gérard 99
Gentileschi, Artemisia 133–135
Gerrig, Richard 21–22
Gillette, Paul J. 147–148
Giroux, Henry 206
Glass, William H. 19, 21
Glavin, John 182–183
Goethe, Johann Wolfgang von 61, 83
Goulemot, Jean Marie 3, 10–11
Gregg, Melissa 16
Grünewald, Matthias 132

Harrison, Nicholas 9–10
hearing 18, 87–88, 93, 103–111, 121, 156, 204, 214
   aural imagery 20, 24, 87–89, 92–94, 98–100, 103, 105–106, 108, 110, 122–123, 168
   inner speech 20, 103–104, 107–108, 213
Heine, Maurice 47, 50, 149–150, 154, 163
Hélvetius, Claude-Adrien 88
Hénaff, Marcel 109
Herder, Johann Gottfried 64–65, 69, 111–112
Holierhoek, Jeanne 166, 172
Holland, Norman N. 13–14
hooks, bell 25, 175, 180–181, 196
Hubscher-Davidson, Séverine 139, 144–145, 166, 168, 171–172
Hume, David 17, 212
Huysmans, Joris-Karl 75

imagination 21, 30, 38, 42–43, 47, 54, 61, 69, 88–89, 101–102, 106, 110,

113, 124, 128, 134–135, 138, 145, 160, 162, 165, 199, 210–213
incest 28–29, 37–38, 42–48, 54, 60, 62, 143, 195
inner speech. *See* hearing: inner speech
Iser, Wolfgang 13, 20, 142

James, Henry 76
Johnson, Geraldine A., 64
Joubert, Joseph 161–162

Kaan, Heinrich 74
Kanpol, Barry 197
kinaesthesis 24, 84, 113–116, 119, 121–122, 124, 126, 168, 178, 180
Kivy, Peter 19–20, 104
Klossowski, Pierre 2
Koskinen, Kaisa 145
Kosslyn, Stephen M. 18
Krafft-Ebing, Richard von 76
Kuzmičová, Anežka 22–23, 99, 103–104, 106, 115, 117

Laclos, Choderlos de 175
La Mettrie, Julien Offray de 42–43, 61
Lamm, Claus 130–131
Langfeld, Herbert S. 113–114
Lanzoni, Susan 114
Lars and the Real Girl (2007) 76
Le Brun, Annie 6–7, 159, 177
Lely, Gilbert 2
Levi, Primo 143
Levin, Kate 182
Levine, Suzanne Jill 150–151
lighting 53–54, 56–57
Lipps, Theodor 112–113, 119, 133
listeners and listening 24–25, 85–94, 96–98, 100, 105–107, 110–111, 126
literary criticism and theory 7, 12, 17, 23, 98, 114, 177, 186, 196, 206
  narratology 21–22, 85, 99
Littau, Karin 12–13
Locke, John 17
Lucian 65–66
Lynch, Lawrence 5

MacKinnon, Catharine A. 79, 217
Maier, Carol 144, 153–154, 168
Manhunter (1986) 173
Marivaux, Pierre Carlet de 90
Marks, Elaine 182
Martin, Christophe 30, 34
masochism 98, 110, 163, 169–170
Massardier-Kelly, Françoise 152
masturbation 34, 52, 62, 68, 78–79, 126, 185, 193
mental imagery 17–18, 21, 24–25, 53, 89, 123, 162, 165, 213
Mercier, Louis Sébastien 161
Miall, David S. 15–16
Miller, J. Hillis 29, 62
Miller, Nancy K. 84, 110
mind 16–22, 24, 30, 32–33, 52, 56, 59, 62, 83, 91, 100, 102, 108, 113, 126, 147, 173, 179–180, 190, 192, 211–212, 217
misogyny 6, 39, 138, 150, 153–154, 193, 195, 199–201
Molière 27, 30, 43
Montessori, Maria 178
Moore, Alan Tonnies 18
Morgan, Benjamin 114
Morgan, Robyn 78–79
motor resonance 22, 115, 117, 123–124
Myrrha 29–31, 36, 38–39, 41–42, 44–46, 48, 50, 54, 60, 72

Nabokov, Vladimir 34
narratology. *See* literary criticism and theory: narratology
narrators and narration 33, 36, 38, 46–47, 49, 55, 59, 68, 80, 87–88, 91–92, 99–107, 119, 123, 146–147, 168
nausea 159–160
Nell, Victor 21–22
neuroscience 14, 17–18, 25–26, 84, 115, 128, 157, 178
Newmark, Peter 152

objectification 59, 81, 121, 126
O'Neill, Patrick 99

Osborn, Jody 129
Ovid 24, 27–30, 35, 38–39, 45, 60, 62, 72, 113

Paglia, Camille 176
pain 29, 33, 88, 97–98, 108, 110–111, 120, 123–131, 135, 146, 155, 167–168, 175, 215–216
painting 31, 37, 55, 57, 62, 64–65, 67, 91, 132–135
Paraskos, Michael 28
Paulhan, Jean 2, 98
Pauvert, Jean-Jacques 2, 200
pedagogy 25–26, 145, 178–181, 183–188, 190, 192–194, 196–198
perspective 30, 32, 58–59, 81, 84, 91, 95, 97, 99, 115–117, 119–122, 130–131, 137, 144, 154, 157, 178, 214–215
   first-person 94, 97, 115–117, 119, 133, 214
   third-person 58, 92, 101, 115–117, 121, 147
Phillips, John 146
Pinker, Steven 123
Plato 17
Pope, Rebecca 182
pornography 9, 12, 25, 28, 62, 74, 78–81, 93–95, 124, 135, 149, 176, 184–188, 194–196, 200–201, 204–205, 207, 213–214, 216–217
Poulet, Georges 140
Probyn, Elspeth 181, 183, 196, 198
Proust, Jacques 1
Psycho (1960) 109
psychology 6, 14, 18–19, 21–22, 76, 84, 94, 100, 111, 113–116, 124, 131, 141
Pygmalion 24, 27–33, 38–39, 41, 45, 48, 54, 56, 62, 66, 68, 72–74, 111, 113, 213
Pygmalionism 28, 74–76

questionnaires 15, 23–24, 28, 52–53, 56, 60, 81, 84, 101, 103, 105, 110, 120–121, 206, 213

Rabelais, François de 149
rape 24, 49, 78, 87, 94–98, 101, 118–123, 128, 130, 135, 143–144, 149–151, 195, 205, 214–217
readers and reading 1–3, 5–29, 46–47, 49–60, 62, 64, 66, 75, 81, 83–84, 88–89, 91, 93, 98–111, 115–119, 121–124, 128–132, 135, 137–138, 140, 142, 146–150, 153–155, 157, 159–160, 162, 165–166, 168, 170–171, 175–177, 179, 184, 190, 192–193, 195–206, 211–213, 215–217
reception 27–28, 62, 73, 78–80, 83, 92, 100, 103, 108, 137, 145, 177, 197, 200, 211
Rice, Marnie E. 95–97, 100, 107, 124, 216
Rimmon-Kenan, Shlomith 99
Robinson, Douglas 139–140, 156–157
Robinson, Ken 178
Roger, Philippe 5
Roscommon, Wentworth Dillon, Earl of 140–143
Rose, Margaret A. 37
Rousseau, Jean-Jacques 38, 54, 69, 109
Ryan, Marie-Laure 22

Sacher-Masoch, Leopold von 76
   Venus in Furs 76, 195
Sade, Donatien-Alphonse-Francois, Marquis de
   120 Journées de Sodome, Les 3–4, 25, 40, 74, 80, 87–90, 92–93, 100, 118, 125, 130, 137, 144, 147–150, 153–162, 165, 170, 172–173, 187, 189, 194, 196, 198–199, 209, 216
   Aline et Valcour 41–42, 45, 71, 86
   Complete Marquis de Sade, The 147
   Crimes de l'amour, Les 24, 27, 36, 46, 195
   'Eugénie de Franval' 24, 27–28, 37–43, 45–51, 54–55, 62, 68, 72, 78–79, 81, 101, 103–105, 107, 119–120, 192, 195

Histoire de Juliette 43, 67, 70, 74, 92, 127, 147, 209, 211–212
'Idée sur les romans' 36–37, 61–62
Justine, ou les Malheurs de la vertu 24, 37, 49, 71–72, 80, 84, 90–93, 97, 101–105, 108, 119, 123, 126–127, 130–131, 145–147, 160–162, 175–177, 192, 194, 198, 202–203, 205
Lettres à sa femme 94, 209
Marquise de Gange, La 37, 137
Nouvelle Justine, La 71, 87, 92, 147
Philosophie dans le boudoir, La 25, 40, 44–45, 47, 127–128, 176, 187–192, 199
sadism 2, 5, 98, 110, 155, 170, 216
Santaemilia, José 156
Sartre, Jean-Paul 19, 21
Scarron, Paul 30
Schiller, Friedrich 64
Scobie, A. 75–76, 78
Sedgwick, Eve Kosofsky 200
Segal, Charles 29, 60
Seigworth, Gregory J. 16
sensations 12, 16, 87–88, 115, 124, 127–128, 135, 139, 145, 183, 209, 213, 217
senses 10, 12, 18, 21, 23, 25, 31, 38, 51, 64, 83, 88–89, 92, 121, 126, 134–135, 138–139, 157, 167, 180, 184, 211, 213
sex and sexuality 1, 8, 10, 37, 46, 49, 52, 58, 69, 71–72, 74, 78–79, 84, 90, 92–98, 100, 107–110, 131, 143, 156, 175–177, 181–182, 184–188, 190–200, 202–207, 212–214, 216
sexology 7, 74–78, 200
Shattuck, Roger 8–10, 165, 177
Shawshank Redemption, The (1994) 159
Shephard, Roger 18
Sheriff, Mary 27, 39
sight and visual imagery 18, 23, 33, 35–36, 52–53, 61, 64–65, 69, 88, 98, 105–106, 116, 120, 160–161, 168, 203

smell and olfactory imagery 4–5, 22–23, 25, 32, 83, 88, 138, 157–162
Smith, Adam 114, 124–125, 128
Smollett, Tobias 66
Soble, Alan 79
social science 97, 184
statue love. *See* Pygmalionism
statues 24, 27–33, 35, 45, 48, 50–51, 54–56, 60, 62–78, 81, 84, 101, 111–112, 126
Steiner, George 3, 12, 143, 157, 170
Stewart, Garrett 100, 107
Stoichita, Victor 62
Strange Days (1995) 213–217

Tasso, Torquato 33
taste and gustatory imagery 23, 28, 34, 62, 80, 83, 88, 93, 127, 157, 159–161
teachers and teaching 11, 13, 25–26, 40, 137, 166, 175, 178–179, 181–190, 192, 194–200, 202, 204, 206
Thérèse philosophe 31–32, 100
Thomas, Chantal 5, 10, 177, 211
Titchener, Edward 113
Tompkins, Jane 13
touch and tactile imagery 18, 23–24, 28, 32, 35, 48, 50, 60–65, 68–69, 81, 88–89, 92, 111, 154, 157, 172, 181, 191, 214
translator and translations 9, 25–26, 42, 47, 52, 66, 121, 137–157, 159, 162–163, 166, 168–173, 178, 193, 195

Urmson, J.O. 20

Venuti, Lawrence 141, 198
violence 1, 3–6, 8, 25, 79, 84, 92–95, 97–98, 106–107, 109–110, 121, 123, 126, 128, 130–131, 133–135, 138, 143–144, 149–150, 153–155, 157, 162, 165, 171–173, 175–177, 186, 193–196, 206, 209, 212–213, 216–217, 224
viscerality 4, 8, 10, 88, 117, 137, 144, 154, 160, 162–163, 177, 195, 206

Vischer, Robert 112
voice 30, 60, 73, 92, 96–97, 99–100, 102–108, 110, 121, 123, 139, 154–157, 170
  female voice 92, 95–97, 102, 104–105, 107
  male voice 95, 97, 102, 104–105
Von Flotow, Luise 151–154

Wainhouse, Austryn 148–149
Walton, Kendall 22
Warman, Caroline 88, 126
Waskul, Dennis 184–186, 196

White, Murray 76–77
Williams, Linda 184, 187, 201, 204
Wilson, Emily 155
Wimsatt, W. K. 12, 15–16
Wittgenstein, Ludwig 19, 53, 83
Wrigley, Richard 63–64
Wynn, Thomas 25, 137, 148

Yeats, W. B. 117

Zayas, Maria de 30
Zoffany, Johan 67
Zuckert, Rachel 65

About the Team

Alessandra Tosi was the managing editor for this book.

Adèle Kreager and Sophia Bursey proof-read this manuscript.

Hannah Shakespeare and Adèle Kreager compiled the index.

Jeevanjot Kaur Nagpal designed the cover. The cover was produced in InDesign using the Fontin font.

Annie Hine typeset the book in InDesign. The main text font is Tex Gyre Pagella and the heading font is Californian FB.

Jeremy Bowman produced the PDF, paperback, and hardback editions and created the EPUB.

The conversion to the HTML edition was performed with epublius, an open-source software which is freely available on our GitHub page at https://github.com/OpenBookPublishers

Hannah Shakespeare was in charge of marketing.

This book was peer-reviewed by Prof Thomas Wynn, University of Durham, and Dr Marine Ganofsky, University of St Andrews. Experts in their field, these readers give their time freely to help ensure the academic rigour of our books. We are grateful for their generous and invaluable contributions.

This book need not end here...

Share

All our books — including the one you have just read — are free to access online so that students, researchers and members of the public who can't afford a printed edition will have access to the same ideas. This title will be accessed online by hundreds of readers each month across the globe: why not share the link so that someone you know is one of them?

This book and additional content is available at
https://doi.org/10.11647/OBP.0488

Donate

Open Book Publishers is an award-winning, scholar-led, not-for-profit press making knowledge freely available one book at a time. We don't charge authors to publish with us: instead, our work is supported by our library members and by donations from people who believe that research shouldn't be locked behind paywalls.

Join the effort to free knowledge by supporting us at
https://www.openbookpublishers.com/support-us

We invite you to connect with us on our socials!

BLUESKY
@openbookpublish.bsky.social

MASTODON
@OpenBookPublish@hcommons.social

LINKEDIN
open-book-publishers

Read more at the Open Book Publishers Blog
https://blogs.openbookpublishers.com

You may also be interested in:

The Atheist's Bible
Diderot's *Éléments de physiologie*
Caroline Warman
https://doi.org/10.11647/OBP.0199

Denis Diderot's *Rameau's Nephew*
A Multi-Media Bilingual Edition
Marian Hobson (ed.), Kate E. Tunstall and Caroline Warman (transl.), Pascal Duc (music editor)
https://doi.org/10.11647/OBP.0098

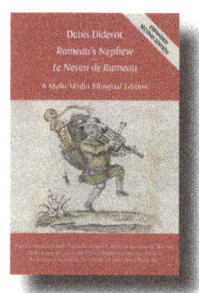

The Philosophes by Charles Palissot
Edited by Jessica Goodman and Olivier Ferret
https://doi.org/10.11647/OBP.0201

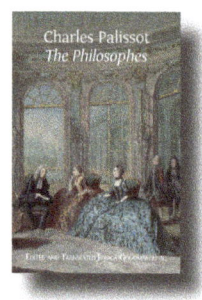

Tolerance
The Beacon of the Enlightenment
Edited and translated by Caroline Warman
https://doi.org/10.11647/OBP.0088

www.ingramcontent.com/pod-product-compliance
Lightning Source LLC
Chambersburg PA
CBHW050900240426
43673CB00050B/1947